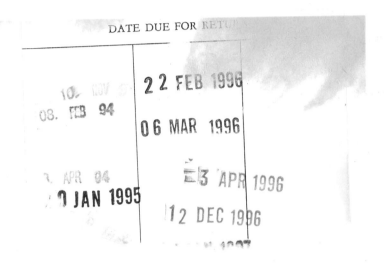

INSIDE THE THINK TANK

INSIDE THE THINK TANK

Advising the Cabinet 1971–1983

TESSA BLACKSTONE
AND
WILLIAM PLOWDEN

WILLIAM HEINEMANN
LONDON

William Heinemann Ltd
Michelin House, 81 Fulham Road, London SW3 6RB

LONDON   MELBOURNE   AUCKLAND

First published 1988

British Cataloguing in Publication Data

Blackstone, Tessa
    The Think Tank : advising the Cabinet.
    1. Great Britain. Government. Policies.
    Formulation. Organisations. Central Policy
    Review Staff, 1971–1983
    I. Title   II. Plowden, William
    354.4109′3

ISBN 0 434 07490 X

Photoset by Deltatype Ltd, Ellesmere Port
Printed and bound by Richard Clay Ltd, Bungay, Suffolk

Preface

THE CENTRAL POLICY Review Staff, always known as the CPRS for short, and often referred to as 'the Think Tank', was set up by the Conservative government of Edward Heath in 1971. Its first head was Lord Rothschild, who had previously been head of research at Shell. The CPRS survived the change of power from Conservative to Labour in February 1974. Rothschild himself resigned before the second general election of 1974; he was succeeded by Sir Kenneth Berrill, an academic economist who had previously been Head of the Government Economic Service. The CPRS, and Berrill, survived the change of Prime Minister in 1975, when Mr Callaghan replaced Mr Wilson, and the replacement of Labour by Mrs Thatcher's Conservative government in 1979. When Berrill resigned in April 1980, Mrs Thatcher appointed Robin Ibbs, a senior manager in ICI, as head of the CPRS. Ibbs returned to his firm in April 1982 and was succeeded by John Sparrow, from the merchant bank Morgan Grenfell. Mrs Thatcher won a second general election in June 1983. Immediately after the election she announced that the CPRS was no longer needed and was to be abolished.

Many of the documentary sources to which we should like to have turned in writing this book were not available. They are subject to the Official Secrets Act. We have therefore had to rely substantially on our memories and the memories of large numbers of ex-members of the CPRS whom we interviewed in the process of collecting material. Relying on memories is bound to lead to omissions, inaccuracies, and erroneous interpretations. This book cannot therefore be a complete picture of the CPRS and its work; moreover the story it tells may sometimes fail to reflect accurately what happened at the time. Wherever possible, where there has been any doubt about people's accounts we have checked these with others. However, we have not by any means been able to double-check everything we have been told. We are aware therefore that we may sometimes have got it wrong.

Nevertheless we believed when we set out, and we still do, that it was worth trying to put together an account of the CPRS's work. But the definitive history of the CPRS will have to wait until thirty years have passed and the records can be opened up. It will not therefore be before the year 2013 that a future historian can complete a study of the life of the CPRS. This is a long time to wait. We thought therefore that it was worth while writing a short book about this unusual organisation in the interim. It cannot, however, be judged in terms of the usual requirements of social science research. The evidence we needed to meet these requirements was not available. It can best be described as a collective memoir.

As such it could not have been written without the help and co-operation of our ex-colleagues and those who joined the CPRS before and after us. Our gratitude to them is immense. Many of them gave up time to talk to us; some gave up even more time to read and comment on our draft. We have quoted them frequently in our text. All quotations without reference to the source are from our interviews or from written comments sent to us on a draft version of the book.

We would also like to thank the Policy Studies Institute and the Rowntree Memorial Trust for their support in helping us complete this book, by providing a Visiting Fellowship for one of us (Tessa Blackstone).

We are grateful to the following for permission to quote material: the late Baroness Sharp (letter from herself to William Plowden); Sir Donald MacDougall ('The Prime Minister's Statistical Section'); Mr Edward Heath ('Report of the Machinery of Government Group'); Mrs Barbara Castle and George Weidenfeld and Nicolson Limited (*The Castle Diaries*, 1974–76).

Contents

Abbreviations

ACARD	Advisory Council for Applied Research and Development
CBI	Confederation of British Industry
CEGB	Central Electricity Generating Board
CRC	Community Relations Commission
CSD	Civil Service Department
CSO	Central Satistical Office
CSSP	Centre for Studies in Social Policy
DES	Department of Education and Science
DHSS	Department of Health and Social Security
DOE	Department of the Environment
DTI	Department of Trade and Industry
FCO	Foreign and Commonwealth Office
GCHQ	Government Communications Headquarters
GDP	Gross Domestic Project
GLC	Greater London Council
GNP	Gross National Product
IBA	Independent Broadcasting Authority
IBRO	Inter-Bank Research Organization
IMF	International Monetary Fund
JASP	Joint Approach to Social Policy
MAFF	Ministry of Agriculture, Fisheries, and Food
M.o.D.	Ministry of Defence
MSC	Manpower Services Commission
NHS	National Health Service
OECD	Organization for Economic Co-operation and Development
OFTEL	Office of Telecommunications
PAR	Programme Analysis and Review
PESC	Public Expenditure Survey Committee

ABBREVIATIONS

PPBS	Planning, Programming, and Budgeting Systems
RIPA	Royal Institute of Public Administration
ROR	Review of Overseas Representation
ROSS	Review of Social Services
RPI	Retail Price Index
SSRC	Social Science Research Council

1

The Origins of the CPRS

BY THE BEGINNING of the 1980s it had become fashionable to scoff at prescriptions of the kind proposed in the White Paper *The Reorganization of Central Government*, published by Edward Heath's government in October 1970. This proposed 'a major reorganisation of the machinery of central government', in line with the government's aims of reducing the burden on industry and on the country at large, of reducing the overload on the government machine itself, and of increasing the efficiency of government. There would be less government and better government: better analysis of policy, greater clarity about objectives, priorities, and strategy. The means to these ends included the merging of government departments into new, larger units; new ways of analysing government expenditure programmes; and a new centrally located review staff. This was not the language of the 1980s. By then terms such as 'analysis', 'priorities', or 'strategy' seemed too ambitious and high-flown, both to those who regretfully believed that governments were incapable of planning and managing the recovery of Britain and to those who insisted, as a matter of principle, that governments should not try to do so. It was also widely felt that the benefits of reorganization had been grossly exaggerated: some argued that if a government's basic policies were right, its structures could look after themselves; others, that there were too many regrettable examples to show that reorganization was as likely to exacerbate problems as to solve them. Local government and the National Health Service were often cited. When in June 1983 the newly re-elected Mrs Thatcher announced the abolition of the Central Policy Review Staff set up less than thirteen years before, on the grounds that it had become superfluous, this was noted with little comment and less protest, inside or outside government. It seemed to be accepted that this was simply the last, logical step in recognizing that the world had changed, that the nostrums of 1970 were irrelevant to the problems of 1983, and that fashions in administrations are as transitory as any other.

1

But what had been striking about the Central Policy Review Staff, or CPRS, when it was set up in 1970 was how long it had been in gestation, how widespread had been the recognition that something like it was needed, and how logical had been its creation as part of the extended process of improving the central management of government business. Not its establishment, but its abolition was the aberration in a process which had begun, in effect, in 1916 and which by the mid-1980s seemed once again as inexorable, if as slow, as ever.

The process began when Lloyd George replaced Asquith as Prime Minister at the end of 1916. Both the office of Prime Minister, and the Cabinet which the Prime Minister chairs, date in their modern form from that moment. The War Cabinet Secretariat then established, under Colonel Maurice Hankey, contained all the essential elements of the modern Cabinet Secretariat. Henceforth the process of decision-making at the centre of British government would be structured, recorded, and promulgated with an administrative efficiency that many other modern states would not match until many years later, if then. The Cabinet Secretariat, however, was then and to a large extent remained later what its name implies: a secretariat, concerned mainly with the processing of decisions rather than with their content or their implementation; and a secretariat for the Cabinet, with no formal acknowledgement that, within the Cabinet, the Prime Minister might have some special claims and requirements.

The modernity of Lloyd George was reflected in his simultaneous establishment of what would now be called a personal 'think tank', or 'policy unit', in the form of the so-called 'Garden Suburb'. This little group of five men was the precursor of an institution which is still not yet fully established in British government—a Prime Minister's Office. The Cabinet Secretariat, then as for many years afterwards, concentrated on the relatively mechanical work of organizing meetings, preparing the papers for them, recording the outcome, and, as part of this, ensuring that chairmen (the Prime Minister, in the case of the Cabinet) were properly briefed. The 'Garden Suburb', by contrast, was very much concerned with policy. Under the leadership of an Oxford don, Professor W. G. S. Adams, it was in effect the earliest of a number of attempts to strengthen the Prime Minister's hold over central government. During its brief life between December 1916 and 1918 the Garden Suburb processed information for Lloyd George, before and after meetings of the War Cabinet; it commented on departmental and Ministerial proposals coming forward to Cabinet or to 10 Downing Street, and acted as 'progress-chaser' after decisions had been taken. Like many similar staff, its members also helped in resolving difficulties and interdepartmental disputes, thus relieving the Prime Minister and the Cabinet of all but a formal responsibility for the outcome (Turner, 1980).

During the closing stages of the war Lord Haldane's Committee on Machinery of Government tried to distil the conclusions of recent experience and of its members' long years of previous thinking. The Committee aimed to apply rational principles to the procedures of governing. It noted, among other defects, the absence of adequate provision

for the organised acquisition of facts and information, and for the systematic application of thought, as preliminary to the settlement of policy and its subsequent administration (Machinery of Government Committee, 1918).

But no notice was taken either of experience or of the Haldane Committee. The Committee's recommendations were completely ignored. Lloyd George's innovations were decried. The Garden Suburb melted away, as its members drifted one by one into other careers from mid-1918 onwards. When the Conservatives under Bonar Law replaced Lloyd George's government in October 1922 the temporary huts in the garden of Number Ten, which had given the secretariat its name, were demolished. (Hostility to the centralizing style of Lloyd George was so great that the Cabinet Secretariat itself was denounced as unconstitutional; during the 1922 election campaign Bonar Law actually promised to abolish it.) Though the Cabinet Secretariat survived, in the years between the wars the Prime Minister's Office evolved slowly into a unit staffed entirely by civil servants. Hankey consolidated the position of the Secretariat and of himself as its founder and head, but did not formally extend the Secretariat's role. He was succeeded as Cabinet Secretary by Sir Edward Bridges in 1938 and himself became, briefly, Minister without Portfolio in Neville Chamberlain's War Cabinet of September 1939–May 1940.

The Secretariat helped to manage the Cabinet's business in orderly fashion, but did little to ensure that the business done was that which most needed doing. In a celebrated critique of the inter-war Cabinet which was still wholly relevant a generation later Leo Amery complained:

The one thing that is hardly ever discussed is general policy . . . There is very little Cabinet policy, as such, on any subject. No one has time to think it out, to discuss it, to co-ordinate its various elements, or to see to its prompt and consistent enforcement. There are only departmental policies . . . (Daalder, 1964).

When Churchill became Prime Minister in 1940 he attempted to impose some central control on the situation. Breaking with evolving practice, and harking back to Lloyd George, he brought with him from the Admiralty a small, entirely personal staff under Professor Lindemann. Lindemann himself had been Churchill's adviser at the Admiralty, originally on scientific matters, but, within a month, on statistical issues as well. Half a dozen young academic economists were recruited. The staff 'was to collect and co-ordinate Admiralty and cognate statistics for the First Lord and also to advise him on wider matters with which he was concerned as a member of the War Cabinet' (MacDougall, 1951. See also MacDougall, 1978, 1987). When Churchill moved to Number Ten, the staff moved with him. Lindemann became Lord Cherwell in 1941, and Paymaster General in 1942, and the staff advised and briefed him as well as Churchill. Staff members also took part in other Whitehall activities, such as interdepartmental committees. But their main task continued to be supplying the information which Cherwell then passed on to the Prime Minister, as their principal client.

The work, and the general approach, of the section were well described in an article written by one of its members shortly after the end of the war. There is much in this that was to be relevant, twenty-five years later, to the new CPRS.

The total establishment was in the neighbourhood of twenty. On the average there were perhaps half a dozen economists; one scientific officer; one established Civil Servant (with economic training) to help keep the amateurs on the rails; some half a dozen [human] computers; two or three typists and clerks; and last, but not least, a number of what were called 'chartists'—about four were fully employed in the early period when there was much drawing of new charts and diagrams.

The staff had contacts with nearly every Ministry, most of all with the Service and supply departments. They dealt with departmental officers at all levels, and Lord Cherwell had much conversation and correspondence with the various Ministers. Work was informal and intimate, and Lord Cherwell spent much of his time in discussion with his staff.

The main method of communication with the Prime Minister, apart from tables and charts submitted regularly, was through minutes from Lord Cherwell supplemented by his frequent discussions with the Prime Minister.

Some of the minutes were comments on official papers circulated to the Cabinet or Cabinet committees; some commented on minutes sent by other Ministers to the Prime Ministers; many were written in response to requests by the Prime Minister for information and an opinion on specific topics; many raised matters which Lord Cherwell, on his own initiative, wished to bring to the Prime Minister's attention.

A minute from Lord Cherwell recommending action might occasionally form the basis of a directive by the Prime Minister, after consultation with the Ministers concerned. More often the Prime Minister would address an inquiry to the appropriate departmental Minister or Ministers, or ask a Minister without departmental responsibility to conduct an inquiry and report. The Ministerial reply would normally be passed to Lord Cherwell for comment. When a new line of policy was settled the Prime Minister would sometimes ask for periodic progress reports which would in turn be examined by the Section (MacDougall, 1951).

This article did not comment on the nature of the working relationships between the Statistical Section and Whitehall. They were not cordial.

4

Cherwell, it was said, 'detested bureaucrats', who responded 'with suspicion, if not disfavour and fear' (Daalder, 1964).

Cherwell himself, a man of acknowledged personal courage, has been described as 'exceedingly self-assured and often vindictive', contemptuous of those who disagreed with him. The Prime Minister's personal minutes, effective though they often were, were resented in Whitehall, and Cherwell's part in composing them was resented even more (Daalder, 1964).

Churchill, like Lloyd George, was an interventionist, authoritarian Prime Minister who came to power in wartime and whose methods were widely felt to be inappropriate in times of peace. When the Conservatives were defeated in July 1945 Lord Cherwell and the Statistical Section went with Churchill, and were not replaced; Attlee's personal staffing arrangements were much more like those of Neville Chamberlain. The Cabinet Secretariat, under Sir Edward Bridges, continued to play much the same neutral or administrative role that Hankey had developed for it before the war.

However, in the early days of the Attlee government one development did for a few months provide Ministers collectively with advice as well as with purely secretarial services, on economic matters at least. Following the serious economic crisis of 1946–7, a new joint interdepartmental planning staff was set up to prepare long-term economic plans and to advise on the adjustment of existing plans to changing circumstances. It was to have a full-time head, supported by his own small staff and secretariat. He would work under the Lord President (Herbert Morrison), who was responsible for co-ordinating domestic economic policy, and would have access to all Ministers concerned with production. The first Chief Planning Officer was Sir Edwin Plowden (father of one of the authors of this book), one of the many temporary civil servants who had come into Whitehall from the private sector at the beginning of the war.

Later the same year, faced with continuing economic difficulties, Attlee appointed Sir Stafford Cripps as Minister for Economic Affairs; Cripps took over the Economic Planning Staff and other supporting staff. But when, in the autumn, Cripps became Chancellor of the Exchequer on the unexpected resignation of Dalton, he took with him to the Treasury the Chief Planning Officer and his staff. Henceforth there was no alternative focus, or source of advice for Ministers other than the Chancellor, on economic and financial matters. After 1947 the arrangements in Whitehall for providing central, i.e. non-departmental, advice and analysis were once again as rudimentary as they had been at all times except during the highly personal regimes of Lloyd George and Churchill. Though the Cabinet Secretary was inevitably closer to the Prime Minister than to other Ministers, he had no formal status as Prime Ministerial adviser, and no staffing support which would have helped him to do such a job effectively. Prime Ministers had individual confidants who sat in Number Ten with titles such as Prime Minister's Personal Secretary. But these were personal arrangements, virtually appointments at court, of a kind that would have been familiar in the eighteenth century. Harold Macmillan's John Wyndham is perhaps the extreme example. Marcia Williams, later Lady Falkender, provided a broadly similar service, though in an utterly different style, for Harold Wilson between 1964 and 1970. But the mere mention of these exceedingly informal arrangements, artlessly recorded in the participants' memoirs, shows how little progress there had been, if any, since the days of the Garden Suburb.

The foundations for something much more systematic were laid during the period of Labour government, and Conservative opposition, between 1965 and 1970. During these years Edward Heath, the new leader of the Conservative party, received and commissioned a great deal of advice on ways of improving the structures and processes of government. An old-style committee, chaired by Sir Edward Boyle, reviewed the Cabinet system; it reported in early 1966, with a range of proposals which had virtually nothing to say about the most central structures of all, 10 Downing Street and the Cabinet Office. The style of the report is perhaps conveyed by its comment on Number Ten: 'We feel it right that it should continue to consist of a small number of high-calibre young men.' More radical was the thinking of the several teams of businessmen and other analysts set up under the nominal oversight of Ernest Marples, who had been Minister of Transport in the previous Conservative government. Prompted by young Conservatives such as David Howell, MP and Mark Schreiber, these advisers came up with the idea of totally restructuring the centre of government; a new 'Central Capability' was to bring together the Cabinet Office, the Civil Service Department, and the public expenditure side of the Treasury. Its task would be to help the new Conservative government to plan its strategy, to link resource allocation to planning, and to monitor the implementation of plans and budgets in all parts of government. At the centre of all this a new 'Crown Consultancy Unit', based in the Cabinet Office and reporting directly to the Prime Minister, would have a continuing task of advising on the modernization of the public sector and its processes, starting in Whitehall.

While all this work was being done under official party auspices Edward Heath had made some much less elaborate arrangements to provide himself with some personal advice on the machinery of central government. In the spring of 1968 there came into being a small working group of former civil servants, chaired by the formidable Baroness Sharp, who had recently retired as Permanent Secretary at the Ministry of Housing and Local Government. Its task was to review the machinery of central government, and its client was Mr Heath.

The origins of the group went back several years; they were rooted in a general dissatisfaction with the working of the centre of Whitehall in particular, based on personal experience. As Lady Sharp later recalled:

In the particular sphere in which I worked—local government, housing, new towns, land use, planning, etc.—the machinery [of government] did not work well. There was a great deal of overlapping between departments and a great deal of friction. I remember bitter arguments between myself and the Board of Trade (responsible for the distribution of industry) about the siting of new towns; and again of course with the Ministry of Agriculture. Sometimes these disputes were taken to the Cabinet for settlement which took up a lot of their time and did not necessarily produce the right result. There was also a lot of chopping and changing in the distribution of responsibilities between Departments . . . But there seemed to be no way of settling the Departmental pattern in the interests of good government. It was nobody's business (Sharp, 1982).

Lady Sharp added that as she watched overburdened Ministers ploughing through the contents of their Ministerial 'red boxes', she wondered if they ought to have more help in considering subjects outside their own departments' fields but on which they would be expected to make sensible comments in Cabinet or Cabinet committees.

Lady Sharp's account continued:

One day . . . Mr. MacMillan, then Prime Minister (whom I had known well at [the Ministry of] Housing and Local Government) asked me to lunch . . . One thing he said was: 'It's a strange thing that I have now got the biggest job I ever had and less help in doing it than I have ever known.' And that clicked with my growing notion that there was a gap in the machinery of government at the centre. Should there be a Prime Minister's Department? Or a staff to serve the Prime Minister and Cabinet Ministers?

Some years later, when the Conservatives were in opposition, Lady Sharp shared these thoughts with their leader Edward Heath. It was agreed that a group of retired senior civil servants should be set up to advise Mr Heath on the machinery of government, and that Lady Sharp should take the chair. The group included Sir Henry Hardman, Permanent Secretary, Ministry of Defence, 1964–6, F. A. Bishop, Permanent Secretary, Ministry of Land and Natural Resources, 1964–5, Sir Eric Roll, Permanent Secretary, Department of Economic Affairs, 1964–6, and James Robertson, a former senior official in the Ministry of Defence who had also been private secretary to the Secretary of the Cabinet. One of the authors of this book (William Plowden), then a lecturer in government at the London School of Economics, acted as secretary.

In November 1968 Mr Heath wrote to Lady Sharp, asking for the group's views on several specific topics, including the organization of a 'Prime Minister's Department'. The group discussed this question in the first of its several reports, submitted to Mr Heath the following February. The report commented on the Cabinet's preoccupation with short-term problems. It noted also the weak position of the Prime Minister himself, who, despite his central role, 'has normally had no agency on which to call for objective advice or for help in evaluating his colleagues' *ex parte* statements, other than the tiny personal staff located at No. 10.'

The report's solution to these problems was the creation of a new 'Office of the Prime Minister and Cabinet', with the basic tasks of 'co-ordination, planning, research and study, management and organization services at government levels'. Its responsibilities were to include the Cabinet Secretariat, Civil Service personnel management and management services and, most important, the planning of priorities—'the crucial task of enabling the Government to identify its main objectives, to relate individual decisions to their wider context and, in doing so, to co-ordinate its own activities'. This task would be performed by a small central staff, alongside the Cabinet Secretariat and headed by a 'Chief Planning Officer' equivalent in rank to the Cabinet Secretary. It was to be supported by a permanent research unit. Its advice would

enable the Government, once its major purposes had been established, to ensure that the means by which these were implemented were compatible with each other; and whether existing activities were compatible with them . . . . and to determine whether apparently unrelated proposals coming forward from departments were consistent with them, in both the short and the long term . . . (Machinery of Government Group, 1969).

Edward Heath discussed this report with its authors, but kept his own counsel about his reaction to its recommendations, including that for an Office of Prime Minister and Cabinet. While the group was at work Heath had in fact had some rather similar advice—which was shown to the group—from another source. Lord Plowden and Lord Roberthall, formerly Chief Planner (see p. 5) and Chief Economic Adviser respectively, sent Mr Heath a short memorandum noting the long-felt need by Prime Ministers and non-departmental Ministers for 'impartial advice on matters with a high context of expertise which come to Cabinet from Departmental Ministers'. Cabinet Office briefing was of little help, being at most 'the quintessence of civil service impartiality—"On the one hand . . . on the other . . .".' What the Prime Minister, and his non-departmental colleagues, needed was a 'relatively small staff of able people who can examine proposals from Departments . . . from the point of view of the whole national interest in the short and especially in the long-term . . . Such a body could also bring out the real issues at the root of a conflict of advice, which can usually be resolved into different views about the aims of policy or different

8

estimates of probability.' This staff would work to a senior Minister, possibly the Prime Minister himself; especially since it would be 'bitterly opposed by existing Whitehall departments', the Prime Minister would need to make clear his own backing for it and to ensure that the Cabinet was agreed on the need for it (Plowden and Roberthall, 1968).

This advice, too, was absorbed by its recipient with little perceptible response. He may have been preoccupied with reading and digesting the bulkier proposals, for more elaborate policy-making arrangements, which were reaching him at about the same time from the official party advisory machinery. The party's thinking was refined—and summarized for public consumption—by David Howell. Also involved was a friend of Heath's, Lord Jellicoe. He was to become Lord Privy Seal and Minister in charge of the Civil Service Department in the 1970 government; Howell became his Parliamentary Secretary. Howell and Jellicoe were still pressing for the 'big bang' Central Capability, and for the inclusion in this of a number of outside appointments from the business world.

While all this advice, official and unofficial, was being generated by the Opposition party, minds inside Whitehall were also thinking along some partly parallel lines. Some, like Sir Richard ('Otto') Clarke, were preoccupied with the reordering of the functions now divided between the Treasury, the Cabinet Office, the Civil Service Department (created following the Fulton Report in 1968), and Number Ten. Almost every possible permutation was considered, as was to happen again in 1980: an 'executive office of the Prime Minister', on the lines of the Office of Management and Budget, which had been established in the United States in 1968; abolition of the CSD and recreation of the old-style Treasury; a massive Prime Minister's department, embracing the CSD, the Cabinet Office, the expenditure divisions of the Treasury, plus central management services; and others. Otto Clarke's own thinking at the time was later reflected in the lectures he gave at the Civil Service College in the spring of 1971 (Clarke, 1971). Implicit in most of these arrangements was an enriching of the neutral approach of the Cabinet Secretariat by bringing it closer to people concerned to think and advise on the substance of policies.

Others, like the Secretary of the Cabinet, Sir Burke Trend, and the Head of the Civil Service, Sir William Armstrong, were more concerned about the lack of any central 'thinking' capacity which could offset the centrifugal tendencies of Whitehall, and about the ease with which departments putting forward proposals on complex and technical issues could secure Cabinet agreement without adequate understanding or discussion—the problem which had worried Plowden and Roberthall. There was no central staff whose task it was to help Ministers to develop a strategy for the government as a whole, to guide the Cabinet's thinking about government as opposed to departmental priorities, and to ensure that the actions of individual Ministers were consistent with each other. In recent years several specialized units had been established at the centre: the Social Services Unit, the Scientific Unit, the Population Unit, and the standing Royal Commission on Environmental Pollution. Another later example was the Information Technology Unit (see Chapter 7). All of them were linked to the Cabinet Office but each operated separately and with quite unrelated objectives. Most of them were established, not so much to provide central thinking as to demonstrate Ministers' concern for, and to devise policy on, issues which were perceived to be of some political importance.

Trend, Armstrong, and others were discussing these questions well before the general election of June 1970 and the arrival of the new Conservative government. Trend's natural interest in strengthening the Cabinet Secretariat was countered by the interest of William Armstrong, then probably at the height of his influence, in enlarging and consolidating the authority of the Civil Service Department. The outcome, perhaps predictably, was a rejection of all the 'big' solutions. When, after the election, officials first got together with Conservative advisers such as Mark Schreiber, solutions such as a 'Central Capability' or a 'Prime Minister's Office' were ruled out. The preferred option was to leave the CSD and Treasury as they were, but to strengthen the Cabinet Secretariat slightly by adding to it some specialized staff to help Ministers to think about priorities. By midsummer this had been agreed in principle. The details were worked out during the autumn. Howell and Jellicoe continued for several months to press the case for something closer to a Prime Minister's Department. 'Some of us', Howell said later, 'wanted . . . a staff for Number 10 for the Prime Minister, rather more like today's Policy Unit which the present Prime Minister has in Number 10, and less a general body to serve all the Cabinet. We thought that Number 10 was under-equipped to deal with the great departments of state' (Hennessy, 1986).

But their view did not prevail. In August John Mayne, a member of the Cabinet Office on secondment from the Ministry of Defence, was given the task of expressing both the principles and the details in official prose. It was his formulation of both which—to the distress of Howell and Jellicoe—appeared in the October 1970 White Paper *The Reorganization of Central Government* (Cmnd. 4506). This announced the establishment of 'a small multi-disciplinary staff in the Cabinet Office . . .'.

2

The Case for Advice at the Centre

THE OFFICIAL CASE for the creation of the CPRS was expressed mainly in terms of the weakness of the central structure of Whitehall in relation to strategic planning and of co-ordinating the multifarious activities of different departments. 'In recent years', said the White Paper,

it has become clear that the structure of inter-departmental committees, each concerned with a separate area of policy, needs to be reinforced by a clear and comprehensive definition of government strategy which can be systematically developed to take account of changing circumstances and can provide a framework within which a Government's policies as a whole may be more effectively formulated. For lack of such a clear definition of strategic purpose and under the pressures of the day to day problems immediately before them, governments are always at some risk of losing sight of the need to consider the totality of their current policies in relation to their longer term objectives; and they may pay too little attention to the difficult, but critical, task of evaluating as objectively as possible the alternative policy options and priorities open to them (*Reorganization of Central Government*, 1970).

This critique, fairly general in tone, avoided singling out any identifiable group (including the Cabinet) for hostile comment. Perhaps partly as a result, it found support among politicians and civil servants alike. Its conclusion was that the small staff mentioned at the end of the previous chapter should work, under the supervision of the Prime Minister, for Ministers collectively. It was to enable them to

take better policy decisions by assisting them to work out the implications of their basic strategy in terms of policies in specific areas, to establish the relative priorities to be given to the different sectors of their programme as a whole, to identify those areas of policy in which new choices can be exercised and to ensure that the underlying implications of alternative courses of action are fully analysed and considered.

These conclusions, and the analysis that led up to them, masked some much harsher critiques both of the working of governments in general and of

11

particular British institutions. Many of those who have pressed for the establishment, retention, or reintroduction of the CPRS have done so from a perspective more sharply critical of Whitehall than the rather bland language of the 1970 White Paper would suggest.

Some of these critics saw the CPRS as a way of correcting defects common to many governments. As a singular collective noun, 'government' implies a comforting unity of thought and purpose. The word, obviously, suggests that governments do indeed 'govern', in a range of senses including planning, steering, regulating, implementing, and generally managing the systems of which they have charge. Governments—except in extreme circumstances— are aware, coherent, authoritative.

Little space need be taken here in explaining that this is rarely so. The reality is much more confused. 'Governments', in all forms of regime in all parts of the world, are pluralistic, divided, under-informed, short-sighted, only partly in control of their own processes, and unable to guarantee the outcomes which they promise. There are enormous gaps, and sometimes no linkages at all, between realities, perceptions, decisions, actions, and consequences. The collective interest is too often dominated and distorted by sectional interests; 'rational' decisions are distorted by political considerations; there is an excessive focus on the short term. The responses to new problems are incremental rather than radical. Individual decisions are often inconsistent with each other, with existing policies, and with any overall objectives that the government may have defined.

The main factors at work are probably the nature of bureaucracies, the fragmented nature of governments, the incongruity between politics and management, and the weakness of leaders in the modern world. Government bureaucracies, like bureaucracies everywhere, are typically large, well-established, hierarchically organized, with their own equally well-established links with other organizations and individuals, their own implicit (and sometimes explicit) sense of priorities and value systems. Certain styles of doing things become customary, and are slow to change. Attitudes and values become strongly entrenched: proposals which are discordant with these are likely to be rejected with little consideration of any merits they may have. The pace of change is constrained not only by internal practices, but also by external relationships: a department of agriculture does not find it easy to risk the wrath of the farmers by cutting back on subsidies, or a department of trade or industry to pursue policies which private firms see as damaging. Departments become locked into relationships and into broad policy stances which often flow from these. Officials at all levels often find it genuinely hard to grasp that a particular cherished policy has failed, and are genuinely reluctant to accept the need for a change of direction.

The Case for Advice at the Centre

The difficulties faced by those at the top wanting to change direction derive partly from their lack of information about what is going on lower down. Sometimes they do not know even the most basic facts about what their departments are doing, about the distribution of departmental resources among the many functions carried out. They often have even less idea about the effectiveness, or otherwise, of those functions—either because no way has been agreed of measuring their effectiveness or because their subordinates prefer to let them believe that all is going as well as possible, whether it is or not.

The problems are exacerbated when these subordinates are permanent officials and those at the top are politicians—and thus, almost by definition, temporary. In virtually all governments of the world Ministers, elected or appointed, are typically laymen in the subject-matter of their departments. Most of them do not get the chance to become experts because they hold any particular post for such a short time—often for two or three years at most. The Soviet Union is a striking exception (Blondel, 1985). Coming into office with a set of objectives, an ideology, a manifesto commitment, or sometimes simply a generalized personal ambition, Ministers then have to apply these to the untidy and confusing real world through the bureaucracy of which they are in charge. Sometimes most of their subordinates are permanent career officials and so know much more than their Ministers about their department's areas of activity. Those of them that have come in with the Minister may know as little as he does about these matters—or even about government. The more nearly Ministers or advisers are professional politicians the less likely they are to have managerial skills or experience. Nor are they likely to possess the skills of analysis and scientific problem solving.

One reason for this is that these are not the skills most useful in the political process, and thus in government. The short-run need for electoral or other forms of popular support, the need to put the best possible appearance on everything, the need to pay debts to old supporters or to give favours to potential new ones, can make it necessary to ignore economic or managerial rationality. The conclusions of analysis can be totally convincing in every sense except a political one, and for that reason alone can be set aside.

In addition, political leaders are always likely to exploit the inherent defects of the system to their own advantage. Often reluctant to subordinate their own sectional interests to overall government policy, Ministers in charge of departments will at times exacerbate the propensity of their own officials to go their own way. One of the chief problems faced by heads of governments is the fragmented nature of the systems they head: the sectional interests of the several bureaucracies—industry against agriculture against foreign affairs, and finance against everybody—overlie and reinforce the political and personal rivalries between individual Ministers.

13

Professor Yehezkel Dror has argued that 'rulers'—a traditional term to which he has given new currency—are so important in modern government that improving their performance is central to any programme of redesigning governmental systems. The performance of rulers—i.e. the quality of decisions that they take—is weakened by factors inherent in the very processes in which rulers are involved: 'overload', stress, and strain, the manipulation of information by colleagues and subordinates, 'court politics', excessive deference on the part of most of their advisers, and so on. One way of counteracting these defects, Dror argues, is by improving the quality of policy analysis available to rulers (Dror, 1984).

These problems are if anything more severe in collective decision-making. This has two weaknesses. First is the implicit assumption, which applies also to the adversarial process in law, that the product of competing sectional points of view will be an outcome which most nearly serves the common purposes of the organization as a whole—and, secondly, the complementary absence of any capacity at the centre with the task of trying to identify what those common purposes might be. In other words, individual departments state their sectional cases as best they can. The Prime Minister, at the centre, adjudicates between these different viewpoints and tries to elicit the most appropriate collective decision. But because the Prime Minister's job is, in theory, not to impose a case of his own but to synthesize those of his colleagues, he is not thought to need a department of his own to help him to make such a case. Hence the absence of anything that could be called a Prime Minister's department. Lord Hunt, formerly Secretary to the British Cabinet, observes of this process:

The theory on which our system of servicing our Prime Minister is based is that advice on any subject is given by the responsible departmental Minister; and, of course, it is his view that the Prime Minister will most want to hear and which will no doubt normally prevail (Hunt, 1983).

When the Cabinet is faced with the need to take a decision about a problem or about a new proposal from one of its members, both it and the Prime Minister in the chair require advice on several different things. They require advice about the basic facts of the existing situation and about the effectiveness of existing policies in dealing with that situation. It should not need saying that advice on situations or policies must include advice on areas for which individual departmental Ministers are notionally responsible, whether or not it is felt that the latter should be left to get on with implementing the relevant policies. The point is, of course, that activities which in a managerial sense are wholly the responsibility of a particular Minister are none the less the concern of his or her Cabinet colleagues in a political sense: first, because the wrong

14

decision can affect the standing of the government as a whole; second, because decisions on even apparently isolated issues can have repercussions for the programmes and policies of other departments.

Advice is also needed on several aspects of new proposals brought forward for Cabinet discussions; about their true costs, about their likely impact, about their side-effects, and about their long-term effects. It follows logically that advice is also needed about alternative options. Such options must include the possibility of spending more, rather than less; even if the overall objective of the government be to contain public expenditure, any government without a totally distorted sense of priorities must be interested in advice about better outcomes and in enhanced effectiveness, whether or not the implications for resources are neutral or negative. The question, in effect, is where the marginal pound will have the greatest impact.

Critics of the collective principle will argue that when considering expenditure decisions, advice is not needed on decisions which have no net effect on the departmental budgets of individual Ministers, adding that if such advice is available it will only encourage other Ministers to meddle in matters which are not their business. It is true that there is a sound managerial case for leaving Ministers, responsible for managing their own shares of the government's resources, to do so without outside intervention from their less expert colleagues. This argument may seem all the stronger where a Minister's decision does not affect his department's total expenditure and thus seems to have a short-run impact on his colleagues' budgets. But this line is no more convincing in relation to expenditure decisions than it is generally. A department's particular current share of governmental resources is not sacrosanct. It is simply a product of history and of decisions taken in the distant past and not corrected. It may be the more or less arbitrary result of generations of incremental increases and decreases in spending programmes. The opportunity cost of an over-inflated, ineffective spending programme in one department may be inability to develop more effective new activities in others.

If it is accepted that collective advice should be available for collective decisions what is the most appropriate source for such advice? From where should the Cabinet get advice on and between economic, social, and other priorities? There are several alternatives. Should it simply be individual Ministers, briefed by their departments? It can be argued, and often is by departments and their Ministers, that it is pointless to have expert departments if their advice does not prevail.

But there are several reasons for not allowing departments to be the sole source of collective advice. First, because they are inevitably sectional interests themselves, representing other sectional interests. Lord Hunt continued that departmental advice

is, however, advice from one point of view only—and one which is inevitably more concerned with the particular problems of the departments concerned than with the government's overall strategy (Hunt, 1983).

Second, even the most comprehensive sum of departmental views will not necessarily cover all aspects of the situation, particularly if it is a new type of situation, nor even take account of all the major interests affected. Third, executive bodies like spending departments find it hard to be objective about their own programmes or about proposals which impinge on these. They prefer to avoid questions which challenge these programmes.

These remarks apply to all departments—including the Treasury. It is sometimes suggested, often by Treasury officials, that the Treasury has a unique claim to be the main source of advice to the Cabinet on its priorities and on the shape of its strategy. Undeniably the central role of the Treasury is of great importance. The Treasury's overall responsiblity for economic policy and for the control of public expenditure gives it an overseeing role in relation to all departments. However, it cannot take on the task of co-ordinating strategy, nor be the sole source of collective advice, because in certain crucial respects it is *parti pris*. Thus, because part of its job is to *control* public expenditure, it has a vested interest in minimizing expenditure wherever it can. It could not therefore be expected to be neutral towards those parts of the government's strategy that involved the spending departments. Its starting-point would inevitably be that proposals for expenditure should be limited, pared down, or constrained in some way. Moreover, to quote Lord Hunt again, 'The Treasury, being primarily concerned with the effect which *total* spending will have on the domestic economy, tends to be neutral as between particular spending plans' (Hunt, 1983). Or as one head of the CPRS put it, 'The Treasury doesn't care much whether it cuts hospitals or defence spending'. We would add that even in relation to total levels of public expenditure the Treasury's advice needs tempering by advice from other sources. To vest in the Treasury further powers in the areas of formulating strategy or co-ordinating policies would not be satisfactory for these reasons.

Hard though it is to envisage any other way of structuring the activities of modern government than through some system of departments, such a structure hampers any effort that a government may make to plan a consistent overall strategy and to see that the parts fit with the whole. There are two main reasons for this. First, the *overall* strategy may not be adequately formulated under a departmental structure: each department is concerned with its own area of government and its own function so cannot take responsibility for it. As a result the objectives and priorities of the government as a whole may never be adequately formulated. Second, even if such a strategy does exist, it may be difficult to impose this on departments. This can be hard enough in a presidential system. In a cabinet system where the Prime Minister is in theory only *primus inter pares* it can be impossible.

The consequence is that powerful Ministers heading important departments can drive the government in directions which the Prime Minister and Cabinet colleagues either do not want or have not fully thought through. The Cabinet can be, in principle, collectively responsible for decisions which, in practice, some of its members do not understand and may disagree with. In such circumstances the doctrine of collective responsibility can look extremely threadbare.

The logic of this analysis is that some source of advice is needed elsewhere than in departments. This must mean at the centre. In presidential systems this source will typically be found in an extended presidential staff or executive office. In some parliamentary systems—for example, Canada or Australia—there is a strong central prime minister's office. Even these are only partial solutions to the problem, since they normally serve only the president or prime minister, not the other senior members of the governments. But in Britain even this partial solution is missing. British Prime Ministers have traditionally been served by minuscule staffs of civil servants, and by the Cabinet Secretary and his staff in the intervals of doing their other jobs. Only in recent years have there been added Prime Ministerial policy units staffed by political sympathizers. Even with these the scale and capacity of the Prime Minister's support system is painfully limited compared with that in most other governments. There has been, commented Lord Hunt, 'in the absence of our system of a Chief Executive with his own supporting staff, a "hole in the centre of government" . . . which an overworked Cabinet seemed incapable of filling' (Hunt, 1983).

Some might argue that this 'hole' should be filled by individual Ministers themselves. Tony Benn told us, 'I am not in favour of the CPRS. Ministers should do their own thinking and *we* should use the *Party* Committees in forward analysis' (Benn, 1982). Mrs Thatcher seemed to share this view when, at the start of her first administration in 1979, she took a very restrictive line towards the appointment of 'special advisers' by her Cabinet colleagues. But can this be realistic in today's circumstances? It hardly seems to fit the facts either of the Ministerial way of life or—overlapping with that—of parliamentary procedures.

British Cabinet Ministers frequently work a twelve- to fourteen-hour day, six days a week. One reason for this is that, unlike their counterparts in countries such as France, they must continue even when they become

Ministers to undertake work for their constituents and to play an important part in Parliament. Constituency demands on a Cabinet Minister will vary. If the seat is held by a large majority, relatively little 'nursing' need be done. By contrast, MPs for marginal seats, whether Ministers or not, will feel the need to put quite a lot of effort into constituency work. If the constituency is hard to reach from London its MP, whether a Minister or not, has the additional problem of long and tiring journeys.

All this is on top of long and tiring hours in Parliament. The British House of Commons sits for considerably longer than legislatures in other democratic countries. The number of sittings ending at or after midnight has grown. Ministers, as members of Government, must be available to vote loyally on all occasions when the Whips require this whatever the time of day or night. In recent years Ministers in both Labour and Conservative governments have been brought back from China in order to vote. Ministers must, of course, also answer questions on the work of their department and take part in debates. They must appear, more often than in the past, before Select Committees. Such appearances require more lengthy and more careful preparation, as the level of information and advice to Select Committees improves. Desirable though this is, it adds to Ministerial burdens; the extra work involved may still further reduce Ministers' capacity to stand back to think about central questions of strategy.

To this must be added a Minister's role as Head of a Department of State. At all times the development of policy and the day-to-day business of a department will require a massive amount of energy on the part of the Minister. At a time of crisis, or when a major piece of legislation is being steered through Parliament, the work entailed becomes greater still. To do the job properly Ministers need to be in frequent and regular contact with their senior civil servants. They also need to be in regular contact with the 'clients' of the department, whether these be industrialists, doctors, local authorities, financial institutions, the professions, or the recipients of social services. There can be a multitude of different 'clients'. The growth of very large departments such as the DHSS, the DOE, and the combined Department of Trade and Industry has certain advantages for the co-ordination of closely associated areas of policy. But the burdens on Ministers in charge of such departments are enormous.

Ministerial burdens are increasingly international as well as domestic. Foreign travel is common. This is true of Ministers responsible for domestic departments as well as those with traditional overseas interests such as the Foreign Office and the Department of Trade and Industry. For Ministers in departments such as Agriculture Britain's membership of the EEC involves frequent visits to Brussels.

18

If it is impractical for Ministers to fill the 'hole in the centre', could the task be performed by the Civil Service? This question raises issues of structure, skills, style, and values. In their most basic form, few of these are peculiar to the British Civil Service, but—in Britain as elsewhere—the precise nature of the issue is shaped by local circumstances.

The problem of 'departmentalism' has already been mentioned. Most British officials spend most of their working lives in the same department. This reinforces their propensity to pursue the sectional rather than the general interest. Departmental officials' first loyalty is, inevitably, mainly to their own department. Their judgements about new policies are affected by the ethos and interests of that department. They can and will advise about the implications of new policies for the department and for its existing policies, and about the position of departmental policy in the overall strategy. But they find it much harder to advise about the government's strategy from a non-departmental perspective, and they often see no need to do so. Lord Rothschild, the first head of the CPRS, used to tell of his dismay, during discussion of some major issue in a Cabinet committee, at noticing that the briefing of the Minister next to him consisted solely of the words 'There is no departmental interest in this item'. Nor is it easy for officials objectively to monitor their own policies to make sure they are consistent with the government's strategy.

Some more fundamental features of the British senior Civil Service cast doubt on its ability to fill the hole in the centre adequately. The senior Civil Service is hierarchical, relatively homogeneous, bound by rigid rules of official secrecy, and generalist rather than expert. It has many strengths but its weaknesses have become increasingly apparent to outside commentators, to those who have worked in Whitehall on a temporary basis, notably as advisers to Ministers, and to some civil servants within the system.

The hierarchical structure has a number of consequences for policy-making. Few people have access to the whole range of information and analysis that is relevant to key decisions. Those who do, tend to be at the top of the hierarchy and consequently have to absorb information, argue and decide about a wide range of subjects of which it is hard for them to obtain more than a superficial grasp. Much time is spent by junior administrators who have done the work on specific problems briefing more senior officials. Ministers as a rule only have contacts with those fairly high up the hierarchy. They infrequently discuss the possible options with those who are likely to be the best informed about them.

The homogeneity of the top echelons of the bureaucracy has been criticized by a number of commentators. Much of this criticism has focused on the narrow social and educational background of its members. It is a predominantly male, upper middle class, public school and Oxbridge educated group. Only in 1986 did graduates from institutions other than Oxford and

Cambridge secure, for the first time, more than half the places in the Civil Service's 'fast stream' entry competition. Recent recruits have been drawn from a somewhat wider background than in the past and there has been a marked increase in the number of women entering the administrative stream. Perhaps more important than the personal backgrounds of senior civil servants are their career experiences. The typical civil servant joins the Whitehall system in his or her early twenties and stays for a lifetime. Associated with this fact are several other characteristics: few civil servants have any experience of other professions or occupational milieux; because few leave, few arrive, so there is little infiltration of the bureaucracy from outside, which might bring in new ideas and new methods. This gives rise to a closed society where the process of socialization which newcomers endure has a powerful effect in imposing conformity which cannot easily be broken down by counter-influences from outside. Few senior civil servants have experience of the provinces; they spend their working lives in the metropolis. Their confinement to the world of Whitehall and the narrowness of their experience seem likely to limit their understanding of some of the contemporary social and economic problems they face, however powerful their intellects.

The inward-looking nature of Whitehall is reinforced by the operation of the Official Secrets Act. Official secrecy is strictly enforced by written codes which lay down general principles and rules of conduct for the Civil Service including regulations about the disclosure of information. Whilst leaks are frequent and are sometimes instigated by officials rather than Ministers, most civil servants feel bound by the rules and are reticent towards outsiders. Indeed, distrust of outsiders and of other cultures could be said to be central to the culture of Whitehall, for the reasons we have already given. But even where individual civil servants believe in greater openness, they must tread carefully for the sanctions against revealing so-called official secrets are considerable. The lack of openness imposed by the Official Secrets Act has a number of disadvantages. Possible options fail to be considered, which might have emerged had there been more public discussion. The consequences of those options which are put forward may well be less well understood because of the lack of any public debate about them. It is frequently difficult to draw on valuable expertise while policies are being analysed and reviewed.

Other characteristics of the British Civil Service inhibit its ability either to do effective policy analysis or to innovate. Relatively few senior officials in what used to be called 'administrative' grades were educated or trained as scientists or social scientists. (The economist and other specialist groupings are obviously different.) A 'scientific' approach to problems does not come naturally to them. Indeed, what might perhaps be called the 'forensic' mode is more common than the scientific, even in internal discussions, where the capacity of a case to prevail will often depend on the ability of its protagonists to defend it in debate with other interests. This kind of ability is high among the skills needed by the 'generalists' who still fill most senior posts in Whitehall. It is now some twenty years since the Fulton Committee recommended that there should be greater specialization by administrative stream civil servants. This was neither accepted at the time nor has it been since. The basic case for specialization has been put by one of us elsewhere.

As governments have become more interventionist and the world in which they operate more complex, the job of civil servants has demanded more expert knowledge about particular areas of policy. In many areas there are large amounts of complicated detail to be absorbed as well as a broad understanding of the role of the various participants. This includes knowledge about the often diverse providers of a public service and their interrelationships as well as the needs of the clients. The capacity to absorb information rapidly, the possession of analytical skills to evaluate existing policies or new proposals, and sufficient creativity and imagination to put forward new ideas on how to meet political objectives are all required. A good deal of attention has been paid to how to find the right people for the job and how to select them fairly and efficiently. Those who are recruited are usually of high intellectual calibre and many of them probably have the right personal qualities to do the job well. How to develop this potential and deploy people effectively once they have arrived and thereafter is perhaps given too little attention. Careful career planning is needed. Further training may have a role. But experience acquired on the job will also be vital. Without specialisation there is a danger that this experience will be so disparate that effectiveness is impaired (Blackstone, 1980).

It can also be argued that if greater specialization led to expertise in particular subject areas, those with the expertise would have the confidence to innovate. An official not wholly master of his subject may well be reluctant to propose radical changes in policy and be uncertain of his ability to assess such proposals by others. He may, as a result, fall back on the safer course of defending and trying incrementally to improve existing policies.

The reply of many senior civil servants to this kind of criticism is to claim that they are experts in the ways Whitehall and Westminster work. This is clearly true, but the riposte is not convincing. It places too much emphasis on the form and not enough on the content. Moreover, it is a form which can be learnt by highly intelligent people fairly quickly. More persuasive is the argument that the peculiar skills of the Civil Service administrator are those needed and esteemed by Ministers in their capacity as Members of Parliament who are weekly or daily—and often unexpectedly—accountable to Parliament for their actions. Only the generalist, it is argued, can draft the statement, speech, or answer in the kind of terms that Ministers need to satisfy their supporters and confound their opponents. If Parliament, and thus Ministers, were less demanding in this way, other skills might be in greater demand. There is something in this, though it implies an extremely conservative view of the possibilities of administrative reform. But as long as it prevails, clinging on to generalism and eschewing expertise in particular areas of policy has a number of undesirable direct and indirect consequences.

Little consideration is given to the 'relevance' of the educational quali- fication of new recruits. Thus no preference is given at the recruiting stage to those who have, for example, studied appropriate social science disciplines. Little emphasis is given to recruiting staff with the specific skills or abilities required for a particular function on which further on-the-job training could be built. This is likely to have negative effects on the quality of policy analysis. In examining the failure of the most sustained attempt so far to institutionalize policy analysis (Programme Analysis and Review, which we discuss at greater length in later chapters), commentators have noted that this work 'often fell to generalist administrators best known for their consummate skills as essayists. Thus the final product was often just that—an essay with little evidence of rigorous appraisal or of prescriptions for action' (Gray and Jenkins, 1982).

Essay writing is in fact a task at which the Civil Service excels. It pays great attention to drafting and to questions of presentation generally. Presentation is clearly important; but if too much attention is paid to it, even more important questions of content can go overlooked. The care taken in drafting and redrafting and in perfecting minor details has opportunity costs. These can include failure to discuss fundamental objectives and to consider the whole range of feasible options for achieving these.

Good policy analysis requires the capacity on the part of the analyst to distance himself or herself from existing policies and methods of implement- ation and to explore radical alternatives. The general tendency of bureau- cracies to support the status quo is reinforced in Whitehall by the overwhelming career basis of the Civil Service. Virtually all positions of any significance are held by officials who have spent their entire working life in the Civil Service. Moreover, the Civil Service itself controls the process of recruitment and promotion. Ministers' role in selecting their own senior advisers has traditionally been the merest formality. It is extremely unusual for the arrival or departure of a Minister, or of an entire government, to be followed by any parallel movements among officials (private secretaries and, sometimes, press officers are the occasional exception). In addition, the number of outside advisers even in temporary positions is still trivial. Few Ministers in recent years have had more than one or, occasionally, two 'special' or 'political' advisers, and even in the mid-1980s some Cabinet members had none at all.

Finally, there is the much more complex and less tangible concept of the

Civil Service's 'culture' and style. The culture of Whitehall is basically written rather than oral. Most arguments are conducted on paper rather than face to face. The culture is also exceedingly polite. One critic has argued that there is too much 'decorum'. Neither of these factors should in themselves militate against good policy analysis but there is no doubt that where too high a premium is placed upon the avoidance of conflict, issues are likely to go inadequately examined and challenging options unexplored. Awareness of the other person's point of view is highly desirable but it can result in minimizing discomfort rather than in optimizing policy.

The moderate style of the British Civil Service derives also in part from its wholly non-partisan composition. It is the boast and pride of the Service that it can and will work willingly and effectively with governments of any political complexion, and that the reason no posts change hand with a change of administration is that there is no need for them to do so; their holders can do as good a job for the Blues in power today as they did for their opponents, the Greens, yesterday. All this is familiar stuff, and well documented. Equally familiar is the argument that a service of this kind must, almost by definition, be professionally moderate. It cannot afford even private—let alone public—enthusiasm for any particular course of action lest that course go suddenly and disconcertingly out of fashion if the government should change. The most celebrated, indeed notorious, expression of this philosophy was uttered in the early 1970s by the former secretary to the Fulton Committee, Richard Wilding. He described the ideal characteristics of the administrator in the following terms:

The belief that the good government of this country is a matter of high importance and the opportunity to contribute to it a privilege; the belief that it therefore demands the best you can give it, in all matters and all the time; a professional pride in making sure, so far as you can, that the objectives that Ministers set themselves are objectives that can in practice be achieved, and that the Government then sets about the job in such a way that they are achieved in fact;
the courage to give unwelcome advice;
the resilience and humour to accept repeated disappointment and frustration without becoming cynical;
the willingness to listen to other people, to learn from your own mistakes and to work in collaboration rather than competition;
two spoonfuls each of honesty, tenacity and obedience; and one spoonful of humility.
Season with common sense, a dash of political judgement and a consuming interest in at least one totally different subject and simmer gently for 40 years (Wilding, 1979).

Much of this is admirable. But what is instructive about this quotation is not what is in it, but what is missing from it. There is no mention of imagination, creativity, enterprise, interest in change, flexibility and adaptability, or knowledge and expertise in particular subjects. All of these qualities, it could be argued, are needed from departmental civil servants if they are to perform the functions we identified earlier at the centre of government.

Some critics of the Civil Service have gone further. They have argued that the ethic so eloquently summarized above is the ethic of an institution that is quite unsuitable for the purpose of governing modern Britain. One such critic, Sir John Hoskyns (a former head of Mrs Thatcher's Policy Unit in 10 Downing Street), stated bluntly that the very moderation of the Civil Service, and its habituation to the repeated failure of its policy prescriptions, have deprived it of the will to succeed. 'The first thing to realise about the civil service, is that few, if any, of its members believe that the country can be saved' (Hoskyns 1983). Hoskyns said this after only two years of the first Thatcher government. Wilding's remarks were made several years earlier still. In the years that followed, a great deal of effort was put into attempts to turn the Civil Service into a more dynamic, thrusting organization, combining managerial skills, the determination to succeed, and, to a small but significant extent, a sympathy with the style if not the ideology of the Conservative government in power. Mrs Thatcher started to take more than a formal interest in promotions to permanent secretary posts. Officials whose personal style did not fit the new age tended to find themselves passed over for promotion. It was symptomatic that in 1984 Wilding himself was moved from a key post in the Treasury to the altogether quieter and less significant post as the senior official in the Office of Arts and Libraries.

The almost lifeless Programme Analysis and Review was terminated and at least partly replaced by the infinitely more vigorous system of 'efficiency scrutinies', led by an outsider brought into government for this very purpose. The new Prime Minister strengthened her personal Policy Unit by bringing in further outsiders. Great emphasis was given to improvements in personnel management, and much greater emphasis than in the past to training: even senior officials were henceforth to be trained, and to have to be trained before they were eligible for further promotion.

It follows that by the later 1980s some elements of the case for having a CPRS to fill the 'hole in the centre' was less strong than it had been in 1970. The Civil Service was being forced to ask itself some very difficult questions indeed, which it might well have preferred to evade. Some commentators thought there was, if anything, too much innovation. But these were changes of degree, not of kind. Much of the description of Whitehall given earlier in this chapter remained as true in 1986 as it had been in 1970. We return to the case for the CPRS in the concluding chapter of this book.

3

The CPRS and how it Worked

THE ANNOUNCEMENT OF the creation of the CPRS in the October White Paper was followed by a long silence. The government had had nobody in mind to head the new unit, and it proved surprisingly hard to find someone suitable. Trend and Armstrong had hoped for someone who had Whitehall experience, and argued for Professor Dick Ross, an academic economist from the University of East Anglia who had been working at the OECD in Paris for some years and who before that had worked in the Treasury. This suggestion was not acceptable to Ministers. Two 'outsider' candidates who were agreed on were Christopher McMahon, then Executive Director at the Bank of England, and Professor Hugh Ford, head of Mechanical Engineering at Imperial College. Both were approached; both declined.

One day in November Lord Rothschild, on the point of retiring as the head of research at Shell, was told by his Dutch secretary that (according to Rothschild himself) 'Someone calling himself secretary of the Cabinet has asked to see you, but I said that you were far too busy saying good-bye').[1] When Rothschild did get to see Trend, he was invited to take the job of head of what Rothschild later described as 'a rather vaguely-defined policy study unit'; his subsequent meeting with Edward Heath, who had not met Rothschild before, left him little clearer about his mission.

Rothschild insisted on a month's holiday before starting the job. On his way through Washington he stopped off to talk to Henry Kissinger, then National Security Adviser at the White House, on the assumption that the CPRS was intended to act as a kind of 'Office of the Prime Minister' in 10 Downing Street. He also talked to senior staff at the Office of Management and Budget including Caspar Weinberger, then the Deputy Director and head of budget. John Mayne, who had drafted the relevant parts of the White Paper, flew out to

[1] A typical Rothschild joke, savouring the fact that both he and his audience would know that the Cabinet Secretary was probably the most significant figure in the Civil Service, while in other worlds such as Shell he might be mistaken for a mere clerical functionary among many others.

see Rothschild while on holiday to explain the meaning of the text. Rothschild and Mayne spent five days arguing about the future role and powers of the CPRS, and about the proper interpretation to be put on Mayne's words.

Rothschild, the third choice for the job of heading—and creating—the CPRS, was in some ways a surprising choice for the job. He was a biologist who for some years had been the Director of Research at Shell, a hereditary peer (who never attended the House of Lords because he disapproved of it), a member of the banking family, and a man believed to be of considerable personal wealth. He was not a member of the Conservative party, nor even known to Edward Heath. Indeed, he was known to be a Labour sympathizer, if not a supporter. He had little or no direct experience of Whitehall and as a scientist could claim no special expertise in the key area of economic policy. The reasons for the choice of Rothschild are obscure. It has been suggested to us that he had become known to Trend when asked, a few years earlier, to investigate security arrangements at the atomic energy research station at Culham. In the event, Victor Rothschild turned out to have been an inspired choice. He had many of the qualities needed to set up this unusual new organization and obtain the respect of Ministers without becoming the poodle of the 'mandarins'. He was independent, iconoclastic, and fearless; as a young man before the war he had played first-class cricket for Northamptonshire and had batted successfully against the universally feared fast bowler Larwood; a few years later, during the war, he had earned the George Medal for defusing German bombs. He was also impulsive, quirky, and touchy—qualities which became much more widely known when the controversy in 1986 and 1987 surrounding the publication of Peter Wright's book *Spycatcher* pushed him into the limelight.[2] He brought to the CPRS, as well as these qualities, a remarkable network of contacts on which he was able to build further in seeking outside advice.

Having successfully insisted on his holiday, Rothschild finally took up his post on 1 February 1971. The first member of his staff, already waiting for him, was John Mayne. Having drafted the CPRS section of the White Paper and done his best to persuade Rothschild of what it meant, Mayne now had the brief of liaising between the CPRS and the Cabinet Secretariat—or, as Rothschild was apt to comment, of making sure that Sir Burke Trend was kept informed of what the CPRS was doing. Mayne also regularly briefed Rothschild on the Cabinet Secretariat's activities.

One of the first decisions to be made concerned the size of the unit. Rothschild had been given no guidance on this point. His own view was that a group of 15–20 people (excluding secretarial and other support staff) was the

[2] Those who are interested in finding out more about him can read his two idiosyncratic books of memoirs (Rothschild, 1977 and 1984).

largest which could operate in the unstructured, 'brain-storming' mode that he favoured. Above this size the full benefits of larger scale would be realized only, he believed, at somewhere between 200 and 300 staff. He therefore decided to limit the unit to not more than 20—which, as it happened, was a number which could be fitted in round the conference table in his office. This number was also small enough to allow the director and his deputy to keep in fairly close touch with all the work being done, and would help to ensure a degree of cohesion among a somewhat disparate group of people. In the event, the CPRS never exceeded 20 professional staff. The support staff were also few in number, consisting of a small number of registry clerks, secretaries, and a driver for the Director.

Selecting the members of his team was Rothschild's first task. Names were proposed both by the Civil Service and by outsiders. Before Rothschild went on holiday, he interviewed Robin Butler, a 33-year-old Principal in the Treasury who had been Secretary to the Budget Committee. He appointed him, and Butler arrived on 1 February. The next member, already designated as one of his deputies, was the Civil Service's rejected nominee as director, Dick Ross. He was given the rank of Deputy Secretary. If Lord Rothschild was the impresario, then Dick Ross was the stage-manager. His capacity for analysing even the most complex of problems on one side of paper was unrivalled. Ten days after he was appointed a fourth member was added to the team, though in a staff rather than a 'line' capacity. This was a young administrator also seconded from the Ministry of Defence, in the traditional Civil Service rung-on-the-ladder role of Private Secretary. Christopher Sandars never succeeded in persuading Rothschild, unfamiliar with this role, that there was a useful job for him to do; he was later able to make a more effective contribution when Rothschild moved him out of his office into the main body of the staff. Rothschild himself chose the fifth member of his initial team, Robert Wade-Gery, an Assistant Secretary in the Foreign and Commonwealth Office, and a Fellow of All Souls College, Oxford. Rothschild's first words when he sat round the table at his first meeting with this group were, 'Well, what the hell are we going to do now?'

The second person appointed from outside the Civil Service was William Waldegrave, one of several names recommended by Lord Jellicoe. Waldegrave, then aged 25, was an active and political Conservative, who had been working in the Conservative Research Department. The younger son of a prominent Conservative family in the West Country, he too was a Fellow of All Souls College, Oxford, and an interesting example of the aristocratic Tory intellectual in politics. He was from the beginning one of the most active 'philosophers' of the CPRS, and the proponent of strong views about its proper role and functions. Waldegrave did two overlapping jobs for Rothschild. First, he was extensively used as Rothschild's trusted emissary and channel of communication with the wider world (a task for which a conventional Permanent Secretary would normally use his Civil Service Private Secretary).

Second, he was used in particular as a link with the Conservative party organization, including the Research Department, and with individual Conservative politicians. Such links did not last. During the period Labour was in government there was little contact with the party organization. Nor were they re-established with the Tory party when Mrs Thatcher took over. Somewhat later some attempt was made to create a dialogue with the Conservative Research Department.

Other members of the staff came variously from inside and outside Whitehall. From the Treasury came Adam Ridley, an economist. Peter Carey, a long-serving member of the trade and industry group of departments came to join Ross as one of Rothschild's two deputies; his task was, in effect, to act as managing director to Rothschild's chairman. From outside came Hector Hawkins, an economist who had been in Barbados with the West Indian Sugar Corporation, Peter Bocock from the World Bank, and, from the London School of Economics, William Plowden, the former secretary of Lady Sharp's group. Rothschild's former employers Shell seconded Dr Tony Fish, the first in a line of appointments from the oil companies whose collective expertise helped the CPRS to build up an enduring capability on energy matters. By the autumn of 1971, the CPRS was 16 strong (excluding support staff).

The mixture of insiders and outsiders was to prove an extremely effective device. The average age of the Rothschild CPRS was low—about 35. The quality of candidates offered by Whitehall departments—though not always accepted by Rothschild—was high. Outsiders came to Rothschild's attention by a variety of means; all were carefully vetted by Rothschild (and, usually, by Dick Ross). CPRS jobs were never advertised; the outsiders, at least, were mostly drawn in from a series of 'old boy' networks whose common property was that at the centre of each sat Rothschild himself. It was a striking, if minuscule, case of personal patronage in Civil Service appointments of a kind which it had been the explicit aim of the Northcote–Trevelyan report of 1854 to eliminate (although Civil Service rules allow temporary contracts of up to five years). It was not true, as the satirical magazine *Private Eye* was later to allege, that the connections were all family ones (although William Waldegrave was for a while engaged to Rothschild's youngest daughter); but it could not be denied that the Rothschild CPRS was largely drawn from a strikingly narrow élite background which contrasted strangely with the greyer, more thoroughly meritocratic, culture of the Whitehall bureaucracy.

So many of the CPRS's working practices took shape during Rothschild's first year or so, even though they were later modified, that the period is worth dwelling on. Thus, until the end, the staff blended seconded civil servants with seconded outsiders. The proportion of the latter dwindled, very slowly, over time, though was never less than a third.

The quality of outsiders remained high throughout. Some observers thought that some Whitehall departments which at first regarded a CPRS posting as a valuable experience to be reserved for their best younger staff, were by the end of the 1970s sometimes trying to transfer those they could most easily spare. However, the scrutiny of potential candidates carried out by the head of the CPRS usually ensured that poor nominees were rejected.

The average length of secondments was about two years. A handful stayed considerably longer than this, most notably the first deputy head, Dick Ross, whose stay lasted from February 1971 until June 1978. Ross was thus for a long time the senior economist on the staff. At most times there were at least two other economists. The handful of other academics included, at different times, a demographer, a sociologist, a political historian, a lawyer, a physicist, and a biologist (of whom more later). The only other 'regular' slot was that filled by the succession of oil industry secondees, all from either Shell or BP. Other outsiders came from the City, industry, and commerce or consultancy. Only after nine years did the CPRS acquire its first member from local government, and only after ten its first from a public corporation. It never had a member from the trade union movement or from the voluntary sector. The civil servants, over time, represented most departments in Whitehall. There was (almost) always someone from the Treasury, the Foreign and Commonwealth Office, and the Ministry of Defence. The few departments never represented included the Department of Energy and the Lord Chancellor's Department.

The essence of the CPRS's working methods was the absence of hierarchy and of specialization. There were in effect three tiers of authority. Rothschild and his successors had an unquestioned authority over the unit as a whole and an unquestioned responsibility for its programme of work and its general role in Whitehall; their special status was reinforced by the fact that they alone had regular personal contacts with the Prime Minister of the day and with the Secretary to the Cabinet. It was also normally they who represented the CPRS at Cabinet committees and other Ministerial meetings. However, this last task was also shared with the two deputies, Ross and Carey, and the others at that level who were recruited later: John Burgh, Gordon Downey, Alan Bailey, and John Caines. These too were in a position slightly different from the rest of the staff. Ross, the academic economist, played a large part in the early days in formulating the CPRS's own working practices; his reflective cast of mind and involvement with macro-economic issues, and thus with the Treasury, tended to cast him in the role of 'resident sage'. Carey, a more pragmatic character, with long experience of the infighting of Whitehall, made an admirable complement to Ross. His shrewd and slightly cynical approach to government business and to the world at large greatly appealed to Rothschild.

When Carey left in September 1972, he was replaced at the same level by John Burgh, a regular civil servant who had worked in several 'economic' departments and who had most recently been working on secondment to the Community Relations Commission (a government-funded body whose task was to improve race relations in Britain). Burgh never established a satisfactory working relationship with Rothschild, who almost seemed determined not to let him fill Carey's place. Although he made important contributions to CPRS activities, most notably in launching and overseeing the major study on race relations (see Chapter 6), Burgh was always something of an outsider in Rothschild's CPRS. After he left, the CPRS operated with only a single deputy secretary between its head and the body of the staff. The exception to this was a period a decade later when David Green from ICI, who was in charge of the Nationalised Industries Review Staff, held the rank of deputy secretary. Ross held this post until mid-1978, when he was replaced by Gordon Downey, a career Treasury official who later became Comptroller and Auditor General. This was a very different kind of appointment; Downey was a more conventional figure who, some CPRS colleagues claimed, was more cautious about challenging Whitehall in general or the Treasury in particular; it should, however, be added that since then, as Comptroller and Auditor General, he showed himself to be very ready to stir up Whitehall with some wide-ranging value-for-money studies. He was replaced in mid-1981 by another Treasury official, Alan Bailey. Bailey left after a year; his successor, who was still in post when the CPRS was abolished a year later, was John Caines from the Department of Industry.

One question about CPRS membership, originally unspoken and later answered pragmatically but leaving the question of principle unresolved, concerned the political affiliations or sympathies of its members. Although the Rothschild CPRS was not, as a whole, predominantly Conservative, several of its members were, or became, avowed supporters of the Conservative party. William Waldegrave later became a political adviser to Edward Heath, a Tory MP, and—in the Thatcher governments of 1983 and 1987—a junior Minister. Brian Reading, who joined the CPRS in November 1971, had already worked briefly for Heath as an economic adviser in 10 Downing Street. Adam Ridley later was an economic adviser to Mrs Thatcher as leader of the Conservative opposition before 1979, and an adviser to Conservative Chancellors of the Exchequer thereafter. But once this first generation had left the CPRS, there was no clear connection between the political beliefs of its members, including its head, and the nature of the government in power. (It is interesting to note that on election day in 1983 in a straw poll taken amongst CPRS members only one admitted to voting Conservative.) Changes of government—of which the CPRS survived two—had no immediate effect on its composition.

This last statement, however, means only precisely what it says. The composition of the CPRS in its last years, under Mrs Thatcher, was undeniably different from that of earlier days. The difference lay not in formal politics but in professional background, skills, and general orientation. Thus at the head of the CPRS Mrs Thatcher inherited and kept on Sir Kenneth Berrill, an academic economist of Keynesian persuasions. When Berrill left he was replaced by Robin Ibbs, a senior manager from ICI; Ibbs was succeeded by John Sparrow, a merchant banker who had been informally advising Mrs Thatcher on financial matters. And while the Rothschild–Berrill CPRS had contained a large proportion—academics and others—of people who might be described as the liberal intelligentsia, broadly sympathetic towards the ideals of the Welfare State, in the Ibbs/Sparrow days there were rather more commercial and financial experts. However they were certainly not hardline monetarists. As one CPRS member put it, 'they had SDP tendencies and were certainly out of sympathy with Norman Tebbit's view of the world'.

It was characteristically British that the lurking question of principle was never squarely faced or resolved. Despite the perceptible changes in the style and culture of the CPRS, over time, in theory all its members were civil servants, temporary or permanent, not political appointees. The corollary was that, whatever their personal beliefs, they would loyally and zealously advise and serve whatever Ministers might be set over them. By the time Rothschild had retired in September 1974, Labour had accepted the case for the CPRS. But when Harold Wilson had to appoint a successor, he had so completely accepted that this was a Civil Service post that he had no candidate of his own to propose and gratefully confirmed the Civil Service's nomination of Sir Kenneth Berrill.

Despite the formal superiority of the one or two deputies to the rest of the staff, the reins of authority were, in fact, fairly insubstantial. Ross, Carey, and their successors represented the CPRS on occasions that seemed to call for relatively high rank, and were responsible for general oversight of current projects. They took day-to-day decisions on whether or not to intervene on a specific issue and, if so, on the final drafting of any CPRS paper on the subject. But most of the work of the CPRS either went on unsupervised or, under Rothschild, was supervised directly by Rothschild himself, leaving his deputies bypassed. This lack of hierarchy troubled some CPRS members from the Civil Service. Below Ross and Carey, neither formal ranks nor seniority counted for much. Rothschild, confident in the quality of a team wholly selected by himself and, perhaps influenced by the familiar experience of scientific research, in the acuity of youth, made something of a deliberate point in using as emissaries the younger members of his team, regardless of the age and seniority of those with whom they had to deal. 'One of my young men will come and see you' was a familiar phrase—although in fact a proportion of the younger members were female. This tradition was continued by both Berrill and Ibbs, although Sparrow attempted to change it by giving under-secretaries more authority.

Though this reliance on younger people was certainly good both for the CPRS and for the individuals concerned, it could produce problems. One of the main criticisms made of the CPRS team on the Review of Overseas Representation (ROR) related to the relative youth of some of its members, as inappropriate to the rank (and, implicitly, self-importance) of many of those whom they were interviewing.

Like most aspects of the CPRS's work, questions such as who should interview ambassadors or others were resolved fairly informally; the outcomes depended upon who was available, on the wishes of the individuals concerned, and on the degree of interest and involvement of the head of the CPRS. Working methods included both a great deal of team-work for some purposes and, at least for some people, much solitary enterprise for others. The guiding principle was an absence of specialization. Although outside experts on information technology or with a background in the oil industry would naturally spend a lot of time working on relevant subjects, they were also expected to lend a hand on quite unrelated projects. (The Nationalised Industries Review Staff under Robin Ibbs was the main exception to this general rule. It became effectively a specialized team insulated from the rest of the CPRS.) Most 'insiders' from Whitehall departments were much less specialized than the outsiders, and logically were employed on a wide range of different jobs; in the course of these some of them acquired considerable expert knowledge, which was often consolidated and exploited in future work in the same subject area, although since few people stayed for more than two years, the scope for effective exploitation in this sense was limited.

Non-specialists could probably contribute most effectively as members of a team. Teams were usually built up to work on major projects (see below) leading to a report. Thus the Review of Overseas Representation team contained five to six members, that on the Joint Approach to Social Policies between four and six, the computer industry team, two (plus three outside 'consultants'), the motor industry team, two (also obtaining help from outside consultants). Any such team would have an acknowledged leader—not necessarily the most senior member of the staff involved—who might spend between 25 and 100 per cent of his or her time on the project. Other members of the team might well be involved in other projects, perhaps as leader, and might spend as little as a fifth of their time on the project. The ROR team was unusual both in its size and in that several of its members worked for some of the period in which the study took place virtually full-time on the project—necessarily, since it was hardly possible to combine frequent visits to posts overseas with any other involvement. Especially in the early days, the in-house members were supported by advisers or consultants from outside, working full- or part-time, as described below.

Whatever the size and independence of a CPRS team, a crucial and usually effective link between it and the rest of the CPRS was the regular weekly CPRS meeting. Started by Rothschild, and continued by his successors, these were held usually on Monday mornings. Every CPRS member not away, or at some other meeting of undeniable importance, was expected to be there. The head of the CPRS would usually describe his activities during the previous week, including any meetings with the Prime Minister or other senior Ministers; he would report on what he had learned, or inferred, both about relatively objective matters such as impending responses to events or changes in policy, and about more subjective issues such as the mood and morale of the government. Other members of the CPRS would do the same for their activities. They might mention developments, inside or outside Whitehall, which could justify a CPRS intervention. They might report on any difficulties which they had experienced on their projects, and might also take the chance to clear with the CPRS as a whole the line that they were taking, or proposing to take, in dealing with a department or in drafting a paper.

Monday morning meetings were one factor which helped to weld the CPRS into the well-integrated team that it was for most of its life. Its members shared the feelings of being both a privileged and a somewhat beleaguered group. On the one hand, they had access, direct or vicarious, to the Prime Minister and Cabinet, of a kind enjoyed by few other civil servants. They had the freedom to think, and advise Ministers, along the lines that they thought best, without being unduly constrained by existing policies, the possible reactions of outside interests, or a cautious hierarchy. On the other hand, they were regarded with suspicion, even resentment, by some civil servants: and they often had to do battle with the official machine if their advice was to have any effect.

The staff, with the exception of the head of the unit or his deputy, was accommodated in a string of offices in the attic rooms on the fourth floor of the Cabinet Office, where the strong sense of solidarity was maintained through the frequent meetings that were necessary to support the work of the various teams. For those like ourselves who came from university posts, the strong mutual support system was refreshing after the isolation common in academic jobs. The staff tended to have lunch together; it avoided the Cabinet Office mess and chose the canteen instead (no waitresses and no senior civil servants from other departments). There was a successful wine-buying syndicate and at

33

one period a duplicate bridge team which competed without distinction in the lower reaches of the bottom division of the Civil Service bridge league. The powerful sense of a special shared experience and perhaps a particular kind of shared vulnerability has continued to be manifested after the demise of the CPRS, in an annual get-together to which all ex-members of the CPRS are invited. This takes place on the lions' terrace at the Zoo on a summer evening after closing time; many ex-members attend, although Rothschild stays away.

Rothschild's own methods of working were, to say the least, idiosyncratic. His style was variously confrontational and conspiratorial. His blunt use of English earned him some enemies among civil servants and Ministers, and his highly selective reliance on particular advisers among his own staff strained some loyalties there. He also tended, until they learnt his methods, to split his staff by assigning two or three individuals the same task, swearing each to secrecy. But, in general, morale and corporate spirit were both maintained by the sheer force of Rothschild's character, and by the entertainment, at his own expense, provided for his staff. Outstanding occasions were dinners to mark the first, second, and third birthdays of the CPRS held at the Mirabelle restaurant. The guest of honour at the first of these—though badly delayed by a political crisis—was the Prime Minister Edward Heath. Rothschild also used personal hospitality to woo specialist advisers and consultants, very few of whom he ever paid, and the bureaucracy. He gave working buffet lunches in his offices to groups of permanent secretaries with a notoriously alcoholic 'cider cup', an ineffective strategem after its secret was blown.

For most of its life the CPRS made much use of outside contacts. Its outside members, in particular, brought with them ready-made their own networks—people and institutions often unfamiliar to Whitehall, who were informally consulted in ways equally unfamiliar. Some of them were more formally involved in specific CPRS projects. The tone was initially set by Rothschild, whose personal network was probably the most extensive of any. An international cast of experts was pressed by him into the service of the CPRS: some became standing members of project teams, others were more intermittently consulted by Rothschild. His scientific background inclined him strongly to the belief that for every subject there were a very few—perhaps only one—generally acknowledged experts, whose advice on the topic was likely to be objectively better than that of other people.[3] The theoretical drawback of this approach in a Whitehall context is that it is often disbarred by the Official Secrets Act; this rarely inhibited Rothschild. There is no evidence that consultation with unlicensed outsiders ever led to unauthorized leaks of

---

[3] As he himself frequently commented when, years later, he was writing his report on the SSRC, the contrast in this matter with the Social Sciences was striking.

34

information. Later heads of the CPRS were considerably more cautious in this respect, and it is arguable that in these circumstances 15–20 professional staff is too small to do a really effective job.

Because of Rothschild's own eminence, he had little difficulty in obtaining advice, often freely given, by world-class experts who were flattered to be asked. Eminent international lawyers advised on legal matters concerning Concorde, the law of the sea, and energy issues. Contacts established with the Hudson Institute by other members of the CPRS led, in due course, to a working lunch in January 1973 in Rothschild's flat for Herman Kahn, the Institute's resident 'thinker of the unthinkable'—a sobriquet which the CPRS liked to use of itself. Kahn's gloomy predictions of Britain's future greatly influenced Rothschild's public speech on the same subject later that year, which led to a serious but temporary rift between himself and Edward Heath (see Chapter 4).

Rothschild did not limit his consultants to well-established experts in middle age. He recruited relatively young people too, including some in their thirties. Indeed one of Rothschild's targets for criticism was the list of the 'Great and the Good'. He remarked that it was impossible to get on to it unless one was 53 or more, had an upper middle class accent and an Oxbridge degree, and was a member of the Reform Club. The result was that the government drew its advisers from an undesirably narrow social group and lost the benefit of help from many able people.

In some of the CPRS's early work it would have been hard to make progress without outside help. A good example was its study of the computer industry where the inhouse team was supplemented by an academic physicist, Professor Sir Brian Flowers—later Lord Flowers—a merchant banker, James Joll, and a data-processing expert (from GCHQ). In other cases individuals provided *ad hoc* advice in a major policy area over a longer period. Michael Posner, an academic economist, played this role on the economy. Walter Levy, an oil economics consultant, played a similar role on oil. Appointing people as general gurus in this way involved certain dangers, for example over-reliance on views which might be idiosyncratic in certain respects. But subsequent reflection has led some ex-members of the CPRS to regret that more outside help was not sought, for example to lend more authority to the CPRS's attempts to pronounce on complex issues such as the expansion of the steel industry.

Under Berrill consultants, individual and institutional, continued to be used. They were employed to especially good effect in two major industrial studies. In the study of the car industry published in 1975 (see Chapter 7 for a detailed description), McKinseys was commissioned to collect and analyse data about the car industry in the UK and Europe. Control of the study remained in the hands of the CPRS, as did the writing of the final report and the drafting of its recommendations. It was the first time that McKinseys had accepted a relationship in which they would not write a report they were centrally involved in producing. The success of the experiment may have been helped by the fact that Hector Hawkins, who led the study within the CPRS, had earlier been an economic consultant himself. The study on the car industry was followed soon by one on the power plant industry (also described in Chapter 7) for which similar use was made of consultants.

The CPRS also made informal contacts with outside experts over social policy, which took up much of the CPRS's time during the Wilson and Callaghan governments. The views of individual directors of social services, for example, and of academics were sought on parts of the Joint Approach to Social Policy. An academic (Chris Allsopp from Oxford University) was also recruited to work part-time on a CPRS review of unemployment (see Chapter 5). In science policy John Ashworth, who was the Chief Scientist in the CPRS and had himself been an academic scientist, drew on his extensive network of contacts in the academic world and elsewhere.

The CPRS was more cautious under Berrill than it had been under Rothschild in its use of unofficial outside advisers. This tendency was intensified when Mrs Thatcher took over in Number Ten, reflecting her personality, her lack of interest in consultation (particularly of groups such as the trade unions), and her strong distaste for leaks. All Prime Ministers are sensitive about leaks. Heath, Wilson, and Callaghan are no exceptions. But during their regimes consultation with outsiders seemed more acceptable. It is true that Mrs Thatcher told one of us, when asked her reasons for abolishing the CPRS, that it ought to have talked more to Marks and Spencer. But her restrictive attitude towards consultation was felt to be implicit in the request from her office, shortly after her arrival, to Berrill to list his staff's contacts outside Whitehall. When Berrill asked each CPRS member whom they had seen during the previous three months, not all replied—some on the grounds that it was hard to define a 'contact', others because of concern about the use that might be made of such lists. One complained, 'I thought it showed complete misunderstanding of the way intelligent and creative people ought to go about their daily business, and of one of the most vital characteristics of an advisory body, particularly one known as a "Think Tank", which was that they should introduce more porousness into the political and administrative establishments'. Another suggested that such constraints upon consultation reflected Mrs Thatcher's lack of interest in what she saw as academic analysis and her wish for practical advice.

In these respects Ibbs, outsider though he was, was more orthodox even than Berrill. He was determined that the CPRS should scrupulously follow the lead set by the Prime Minister.

Rather different issues were raised by the varying extent to which the CPRS informally consulted outside interests in the course of its work. Two closely linked questions were whether or not the CPRS was publicly known to be working on the subject concerned, and—if not—how far an outside contact could be relied on to keep the CPRS's confidence. Life was obviously much simpler for everybody if the fact of a CPRS study could be acknowledged. But inevitably, once it became known that the CPRS was working on a topic and was seeking views from outside Whitehall, there were pressures for the final results to be published. Neither Ministers nor departments nor, consequently, the CPRS always welcomed these pressures.

In general the CPRS found no difficulty in making contacts: most organizations were anxious to present their point of view. Its industrial contacts—often established through the CBI, the NEDO and its sector working parties, individual firms, and public corporations—tended to be with management rather than with the unions, and with senior management at that. One former member of the CPRS commented to us that contacts at more junior levels were often more valuable since people there felt less constrained to remain committed to the lines adopted by those at the top. The CPRS had fairly extensive contacts with the unions at some times, for example during the studies of the motor industry and, in particular, of the power plant industry; during the latter, mass meetings were held at each of the major plants concerned. A union official was also briefly co-opted to help with a study of unemployment in the late seventies. The CPRS continued to consult the unions, as well as other interests, even during the Thatcher and Ibbs years—for example, during the 1981 study on cashless pay.

More important than CPRS membership and its use of outside help was the nature of its work. It can be argued that this fell into several quite clearly defined groups, as well as embracing a range of miscellaneous activities which are less easily categorized. The first group was for some CPRS members the most fundamental of all, the activity which could by itself justify the existence of the CPRS and to which all its other activities should be in some way related. This was its work on 'the government's strategy'. Although over the years 'the strategy' played a diminishing part in the formal activities of the CPRS, the concept remained fundamental to its rationale. It continued right to the end to be interested in strategy, though under Mrs Thatcher felt obliged to modify the form its interest took. It was Mrs Thatcher's view that if short-term decisions are made correctly, the long-term will tend to look after itself.

Work on strategy was so important, formally as well as informally, in the early years that it is a logical point at which to begin. Cmnd. 4506, as drafted largely by John Mayne, had repeatedly used the words 'strategy' and 'strategic', centred on the comment that governments, in order to govern effectively, needed 'a clear and comprehensive definition of strategy', without which they were 'at some risk of losing sight of the need to consider the totality of their current policies in relation to their longer-term objectives'. One of the main tasks of the CPRS was to fill this gap. In the earliest days of the Rothschild era, the CPRS started to plan for a special meeting of the Cabinet, at which Ministers would discuss a paper on 'the strategy' by the CPRS. Perhaps not surprisingly, major differences developed at once between members of the CPRS as to what it was useful and proper to say in this context. One approach was to stick closely to the terms of the Conservative party manifesto of the year before; to focus on the central objectives which were set out there; to take them more or less as given and to advise the Cabinet both on how far the objectives were being achieved and on what more they should do to achieve them.

The alternative approach started with the proposition that manifestos and political pronouncements were not enough. Ministers needed help in thinking through their aims in the light of the harsh realities of office. They also needed to be encouraged to define objectives for all the main policy sectors, and to do so in terms which made sense to their departments. The whole process was iterative, rather than 'declarative'—that is, the CPRS should ensure that Ministers agreed with its own statement of what their objectives were before drawing any policy conclusions from these.

This difference of view also extended to the rest of the CPRS work programme, as will be discussed later. Briefly, those backing the first approach felt that the CPRS should tackle only topics that Ministers agreed were of integral importance to achieving their major objectives; others, that the CPRS could and should launch itself into areas which its own members found interesting and important, regardless of Ministerial views. This was for the CPRS a central dilemma throughout its existence.

When it came to the point, the CPRS paper presented to the first 'strategic' meeting of the Cabinet, held at Chequers in October 1971, was a compromise between the two approaches. It both made some bold declarations about the government's strategic objectives, and presented a great deal of detail about other subsidiary policies. This meeting set the tone for several which followed, at approximately six-monthly intervals, under the Conservative administration. A small group from the CPRS, led by Rothschild himself, attended the meeting, along with members of the Cabinet Secretariat whose task was to record the discussion. Members of the CPRS team, with the help of visual aids such as charts and slides, separately presented different sections of the paper. The Prime Minister chaired the meeting; there was general discussion, but no decisions were taken. The meeting lasted all day, punctuated by lunch. During lunch and tea-breaks the CPRS members moved discreetly among the

Ministers and subsequently reported back titbits of gossip and insight at the next CPRS weekly meeting. The two earliest Cabinet meetings of this kind were each followed by two successive meetings, at which the CPRS presented the same material: first to second-ranking Ministers–departmental Ministers not in the Cabinet and Ministers of State—and then to the third tier— Parliamentary Secretaries. Once again the Prime Minister took the chair.

Strategy meetings were divided into three parts: economic policy; the labour market and labour relations; and social policy. The meetings lasted until early 1973; thereafter, first the oil-price crisis and then the political crisis of 1973–4 distracted Mr Heath's government from such longer-term thinking. The subsequent Labour government held one strategy meeting. One or two meetings with broadly the same aims, but in specific policy areas—the nationalized industries, or social policy—were held later in the lifetime of the CPRS, but none of these attempted the same panoramic coverage, or the same style of 'mid-term report' on the government's overall success in achieving its objectives. While they lasted, strategy meetings took up a great deal of CPRS time, especially the time of Rothschild, his two deputies, and an informally but carefully selected team.

The purpose of the strategy exercise was to make Ministers look ahead and to think how—if circumstances allowed—they would like their policies to develop in the medium to longer term. The weakness in practice of this approach is that circumstances all too often do not allow policies to develop as governments would wish—and that circumstances and their consequences frequently come as a complete surprise to the governments whose plans are thus disrupted. Moreover, events tend to be dealt with in isolation as they occur. In theory, it ought to be possible and useful to consider the relationships between different future events: could a 'controllable' event—for example, the timing of a foreign policy initiative—be manipulated to offset the damaging consequences of another controllable or even uncontrollable one?

The antidote which the CPRS tried to develop to these problems was, logically enough, called the 'early warning system'. Work on it started in the first weeks of the CPRS's life. Its aim, as expressed within the CPRS, was to 'give Ministers the chance to think about problems before they became problems'. More succinctly, this approach was summarized as 'Mr Whitelaw's bath'—Mr Whitelaw being at that time Lord President of the Council, a non-departmental Minister whose role, it was felt, included reflecting (possibly in his bath) on his colleagues' areas of responsibility and on the problems which might emerge in any of these and knock the government off course.

The principle of the early warning exercise was approved by the Cabinet in the spring of 1971. During the summer the CPRS asked departments to let it have lists of events likely to occur in 'their' areas before the end of the year, and (separately) during the first half of 1972, as well as those that could happen at any time during the following twelve months. They were asked to distinguish between events that were in some sense controllable by the government, such as decisions on public expenditure totals or on the future of the Concorde programme, or the publication of reports of official committees of inquiry; and events that were outside governmental control, such as changes in oil prices, or excessive pay-claims by public sector unions. When the CPRS felt that a department was unimaginatively, or perhaps disingenuously, suppressing mention of a ticklish issue which might develop on its patch, it would suggest that this should be added. In extreme cases, the CPRS would add the item on its own initiative.

These items were assembled in an enormous list, which was then circulated to Ministers and their departments for information and possibly for action. The list was subdivided among the Cabinet and Cabinet committees, according to which of them was likely to find itself discussing each event. In theory, this warned both the Cabinet Secretariat and the chairmen concerned, so that they could start to think about the decisions that would have to be taken.

The first early warning paper was discussed by the Cabinet in the autumn of 1971, and the principle of the exercise once again broadly approved. The CPRS carried on updating the list and refining the methodology of the approach. The hope was that this addition to the wider-ranging, more discursive strategy papers would make possible Ministerial discussions which both looked beyond immediate, detailed problems and yet took account of the vagaries of actual events. However, the main participants involved—apart from the CPRS—disconcertingly declined to behave in the ways predicted and required. On the one hand, the issues underlying the 'controllable' events had to be expressed in such general terms, many of the details being unknown, that they did not seem worth discussing (for example, the impending report of a Royal Commission might, reasonably but uninterestingly, prompt a comment such as 'Need to consider possible legislation'). On the other, in relation to 'uncontrollable' events, departments would not commit themselves to identifying problems more than a month in advance; in any case, they always preferred to err on the side of optimism, and so failed to mention some possible problems in the hope that these would not occur. The result was that the early warning document gave nothing like the comprehensive picture of a possible future that had been intended; it was also both too speculative and too bland to provoke any useful discussion among Ministers.

More damaging still, however, were two overlapping objections to circulating certain sorts of information at all. The Treasury from the beginning took the line that some events, however important and however 'controllable', were far too sensitive to be mentioned even as hypothetical possibilities. In addition, senior Ministers in much the same vein felt that the document as a whole, even if vetted by the Treasury, was potentially too explosive to circulate to all their colleagues in all departments. It has also been suggested since that the Prime Minister found the document too depressing and wanted this approach to be discontinued. It was therefore proposed that the paper should be shown only to the few who were members of the restricted Cabinet Committee on the Central Capability. However, since all departments had contributed to the list of items and therefore knew of the existence of the paper, this would clearly have been an unworkable arrangement. In any case, the early warning exercise had been meant to complement the strategy and meetings—and it had been accepted without question that these ought to involve all Cabinet Ministers (and later, junior Ministers). The CPRS, faced with this dilemma, took the obvious way out. In the autumn of 1972 the early warning exercise was abandoned altogether. A modified and more limited version was revived three years later in the context of social policy (see Chapter 6).

In parallel with work on strategy, the CPRS also saw as part of its role the attempt to get departments to be more explicit about their priorities, particularly for public expenditure purposes. The hope was to get departments to think aloud about these with the CPRS in a way they would never do in front of the Treasury. For the most part it failed. But in spite of failure in this respect, contacts with policy planning divisions in departments and pressure on them to think more about priorities did sometimes pay dividends. There was a tendency, at least until Mrs Thatcher arrived, for spending departments to assume that their programmes could grow considerably in excess of the rate of growth of the economy as a whole, and as one member of the CPRS put it 'that somehow Allah would provide'.

The secondary importance to the CPRS of its concern with the government's strategy was that this both provided a test—admittedly, rather crude—for deciding whether or not a specific topic was suitable for a CPRS initiative or intervention, and that it could be used to justify such intervention if this took place. One perennial problem for the CPRS was the question of whether and when to intervene in the literally almost infinite list of issues which either were—or, sometimes more significantly, were not—on the agenda of government. Cmnd. 4506 gave no guidance on this matter. At the very beginning there was a special Ministerial Committee on the Central Capability, whose task was to oversee the new central administrative innovations introduced by the government, including the PAR programme and the work of the CPRS. It was envisaged that the CPRS's work programme would be well enough defined to be discussed, amended if necessary, and approved by this committee. In the event, the committee had too little to do to maintain its momentum and the interest of its members, while the CPRS programme, strategy meetings apart, soon became so pragmatic, and, at the margins, ill-defined, that there seemed no profit in trying formally to agree it with Ministers. The CPRS quickly became the arbiter of its own activities. This meant, in practice, that it rarely consulted anybody about small-scale interventions, such as passing comments on current policy issues; since these did not constitute major assaults on established policy positions, nor called for a great deal of departmental help in assembling the relevant facts and figures, Ministers and officials alike acquiesced in allowing the CPRS this much licence.

The situation was quite different, however, in the case of the large-scale CPRS inquiries. These inquiries in fact took up considerably more of the time of the unit than its work on strategy. Over the CPRS's lifetime there were probably about fifty of these in all. Best known to the world at large were those, about a third, that were published, for example: *Energy Conservation*; *A Joint Framework for Social Policies* (and other reports connected with this); *The Future of the British Car Industry*; *The Review of Overseas Representation*; *People and their Families*; and *Education, Training and Industrial Performance*. (In Chapter 4 we discuss policy on publication.) The first of the major studies of this kind, and the first to be published, was Government R. & D., though this was unusual in being written by Rothschild himself (in close collaboration with John Mayne, who redrafted much of the text to make it less acerbic). Many other reports, although not all dealing with intrinsically more sensitive matters than did the published reports, were never published: Concorde, Energy Policy, The Computer Industry, Race Relations, Nationalized Industries. (All published and some unpublished reports are listed in Appendix 1.)

The topics for these reports originated both inside the CPRS and with Ministers or officials. Many of them made their first appearance on the long list of issues suggested for the CPRS work programme by Ministers and others in the course of a long 'trawl' round Whitehall by Ross and Rothschild in the first days of the CPRS. Others emerged spontaneously in Cabinet or Committee discussions. Many proposals, however, were developed by members of the CPRS, either alone or in consultation with the CPRS's outside advisers and consultants. In almost every case, though, before the CPRS formally embarked on a study of the issue in question, approval for the project was obtained either from Ministers collectively, or from the Prime Minister, or from the Minister(s) most closely affected by the issue. Thus the study of the Foreign Office, subsequently broadened as 'overseas representation', was initially a CPRS initiative. But it was thought, rightly, that such a study could never get off the ground without at least the acquiescence of the Foreign Secretary. As Chapter 8 showed, this did nothing to commend the report's conclusions to the Foreign Office and others; but it was essential for securing the CPRS access to data, people, and places needed for the study.

One concept which the CPRS needed to keep in the forefront of its mind, when considering proposals for CPRS studies emanating from elsewhere, was that of the 'poisoned chalice'. Especially in its early days, a body such as the CPRS is eager to oblige its clients, and glad when they spontaneously propose commissions to it. But there is a perennial risk that such commissions will turn out to embody the impossible tasks that have defeated all previous inquiries, or the politically explosive issues that nobody else dares touch. In either case they are likely to damage whoever is rash enough to accept them. The CPRS had to look carefully at any external proposal for CPRS work, whether made by officials or Ministers, lest it might turn out to be such a poisoned chalice.

But 'big studies' were only part of the CPRS work-load. These could, arguably, have been done by outside committees of inquiry, reporting privately if need be (although difficulties in obtaining access to all the information required could reduce their effectiveness), or by internal task forces—both set up *ad hoc* for the purpose. It would be something of a luxury, and probably not very efficient, to have an all-purpose standing body with the sole task of producing big one-off reports on any topic that might be given to it.

More important for the CPRS as a whole was its even more open-ended responsibility for monitoring, as far as it could, developments both in the world at large and in government policies, and for intervening when it thought fit with advice to Ministers. The technique developed by the CPRS was directly addressed to the problem which had been pointed out by Lords Plowden and Roberthall (see Chapter 1): that for almost every issue raised in Cabinet or Cabinet committee, one or more Ministers, advised by their relatively expert departments, would circulate a paper arguing their own special case in whatever terms seemed likely to be persuasive; while the chairman would have a broadly neutral (and sometimes not very expert) brief provided by the Cabinet Secretariat; and the rest of the group might be lucky enough to have some departmental interest and thus some departmental briefing—or might not, in which case they would simply have to do as best they could on the basis of their native wit, or remain silent. The result was that Ministerial discussions always risked being dominated by special interests, with no certainty at all that the national or even the collective governmental case would be argued, let alone prevail. The CPRS dealt with this problem by producing what it called 'collective briefs'. These were, literally, papers on the issue which aimed to look at it from a collective point of view and which were circulated collectively, i.e. to all the Ministers involved, and not to the chairman alone. A hypothetical but familiar type of case might thus see a paper prepared by a 'spending' department describing a situation and arguing for more resources to deal with it, and a counter-paper from the Treasury claiming

43

that public spending was already far in excess of the budget and that consequently nothing could be done that cost money—and a third paper from the CPRS, trying to set both the issue and these two responses to it in the context of the government's current strategy and of likely future contingencies. Collective briefs frequently also posed what the CPRS saw as key questions that needed answering before a rational decision could be taken. Whatever that decision might be, a collective brief could be said to have achieved its objective if it at least prevented a Minister from steamrollering his colleagues through his own unexamined assertions.

When a CPRS collective brief was circulated to a Cabinet committee or other group of Ministers either the head of the CPRS or one of his deputies would usually go along to present the paper or to answer questions on it. This did not apply at meetings of the Cabinet itself. There the CPRS paper had to make itself noticed as best it could without any formal sponsor. Lacking one, it was always at risk of going unnoticed, especially if its conclusions were uncongenial to Ministers present.

This account of course assumes that a CPRS paper was circulated. This was not always possible, however important the issue or misguided the departmental papers. One of the most familiar ploys in bureaucratic infighting is the 'bounce'. This can fall into two parts. The advocate of a particular course of action will first delay his advocacy till the moment when, he claims, a decision must be taken at once and without reflection if disaster is to be avoided. He will secondly delay revealing the terms of his argument until so close to the moment of decision that his opponents have no time to develop a counter-case.

The CPRS suffered greatly from this ploy, for the basic reason that its own interventions were almost always made in response to some line taken by a Minister. The latter would often not send his paper to the Cabinet Secretariat for distribution until just before the 48-hour deadline on which the Secretariat insists. The CPRS thus had the difficult task of both deciding its own line, preparing a paper, and circulating this round Whitehall within the required time-scale. The problem could be, and sometimes was, got round both by building up an inventory of draft briefs on subjects known to be coming up and quick thinking and even quicker drafting, a task which was performed with unsurpassed brilliance by Dick Ross, the master of the collective brief. But because of the 48-hour rule the problem was never wholly solved. It was made worse by the fact that many people did not regard the CPRS as having a legitimate role at this stage. This applied not only to departments and Ministers who did not want their case challenged, but also to the Cabinet Secretariat whose task was the easier, the fewer papers were on the agenda on which they had to brief the chairman. 'You are making a lot of extra work for very busy people', said a member of the Secretariat on one occasion; and years later, at a conference on ways of advising heads of government, a senior member of the Secretariat said bluntly that by the time issues had reached the level of Ministers a body like the CPRS had no part to play and could only complicate the taking of decisions by hard-pressed politicians (Plowden, 1987).

One way round this problem was for the CPRS to side-step the formal processes altogether. If the deadline had passed for having its advice distributed as an official Cabinet document, it could and very often did informally advise either the chairman—who was often the Prime Minister—or selected key members of the committee. This could be quite effective. The disadvantages were that such informal briefing had even less claim to be discussed than a CPRS paper, and that other Ministers involved might be quite unaware that the CPRS had contributed to the discussion at all. Over time, therefore, the CPRS could seem to be far less active in helping Ministers to take decisions than was the case. A particular version of this dilemma arose in the general case of a choice between briefing Ministers at large and the Prime Minister individually. A well-aimed word in the latter's ear could be the most cost-effective of all forms of intervention. But too much of this detracted from the CPRS's task of advising Ministers collectively. The CPRS thus risked losing credibility in other Ministers' eyes. It sometimes happened that the CPRS advice would reach the Prime Minister not as an independent document with a CPRS byline, but as an anonymous passage in the briefing prepared by the Cabinet Secretariat. In such cases the CPRS got no credit at all from any of its Ministerial clients.

It is worth dwelling for a moment on this alternative relationship. Close links with, and the goodwill of, the Prime Minister of the day were always seen as important by the CPRS. When the goodwill finally ran out, the CPRS went with it. All the heads of the CPRS did their best to keep this relationship in good repair. Rothschild from the beginning secured an effective right of audience with Heath; the right to send him personal minutes was equally established. Both Ibbs and Sparrow had 'agenda meetings' with Thatcher at which proposals for CPRS work emerged. Jobs could be done for Prime Ministers personally which never formed part of the CPRS's official work programme, and which sometimes were not admitted by the head of the CPRS to any or some of his colleagues. Some of Rothschild's forays into the areas of defence and foreign policy fell into this category, as did work on Northern Ireland. Ibbs, in particular, took on a number of tasks for Thatcher, mainly on industrial matters. A typical example was work on the future of the Invergordon Smelter (see Chapter 7).

It should not be forgotten that some important issues are not discussed in Cabinet committees but instead resolved through personal correspondence between Ministers. Throughout its existence the CPRS frequently intervened in Ministerial correspondence in order to steer decisions on issues of this kind.

Contacts with Ministers and particularly with the Prime Minister were mainly kept to the head of the CPRS or to his one or two deputies. The head of the CPRS, too, had a great deal of parallel contact both with the Cabinet Secretary and with the other permanent heads of Whitehall departments. Individual members of the CPRS also had close relationships with the heads of sectors in the Cabinet Secretariat, and their staffs. One of the main tasks of the Secretariat is to brief the chairmen of Cabinet committees on their agenda, whether they be the Prime Minister, the Chancellor, the Home Secretary, or a junior member of the Cabinet. The CPRS used these briefings as an opportunity to put forward a view which it believed important or to include some factual information omitted from the departmental papers circulated; they also allowed the CPRS to raise criticisms about departmental papers when it did not wish to put in a separate paper itself. The quid pro quo for the Cabinet Office Secretariat was that it could draw on the CPRS for help and advice in briefing, particularly when it was not certain what line to take. The Cabinet Secretariat also prepares the weekly timetable for Ministerial meetings and to this extent programmes the government's work. Early knowledge of the programme was clearly helpful to the CPRS in planning its own work.

Another major responsibility of the Cabinet Secretariat is the setting up, chairing, and distribution of papers for official committees. When the CPRS took part in such committees, again it tended to have a close relationship with the Cabinet Office chairman, who often discussed with the CPRS representative the best line to take in sorting out conflict between the departments represented and might also seek advice in drafting the report which the committee would eventually submit to a Ministerial committee.

As this account implies, regular and *ad hoc* contacts with senior officials were an important channel for CPRS influence. The CPRS took part in many activities at official levels: not only official Cabinet Office committees, but also departmental and interdepartmental working groups and so on. It was always tempting to accept an invitation to take part in the process whereby officials prepared policy proposals for Ministers, since this offered a chance to influence policy whilst it was still fluid and options were open. It was equally tempting to take part in the subsequent processes, when Ministers had made a decision and had remitted to officials the job of working it out in detail; this reduced the likelihood that any surviving aspect of the CPRS point of view would be eliminated by departments.

The problem with both types of involvement was shortage of CPRS resources; someone spending half a day per week on an interdepartmental working group was obviously that much less available for other activities. In addition, the CPRS member of an official group preparing advice for Ministers often found it hard to decide what line to take. First, was there 'a CPRS view' on the topics under discussion and, if so, how far did the CPRS representative need to stick to this and to clear with colleagues any departures from it? Secondly, and more fundamentally, ought there to be a CPRS view in any case? Given that the task of the CPRS was to help Ministers to think through their own strategy and to take decisions accordingly, could it legitimately develop and express a view of its own before Ministers had considered the matter? Could it continue to press its own views even if these had not been unambiguously endorsed by Ministers? These questions were of practical as well as theoretical interests; departments were quick to point out if a CPRS argument uncongenial to themselves seemed not to have been sanctioned by Ministers. As one member of the CPRS commented, 'A favourite trick of Treasury officials was to fix one with a baleful glare and ask, "Has the CPRS a view?" If you said "no" you sounded feeble. If "yes", what was it, and how did it leave options open?'

The question of whether there was, or should be, a collectively agreed 'CPRS view' on major policy issues was never conclusively resolved. In theory, the CPRS was a group of neutral analysts, helping Ministers to think through their own ideas and to turn their broad policy commitments into specific programmes. In practice, as Donald MacDougall had observed of Churchill's Statistical Section years before, such 'an organisation . . . may give undue influence to people who develop prejudices. It is inevitable that such a section, and its head, will come to take a certain line on a number of matters—it could hardly fail to do so and avoid inconsistency . . .' (MacDougall, 1951).

This was likely to be true whatever the nature of the CPRS work programme. It was made completely inevitable by two things. First, Rothschild, like Cherwell before him, felt strongly that CPRS papers ought to end with firm recommendations. Secondly, the big reports in the programme, alongside the more analytical collective briefs, tended to develop in the teams working on them quite strong views one way or another. They needed to have such views, if they were to act as effective advocates for their report's conclusions in the face of an often sceptical and sometimes hostile Whitehall. For the CPRS, having delivered a report, the question was at what point to abandon advocacy and return to analysis. It could be deeply frustrating to watch a package of conclusions being gradually dismantled by, say, an interdepartmental committee of officials from the departments whose points of view the report had in effect been intended to challenge. For the individual, the comparable question was whether, when in future the issue discussed in his report came up again, he could or should ignore his earlier recommendations and act as a totally dispassionate analytical adviser to Ministers.

Examples of other types of CPRS activity will occur throughout this book. One final major activity worth mentioning here was the CPRS involvement in Programme Analysis and Review ('PAR', as it was always known). PAR was introduced in 1971, in parallel with the CPRS, as part of the package of Conservative reforms aimed at increasing governmental efficiency and effectiveness. It was, in effect, a modified and less radical version of Planning, Programming, and Budgeting Systems (PPBS), which had recently been introduced amid much publicity by the Johnson administration in Washington.[4] PAR was, in the end, a failure, though not for the reasons given by official spokesmen either in the Treasury or in departments (who tended to emphasize the alleged irrelevance of PAR's techniques to the 'real world'). Summarized, the formal procedure was that programmes to be reviewed were selected jointly by the Treasury, CPRS, and departments; choices agreed by officials were then ratified by Ministers. The main work on each review was done by departmental officials, but findings were again discussed jointly with the Treasury and CPRS as they emerged. The final reports and recommendations were presented to Ministers for discussion. Ministers were also presented with a CPRS collective brief, commenting on the review and its conclusions and suggesting to Ministers decisions which they might want to make.[5]

There were undeniable defects in the PAR process. Departments had too much influence over the choice of programmes to be reviewed and naturally often put forward candidates of only minor importance. The bulk of the work was usually left to departmental line officials who, equally naturally, tended not to make radical judgements about their own programmes. This was exacerbated by the fact that politicians were not involved at any stage between the choice of programme to review and the presentation of conclusions. Putting a junior Minister in charge of each PAR would have helped. Finally, the Treasury was determined to treat PAR as an expenditure-reducing exercise rather than as an open-minded enquiry into the effectiveness of a programme, which might easily conclude that more resources were needed rather than fewer. But the CPRS put quite a lot of time and effort into PAR until the process was abolished by the Thatcher government in 1979, after a long, slow decline under Labour. The CPRS tried, both in the choice of programmes for review and in the analysis brought to bear, to ensure that radical questions

[4] Mark Schreiber, an adviser in the Heath administration, illustrates one of the purposes of PAR—to examine particular areas of expenditure in terms of their relevance to current policy objectives—with an anecdote from the days of the Austro-Hungarian empire. For many years in Vienna a sentry stood in the park on a particular spot. No one had any idea why he stood there. When further enquiries were made, it eventually emerged that a long time before, the Empress had ordered a sentry to guard the spot where she had noticed the first violet of the spring blooming.

[5] For an evaluation of 'PAR' see an excellent article in *Public Administration* by two academic political scientists (Gray and Jenkins, 1982).

really were asked about the objectives and the achievements of programmes about, for example, the cost-effectiveness of the prison-building programme or about the relative effectiveness in road safety terms of motorway crash barriers as compared with speed limits. Some PARs, such as the one on Urban Deprivation and the one on Preparation for Work, turned out to be fairly influential with respect to later policy thinking. Referring in particular to the PAR on Preparation for Work, a former CPRS member still working in central government said, 'my impression is that the Department of Education and Science in the later 1970s and 1980s is a changed animal from the inward-looking organism of the early 1970s and that PAR's and the CPRS's part in them played at least some small part in bringing this about'. Despite its weakness, PAR offered scope for asking questions of a kind which, ten years later, were still not integral to the resource allocation process: such questions, relating to impact and effectiveness, were very close to the *raisons d'être* of the CPRS itself. After the abolition of the CPRS, the Conservative government's Efficiency Unit, with its programme of scrutinies, was much narrower in objectives and in achievement. A later head of the Treasury, Douglas Wass, was to comment that the demise of PAR 'was not due to any inherent flaw or defect and a new generation of officials, and a firm commitment by ministers, would make it a success' (Wass, 1984).

In terms of its approach to problems, the CPRS was not outstandingly innovative. Its analytic techniques owed more to common sense and quite a lot of applied economics than to the more sophisticated skills of policy analysis.

CPRS documents were unusual, however, in the relative clarity and conciseness of their style and presentation. Spared the perennial bureaucratic need to disguise lack of agreement on objectives, or inadequacy of policies, through obscurities of prose, the CPRS usually managed to take advantage of this and to write in a crisp, no-nonsense style sparingly illustrated with figures, that contrasted well with the tortured and inflated verbiage produced by the Civil Service departments. Until 1980, whether published or not, all major CPRS reports, after the first one on R. & D., had a common format. At Rothschild's insistence, they were made recognizably different from normal departmental documents by being printed (by the Foreign Office press) and bound in distinctive red covers. Their large format and bold appearance made them instantly recognizable among other internal reports and publications. Under Ibbs and Sparrow the tradition of a common format broke down.

At least as significant, on specific occasions, was the use made by the CPRS of oral presentations. Whitehall, as has often been observed (see Howell, 1981), is a paper-based culture, in which almost every important argument is written down and communication is principally, and sometimes exclusively, on paper. High among the skills which take civil servants to the top is the skill of drafting. This applies right up to, and perhaps especially so at, the top. When Cabinet committees, and even more so the Cabinet itself, meet to consider a Minister's proposals, these are presented in the form of a short memorandum (two or three pages has usually been the upper limit), supported where necessary by detailed annexes. This is circulated a day or two before the meeting. Although most of the background work, and often the drafting as well, will have been done by the Minister's officials, the Minister presents the paper single-handed, and only he takes part in the discussion. No officials, other than the Cabinet Secretariat, are present. As a means of conveying often extremely complex issues to busy people this can be grotesquely inadequate.

Rothschild strongly believed in the importance of presentation, in persuading Ministers both that particular pieces of analysis needed doing and that their conclusions should be taken seriously. From the beginning, the CPRS took advantage of its own special status to innovate ways of making major presentations to Ministers. At the earliest strategy meetings, three or four members of the team, including Rothschild, were present; each presented those sections of the CPRS paper about which he or she was relatively expert. Equally important was the use, from the earliest printed CPRS documents, of graphics, graphs, charts, diagrams, and, on one occasion, a caricature produced by a professional for the purpose. These both lightened and clarified the words and figures in which they were set. It was only a logical step from this to supporting the printed presentation with an oral account. Both at the early strategy and at later meetings members of the CPRS stood before Ministers with screen, slides, and pointer, and took them through the cases that the CPRS wanted to put across.[6] Such oral presentations petered out in later years. One member of the CPRS commented that 'had they continued, the CPRS might have had more Ministerial support at the end'.

The use of graphics and, still more so, oral presentations were distinctive trade marks of the CPRS. The example had some impact on the rest of Whitehall, where oral presentations have become more common. However, tired Ministers still have to plough through grey pages of leaden prose, buttressed by statistical appendices, and then listen to their colleagues reading from the Civil Service briefs and dealing, as best they can, with questions on unfamiliar points of detail.

In describing the way the CPRS worked, we have perhaps presented a picture of a smoother and more conflict-free operation than existed in reality.

---

[6] Rothschild invited George Rylands to the Cabinet Office to show members of the CPRS how to do it. It is not clear whether the style of delivery was to be decisively Hamletish, indicating an awareness of all the options, strong on oratory and sex appeal like Mark Antony, or Portia-like in appealing to Ministers' sense of moral duty. Advice was also given by McKinsey's on how to structure and write a report and how to present it face to face with the 'client'.

Questions about how the CPRS should operate were always informally on the CPRS's own agenda, and were never answered in a way that finally satisfied all its members. As already mentioned, uncertainty about the terms of reference of the CPRS combined with the strong views of some of its members to provoke sometimes furious debates about the proper substance and style of CPRS activities. These issues were important not only in the short-term, and not only because they were relevant to the impact and effectiveness of the CPRS; they affected the unit's prospects of survival in the longer term. There were also frequent debates about whether or not a particular problem should become the subject of a major study by the CPRS. Sometimes proposals which had a lot of support inside the CPRS were rejected by officials. One example was a study of departmental policy planning units, which was vetoed by the then head of the Civil Service. Sometimes the head of the CPRS applied the veto. An example was a study of the role of government in the national diet. It was a classic subject for the CPRS: trans-departmental in its own right, littered with pressure groups and special interests, and generally conspicuous for a lack of clear information. But the head of the CPRS thought it too far from Ministers' central interests. If the CPRS work programme contained too many projects which did not interest Ministers, or which led to conclusions with which they disagreed, the CPRS was liable to seem a tiresome irrelevance. The CPRS was always operating on something of a political knife-edge, soliciting the support of one or other Minister or faction of Ministers, one or other department or the bureaucracy as a whole, the Prime Minister, the Secretary of the Cabinet, in varying permutations.

Some Ministers seemed to object to the CPRS in principle. Although Tony Benn was a staunch advocate of the publication of CPRS reports while he was Secretary of State for Industry, when he went to the Department of Energy as Secretary of State he appeared to develop the view that the CPRS was part of a bureaucratic conspiracy against him as a Labour Minister (Benn, 1980). Others, and their officials, could easily become enemies if they felt that the CPRS was intervening disproportionately in their areas of responsibility, or was being unreasonably critical; for much of its life, the CPRS found itself on the other side of the barricades from the Home Office, which frequently opposed any departure from the status quo.[7]

Strategies for CPRS procedure, and for CPRS survival, were thus a recurrent topic of discussion. In the early days Rothschild's somewhat capricious approach to the CPRS work programme, and his heavy reliance on

---

[7] Events sometimes proved it right. One example was reforming the law on Sunday opening for shops which the CPRS argued was self-evidently desirable. The Home Office opposed it on the grounds that it would never get past the back-benchers; the Shops Bill was in fact rejected by the House of Commons in 1986.

some members of his staff to the exclusion of others, caused misgivings and some resentment; shortly before Rothschild finally left, some of the latter group held several unofficial meetings with the aim of trying to think more systematically about what the unit should do and how it should do it. Berrill later found himself facing the demand that he should discuss this with all his colleagues. Rather reluctantly, he acquiesced. The result was that in several successive years the whole CPRS spent a winter weekend at the Civil Service College at Sunningdale, reviewing its activities for the past year and trying to plan for the period ahead. Berrill was never wholly reconciled to this 'scab-picking' or 'navel-gazing', as he somewhat disgustedly described it. But it undoubtedly did help the CPRS, including Berrill, to think about the kinds of resources it needed. Should it, for example, recruit more or fewer economists, and how should they be used? It also helped to maintain a corporate identity which had become a little weaker with the departure of Rothschild and was always threatened by the constant dilution of the CPRS membership through frequent departures and arrivals. Ibbs held only one such meeting, Sparrow none at all. The absence of such corporate thinking, plus Ibbs's own markedly less collegial operating style may have contributed to the CPRS failure adequately to adapt to the Thatcher regime and to its eventual downfall.

4

The Rest of the World and the CPRS

THE CPRS SAT at the centre of the government machine but to do its job it had to be in touch with many different parts of the machine including those at the periphery. It also had to make contact with many organizations outside government. This chapter examines the CPRS's relationships in Whitehall, Westminster, and the world beyond. It begins with the most important group, the Ministers for whom the CPRS worked.

As already stated, the Prime Minister was formally responsible for the CPRS and answered questions on it in Parliament. The CPRS's relationship with the Prime Minister was always closer than with the other Ministers. The relationship was not the same throughout the CPRS's life: it varied between Prime Ministers and within the period of office of individual Prime Ministers. However, each Prime Minister saw the CPRS to some extent as his or her own instrument as well as a body which worked collectively for all Ministers. The CPRS also tended to see itself as having a common interest with the Prime Minister in trying to create a coherent policy out of the often disparate policies of the other Ministers. It felt itself to be 'on the side' of the Prime Minister even though it might differ with him/her on specific issues of policy.

At the same time—as events ultimately showed—the CPRS's survival was entirely dependent on the Prime Minister, the one person who could abolish it at a stroke. The fact that it survived under four very different Prime Ministers was due to its usefulness to four very different individuals and partly to its own ability to adapt to change. If it had lacked that ability it might have gone much earlier.

However, the CPRS's formal role was to work for Ministers collectively. This made its relationship with the Prime Minister slightly ambiguous and one which needed sensitive handling *vis-à-vis* other Ministers. For example, for whom did the CPRS speak in interdepartmental meetings of officials? Should its representatives speak on behalf of the Prime Minister, as departmental officials speak on behalf of their Ministers? In practice, CPRS members spoke at such meetings for the CPRS; only in rare cases where it was asked to do a specific job by the Prime Minister was there any departure from this. In any case, under both Wilson/Callaghan and Thatcher governments, the Prime Minister's Policy Unit was often represented separately on official (and sometimes Ministerial) committees.

The head of the CPRS nevertheless had more contact, even if often indirect, with the Prime Minister than with other members of the Cabinet. The staff at Number Ten is very small and Cabinet Office officials have many other preoccupations (see Chapter 2). Even taking account of the Policy Unit in its different forms, the CPRS was thus the largest group of civil servants available at the centre to provide advice and analysis to the Prime Minister.

Direct contact between Prime Minister and head of the CPRS was probably greatest when Edward Heath and Victor Rothschild occupied these positions. Heath worked closely with Rothschild and found it particularly helpful to have early warnings of problems that might arise later. But he also stressed the value of obtaining this advice informally and maintaining the formal position that the CPRS worked for Ministers collectively. The relatively close relationship between Heath and Rothschild was possibly due partly to Heath's commitment to the CPRS as its creator and partly to his lack of alternative sources of advice; alone of the four Prime Ministers for whom the CPRS worked, he did not have a formal policy unit of his own. Rothschild's confident style and strong personality may also have helped to open the green baize door between the Cabinet Office and Number Ten. However, even Rothschild did not have as much access to the Prime Minister as he would have liked; he is reported to have said that Heath was sometimes cocooned in his close relationship with Trend and Armstrong and that it was not always easy to 'break in'. In addition, Heath was at pains not to institutionalize his own relationship with the CPRS; he emphasized the formal position, that the CPRS was to work for Ministers collectively.

Rothschild's difficulties increased during the last months of the Heath government. The immediate cause was Heath's displeasure at a speech at Wantage in which Rothschild spoke of Britain's appalling economic performance. 'Unless we take a very strong pull at ourselves', he said, 'and give up the idea that we are one of the wealthiest, most influential and important countries in the world—in other words that Queen Victoria is still reigning—we are likely to find [that] . . . in 1985 . . . the GNP of the United Kingdom will be half that of France or Germany, and about equal to that of Italy' (Rothschild, 1977). It was particularly unfortunate that on the same day Heath in a speech elsewhere had tried to put across a quite different message. Rothschild's speech hit the headlines. Heath's speech received little coverage. In *The Times*, for example, whereas Rothschild's speech was the page one lead, with a large photograph of him, Heath's speech was reported briefly and tucked away on page two. The following day *The Times* drew attention to the inconsistency between them: 'The gloomy forecast by Lord Rothschild contrasted bleakly with the optimism of Mr Heath's speech' (Clarke, 1973).

Whether or not Rothschild's speech was fair comment, it was additionally unfortunate that he had failed either to get official permission to make a public statement or to clear the text with the Cabinet Office or 10 Downing Street. This was unquestionably a major breach of the formal and restrictive rules that govern civil servants in these matters. Heath himself clearly felt that Rothschild had gone much too far. Rothschild was reprimanded both by Heath and by the Cabinet Secretary Sir John Hunt, and the fact that he had been reprimanded was made known to the press (Bourne, September 1973; Clarke, 1973).

Opinions vary about the significance of this episode. In the months that followed it there developed the miners' strike and the accompanying political crisis which in the end brought down the Heath administration. In this crisis the CPRS was largely excluded from centre-stage; at official level, public and private attention was mainly focused on Sir William Armstrong, the head of the Civil Service, who acted in effect as chief of staff and temporarily supplanted all other official advisers.

It can be argued that this was inevitable in the circumstances and that it had no connection at all with the speech and its aftermath. Rothschild and Heath subsequently asserted that their working relationship had been unaffected by the speech or by the reprimand. As Rothschild recalled:

once the matter of my Wantage speech was over and done with, my relationship with Mr Heath was just as it was before. To be more precise, Mr Heath gave me a severe ticking off at No. 10 for having made a speech without getting it cleared first by the No. 10 Press Office. The mistake was entirely mine and I apologised to Mr Heath for it. Characteristically, at the end of the ticking off which was very unpleasant, he said 'Well, that's that, now let us return to nuclear reactors.' By the same token, when asked about the matter in the House, Mr Heath said that I had apologised and the matter was closed (Rothschild, 1986).

Rothschild added that the CPRS had, in any case, given no advice about the miners' strike and its resolution—'not a suitable subject for the CPRS'. Others, however, have seen the episode differently. Some former CPRS members believe that the relationship between Prime Minister and head of his review staff was indeed badly damaged; that had this not happened, the CPRS would have been much better placed to deploy its members' views on the handling of the strike; and that had some attention been paid to these views, the government's conflict with the miners could have been resolved, the February 1974 election avoided, and the administration saved.

When Harold Wilson replaced Heath his relationship with Rothschild was cordial if not especially close. Although Wilson greatly admired senior civil servants, he none the less set up his own policy unit of political appointees under Dr Bernard Donoughue. Perhaps partly because of this his initial intention in February 1974 was to dispense with the CPRS; he did indeed issue instructions that it should be abolished. However, both John Hunt and Bernard Donoughue advised Wilson to retain it. After 48 hours the CPRS was reprieved. But Wilson's approach to the CPRS was passive: if it did some useful work, he supported and adopted its conclusions. He did not, however, commission much work from it.

When Wilson was succeeded by James Callaghan there were again uncertainties about the role of the CPRS. Whereas Wilson had a reputation, which he himself cultivated, of having a voracious appetite for reading and background facts, Callaghan was said to be a non-reader, 'a seat-of-the-pants' politician, who was impatient of too much thinking and analysis. There were fears within the CPRS that his arrival would herald its demise. Such fears turned out to be unjustified. If anything, Callaghan made more use of the CPRS than Wilson had.

When he arrived in Number Ten from the Foreign Office he said that he had been abroad for two years and needed to be briefed on many key areas of domestic policy. One form of briefing was a series of individual talks with Ministers in charge of Home departments. The Cabinet Office was requested to provide briefing papers for the Prime Minister's discussions with his colleagues. Sir John Hunt involved the CPRS in this exercise from the start. It was in fact the CPRS which provided much of the substance of the briefs, although its contribution was not revealed to Callaghan.

Callaghan later told us he found it helpful to have a variety of views from different sources. He liked, as he put it, 'to hear all the arguments, to establish the facts' and then to decide what to do. In this respect he was very different from his successor Mrs Thatcher. On the whole the CPRS found it easier to work for a Prime Minister who had not made up his or her mind on too many issues and who, like Callaghan, did not regard himself as an intellectual or a creative thinker but was open to ideas and suggestions from others.

Callaghan told us that he thought the CPRS should have four roles: 'to think the unthinkable; to give a global picture through assessments in the round; to fulfil particular assignments in problem areas; and to inject a new angle in agreed interdepartmental papers'. He regarded the CPRS as most useful in the latter two roles, and especially in undertaking special assignments. It is noteworthy that Heath gave us a similar description of the CPRS's tasks: 'to examine interdepartmental issues which came to the Cabinet including the exposure of fallacies in departmental papers; to carry out particular investigations; to look at the government's overall strategy and report whether it is off course.' Heath, however, unlike Callaghan, attached more importance to the strategy function, which he regarded as extremely useful, although he also said that the CPRS's work on interdepartmental issues was 'admirable'. Both Heath and Callaghan also went out of their way when in office to compliment the current head of the CPRS and gave the impression that they valued the relationship that they had with him. Heath referred to Rothschild's enormous distinction; Callaghan to the Prime Minister's isolation and the support and advice he received from Berrill in particularly difficult areas.

The whole style of government, and the role in it of the CPRS, changed again with the arrival of Mrs Thatcher in 1979. Some of her former colleagues have said that, at least for the first couple of years, she allowed genuine debate to take place in Cabinet. But it is widely agreed, to quote one of her ex-colleagues, that her style and attitude developed into ' "This is what I want to do, this is what the country needs and that's it", and any argument to the contrary, tends to get brushed aside' (interview with authors). As her former Permanent Secretary at the DES recalled, 'She never seemed to need any help. She just needed the facts' (Young and Sloman, 1986).

These attitudes on the part of its main client meant that the CPRS had urgently to rethink its role. It had spent much of the previous decade providing just the kind of 'help' that the new Prime Minister seemed not to need, and providing it to Prime Ministers and Ministers collectively. Moreover, for the past five years it had been providing these services for a Labour government.

Ken Berrill suspected that he was perceived as 'a tired old Keynesian'. The transition was difficult. However, Berrill took advantage of his previous acquaintance and relatively good relationship with the new Prime Minister (his chairmanship of the University Grants Committee had coincided with Margaret Thatcher's tenure at the DES, although he had been appointed by her Labour predecessor, Edward Short).

Eventually, he and others persuaded her that alternative advice might be useful, if only to help her in battle with Ministers with whom she did not agree. So she soon began to make use of the CPRS, particularly on industrial policy. And when Ken Berrill resigned in April 1980 she appointed an industrialist, Robin Ibbs, the head of corporate planning at ICI, to replace him. After this the CPRS focused increasingly on industrial policy, notably on the national-ized industries. This was a reflection partly of Ibbs's interests and expertise and partly of the lack of demand from the 'client' for CPRS initiatives in other areas of policy. In either case, it represented a further and, as it turned out, final shift away from the original concept of the CPRS as having some particular concern for the government's overall strategy.

During its lifetime the CPRS was undoubtedly given more tasks by the

Prime Minister in each of the governments it served than by any other individual Minister. Indeed it probably received almost as many remits from the Prime Minister as from Ministers collectively, especially under the Callaghan and Thatcher administrations. Correspondingly, its perceived value was greater to Prime Ministers than to their colleagues. James Callaghan, interviewed in 1981 could not, unprompted, remember anything the CPRS had done whilst he was Foreign Secretary from February 1974 to April 1976. In contrast, he cited a number of different reports the CPRS undertook during his premiership.

The CPRS thus had a special relationship with successive Prime Ministers. It is more difficult to generalize about its relationship with other senior Ministers. That relationship changed over time and varied from Minister to Minister. Only the head of the CPRS and his deputy had close and frequent contact with Ministers; most other members of the unit rarely saw them. The main means of contact with senior Ministers were the Cabinet committees on which the Director and Deputy Director of the CPRS sat.

These provided the head of the CPRS with the opportunity to catch Ministers before or after the meeting and communicate with them informally. More formal meetings with individual Ministers were relatively infrequent, though occasionally they were sought either by a Minister or by the CPRS. An example of the former was a request from David Owen when he was Secretary of State for Foreign and Commonwealth Affairs to discuss with the CPRS team concerned the recommendations they had made in the Review of Overseas Representation. An example of the latter was a request from the CPRS to talk to Barbara Castle when she was Secretary of State for Health and the Social Services about the CPRS's ideas for a 'Joint Approach to Social Policy'. As the examples show, such meetings often took place when the CPRS was undertaking a specific piece of work which related closely to the responsibilities of a particular Minister.

One of Rothschild's first initiatives when he became head of the CPRS was to visit Cabinet Ministers to find out their views about the CPRS's work programme. Few of them had any ideas or suggestions to make. Rothschild repeated this exercise when the Labour government took office in 1974. Again he encountered few ideas; he commented tartly to us that only three of them knew what the Retail Price Index was but that was three more than amongst the Tory Ministers. These experiences led him to the view that by and large the CPRS had to define its own work programme and then persuade Ministers to accept it.

Some Ministers were more interested than others in the CPRS's work, were more accessible to its members, and made more use of it. This could be a matter of temperament or of responsibilities. During the Labour government

58

Harold Lever was one of those, partly because he was just down the corridor in the Cabinet Office, partly because as Chancellor of the Duchy of Lancaster he lacked both the departmental responsibilities which take up so much of the time and energy of most Cabinet Ministers and the official support which is available to them, and partly because in certain areas of policy he took a relatively open-minded attitude to the party's manifesto and was interested in new policy initiatives. In the same administration, Tony Benn was also at first seen as a potential supporter, as was Shirley Williams. Relationships with both were initially cordial. Many Ministers in successive governments have probably been indifferent to the CPRS. Few, however, have been overtly hostile. Benn is one of the few. The reasons for his hostility are complex and relate in part to his constitutional views on the role of party and government in policy-making (Benn, 1980). Benn's battle with the CPRS over nuclear reactors in 1978, described in Chapter 5, may also have contributed.

By contrast, Barbara Castle's diaries show her as moving from early doubts about the value of the CPRS to grudging respect for some of its contributions and something close to enthusiasm when these seemed to support the DHSS against the Treasury and other departments (Castle, 1980).

An individual Minister's relationship with the CPRS and his or her general view of its value and legitimacy could be affected by the CPRS's attitudes to policies favoured by the Minister. Ministers probably preferred to see the CPRS working in areas outside their own responsibilities but of interest to them rather than on issues for which they were directly responsible. No doubt they were encouraged to take this view by their civil servants, who were usually happy for the CPRS to comment on the policies of other departments but reluctant for it to investigate their own. Sometimes, though, Ministers used the CPRS to get things done when their own civil servants were uninterested or resistant or proving inadequate in combat with other departments. An example of the first was the study of the motor car industry which Eric Varley asked the CPRS to undertake; an example of the second was a request from David Owen that the CPRS should look at aid policy, which involved the Foreign and Commonwealth Office, the Treasury, the Overseas Development Ministry, and the Departments of Trade, Industry, and Employment (though the CPRS did not in the end undertake this study).

For much of the life of the CPRS, few of its members concerned themselves with Parliament or had many contacts there. Rothschild had good contacts with Ministers of all parties, and did not discourage his colleagues from exploiting and developing their own links with Parliament, and with the party organizations. Under Berrill, and subsequently, there were many fewer contacts of this kind, although one or two members with previous acquaint-ances among Ministers occasionally discussed issues with them or suggested topics for parliamentary questions. All this contrasted sharply with the Number Ten Policy Unit, which under Labour and Conservative governments was much more effectively plugged into a party political network.

Parliament itself took an intermittent interest in the CPRS. There were occasional parliamentary questions about its activities and its cost. The CPRS several times gave evidence to parliamentary Select Committees. The first occasion was when in 1972 Rothschild—rather quaintly 'by leave of the House of Lords'—discussed with the Select Committee on Science and Technology his recently completed report on government R. & D. (House of Commons, 1972).

The most extended official public appearance of the CPRS took place in December 1976, when its head and two other members gave evidence to a House of Commons Select Committee. The general subcommittee of the Expenditure Committee was inquiring into 'Developments in the Civil Service since the Fulton Committee Report of 1968' (House of Commons, 1977). The CPRS was invited to submit a paper about its work and to give written evidence.

This request led to a great deal of activity within the CPRS. Though in some ways the unit was flattered to be taken seriously in this way, there was also an acute sense of the need for damage limitation; even the most apparently innocent revelations about the inner workings of Whitehall might be blown up by outsiders and treated by insiders as evidence that the CPRS was unfit to be trusted with secrets. There was much conferring between Kenneth Berrill and senior CPRS colleagues, the Cabinet Secretariat, the Civil Service Department, and the subcommittee's Special Adviser, himself a former Treasury official. Throughout this, the main theme was how little the CPRS could reveal without causing offence.

In the event, little was revealed, and little light shed on the darker parts of Whitehall. The CPRS submitted a bland memorandum about its role and activities. (This is reproduced in full in Appendix 2.) Needled by the subcommittee and in particular by its chairman Michael English ('Would it be true to say that your recruitment processes are a method of short-circuiting the Civil Service Commission's appointments to the higher Civil Service?'), the CPRS witnesses stonewalled cautiously ('I do not think that I can go beyond those of our reports which were published.'). The MPs, in their questions, were mildly critical of the small size of the CPRS and of the consequent danger that it might become something of a 'butterfly system which flies from one thing to another, looking at them, making interesting reports, not really following them up, and then moving on to something else because you have not got the resources to follow them up.' This was a fair comment. Kenneth Berrill resolutely refused to say who had advised him to reply along these lines, or who—if not the CPRS—gave advice to Ministers on machinery of government issues.

It was, perhaps, because the CPRS succeeded in revealing so little about itself or about the rest of Whitehall that neither it nor any of its evidence was mentioned in the subcommittee's ultimate report (House of Commons, 1977).

In 1977/8 the CPRS was asked by a Select Committee to give an account of a specific piece of work. The Defence and External Affairs Sub-Committee of the Expenditure Committee decided to devote its work for the 1977/8 Session of Parliament to an investigation of the CPRS's Review of Overseas Representation (House of Commons, 1978). (A full account of this is given in Chapter 8.) The Committee took evidence from most of the organizations covered by the Review, including the main government departments, the British Council, and the BBC External Services. Most of the evidence it received was critical of the Review's findings, perhaps partly because the organizations concerned were naturally anxious to defend themselves against criticism. By the time it was the CPRS's turn to give evidence, most members of the Committee had apparently been persuaded that many of the review's recommendations should not or could not be implemented.

In these circumstances the CPRS had to make its case as best it could. Outside the formal hearing individual members of the CPRS team talked to a couple of the more sympathetic MPs in order to explain their views. These Members were, however, outnumbered by colleagues hostile towards the CPRS's proposals for change. The Committee's report endorsed most of the existing structures and policies and rejected most of the CPRS's recommendations.

If the CPRS had few contacts with Westminster, the reverse was true of its contact with Whitehall. All members of the CPRS were in daily contact with civil servants in government departments. Indeed without such regular contacts the CPRS would have been unable to do its work, because it would have lacked the constant flow of information it needed from departments.

One of the criticisms frequently made of the CPRS, especially after Rothschild's departure, was that it had become incorporated into Whitehall, had lost its independence, had become a tool of the mandarins rather than of Ministers, and had lost its separate identity. These criticisms beg many questions about how the CPRS ought to operate and what is meant by 'independence'. It is clear, on the one hand, that the CPRS would not be effective if it worked wholly 'outside' the Whitehall machine or was engaged in a constant battle with it. It is equally clear that a CPRS which never investigated anything without the whole-hearted concurrence of senior civil servants, or which trimmed its conclusions to avoid offending their susceptibilities, would not be doing its job properly. Even taking part in the normal deliberative processes of Whitehall had dangers for the CPRS. It could be flattering to be invited to join, say, an interdepartmental working group considering some major issue. But in doing so the CPRS risked becoming prematurely enmeshed in a Whitehall consensus, weakening its ability later to make an independent contribution at Ministerial level. It was a continuing problem to know where to strike the right balance.

Throughout its life the CPRS was physically located in the Cabinet Office building at number 70 Whitehall. The Cabinet Secretary was technically responsible for aspects of CPRS administration such as pay and discipline. In an equally technical sense, the CPRS was independent of the Cabinet Office in its operations.

In practice, the relationships between the CPRS and the Cabinet Office, and between the head of the €PRS and the Cabinet Secretary, were among the most immediate and the most important of all. The Cabinet Office in the 1970s and early 1980s, before it absorbed the rump of the former Civil Service Department in the form of the Management and Personnel Office, was a small department. Indeed, apart from the Central Statistical Office, it was very small, consisting only of the CPRS, the Cabinet Secretariat, and other specialist units such as the European Unit, the Assessments Staff, and the Joint Intelligence Committee, none of which had large staffs. Among these, the CPRS's closest contacts were with the Secretariat, headed by the Cabinet Secretary. For the CPRS, the Cabinet Secretary was second only to the Prime Minister in influencing how the CPRS worked, what it worked on, and whether it survived at all. For the Cabinet Secretary, the CPRS was an addition to his empire and a potentially valuable resource; it was also an unpredictable genie only uncertainly contained within the bottle of Cabinet Office corporate management and liable to go off in unexpected and possibly embarrassing directions.

Successive Cabinet Secretaries understandably wanted to exercise fairly close control over the CPRS and to use it for their own purposes. For the head of the CPRS there was a difficult balance to strike between collaboration with the Cabinet Secretary—who controls most of the crucial information flows within Whitehall as well as the locked door between the Cabinet Office and 10 Downing Street—while preserving the CPRS's own independence to choose its own areas of work and to tackle them as it thought best.

The four heads of the CPRS worked with three successive Cabinet Secretaries—Sir Burke Trend (1963–75), Sir John Hunt (1975–9), and Sir Robert Armstrong (from 1979). Each head of the CPRS handled the relationship with the Cabinet Secretary, and the Cabinet Office, differently. Though some members of the CPRS were suspicious of Trend and felt that he was liable to accept the exclusion of the CPRS from certain topics and discussions, he was undoubtedly a strong supporter of the CPRS in principle, and had indeed argued that something on these lines should be set up. Rothschild and he met regularly, and established a cordial and effective working relationship. However, Rothschild was determined to preserve the independence of the CPRS from any part of the Whitehall machine; he saw the CPRS as an instrument, and himself as a confidant, of Ministers, with its own power-base firmly rooted in its successful service to the Prime Minister and Cabinet. It was symbolic that in his day the CPRS writing-paper was headed

CENTRAL POLICY REVIEW STAFF
CABINET OFFICE

Rothschild never achieved the same rapport with Trend's successor Hunt. One of Rothschild's colleagues detected a certain nervousness in his dealings with Hunt, and added, 'In addition, he wanted (the CPRS) to be involved in defence and international affairs, and didn't want to jeopardize his contacts with top military people, and so pulled his punches.' It was Hunt, recalled the same witness, who after Rothschild's pessimistic lecture sent Edward Heath a cable saying, in effect, 'you will want to be aware that Lord Rothschild has made a speech critical of government policies'. It was Hunt in whose room Rothschild was subsequently carpeted and admonished, on Heath's instructions, for the lecture. 'It was never worth appealing to the Prime Minister over the Cabinet Secretary's head', said one former head of the CPRS—and if this was true even when Heath and Rothschild were so relatively close, it was much truer at various times subsequently. Kenneth Berrill, much more of an official than Rothschild, cultivated relationships with senior officials rather than with Ministers.

As he put it to us, 'You have to make up your mind whether you are a chum of Ministers or a civil servant.' He decided that he was to be the latter—partly for pragmatic reasons, since when he took over the CPRS he knew few Ministers. He saw his role at meetings as being that of an official, not as a confidant of Ministers; though the CPRS should always say what it thought, it should not let itself be regarded as a 'sub-mafia of the Cabinet'. Berrill agreed with Rothschild on the importance of a power-base but believed that this should be the Cabinet Secretariat. The result was that neither Berrill personally, nor the CPRS as a whole, were as close to the Labour governments of 1974–9 as Rothschild's CPRS had been to the Heath administration. At the same time, the CPRS was less plainly independent of the Cabinet Secretariat. It was, once again, symbolic that under Berrill the CPRS writing-paper was headed:

CABINET OFFICE
CENTRAL POLICY REVIEW STAFF

In fact the relationship between Berrill and Hunt was less one of subordinate and superior than of mutual dependence; for example, Hunt frequently sought Berrill's advice on economic matters.

When Ibbs replaced Berrill, the relationship changed again. Ibbs felt if anything more strongly than had Berrill that he was not a 'chum of Ministers' (whom he always scrupulously addressed in letters as 'Dear Minister/Secretary of State'), and was even more prepared to accept that he was subordinate to the Cabinet Secretary, and the CPRS to the Secretariat. Nor did he achieve his predecessors' close relationships with the Cabinet Secretary, especially after Hunt had been replaced by Armstrong. 'Armstrong was much more secretive and hierarchical [than Hunt]', said a CPRS member. 'Ibbs didn't realize the importance of this relationship. Perhaps because of his good relationships with the Prime Minister and senior Ministers he wrongly thought he didn't need the Armstrong relationship.'

John Sparrow, coming in as the Prime Minister's former personal adviser on financial issues, seemed inclined to revert to the original Rothschild style, and to cast himself as a friend to Ministers. Unfortunately time and circumstances prevented him from developing this role effectively.

If the CPRS working relationship with the Cabinet Office was on the whole close and effective, this was less true of the Treasury, with which there were important differences from time to time. The Treasury, as a key central department, was an ally the CPRS wanted to have, if possible. The two worked closely in such areas as the PAR programme (see Chapter 3), and often found themselves on the same side in interdepartmental arguments. As it monitors the spending departments, the Treasury could provide the CPRS with information and opinions about their activities. The CPRS was quite often able to reciprocate. It shared with the Treasury a critical and sceptical attitude to the claims other departments made for their policies. Consequently, though for different reasons, the CPRS often supported the Treasury, with its overwhelming concern to keep down public expenditure. As a result, the CPRS was sometimes perceived by spending departments as the Treasury's fifth column—particularly during the Berrill period, given Berrill's previous position as Chief Economic Adviser at the Treasury. Nevertheless there were many cases where the CPRS did not support the Treasury in opposing policies which required increased expenditure, notably during the Heath 'U-turn' of 1971–2, when the role of the CPRS was described by one jaundiced ex-Treasury official as 'whooping up public expenditure'. The CPRS also sometimes opposed the Treasury on macro-economic and fiscal policy (though not under Ibbs, who took a conscious policy decision that the CPRS should not challenge the Treasury on these matters). Various cases of CPRS and Treasury collaboration and conflict will be discussed in later chapters.

The Rest of the World and the CPRS

The CPRS had to maintain contacts with almost all other departments in order to be able to advise Ministers adequately, especially on issues which cut across departmental boundaries. This involved finding civil servants, typically at Under-Secretary but sometimes at Assistant Secretary level, who were both knowledgeable and reasonably objective about their department's work and willing to share their thoughts with members of the CPRS. Such people were often found among the economists, perhaps both because of their analytical training and because they were usually slightly to one side of the main-line processes of advising Ministers and justifying the consequent policies. Officials of this kind saw the CPRS as a potential ally which could be useful in conflicts with other departments (especially the Treasury) or sometimes within the department—or at least as a potentially influential body with whom it was worth being on good terms rather than bad. They tended to accept the need for a body such as the CPRS and to support its endeavours rather than undermine them. The quality of the CPRS's collective relationships with departments depended very much on its members' success in establishing personal contacts with individual civil servants.

The CPRS often turned for advice and information to departments' economic sections or policy planning branches, both for the reasons just given and because people in these units usually had a good overview of what was going on in their departments. However, when the CPRS undertook a particular study, for example it needed also to talk to officials with direct operational responsibility for the formulation and execution of policy in specific areas. It also needed to see departmental papers and sometimes to ask departments to prepare special papers with the information it required. Overt refusal to provide such information was rare; the risks were presumably not thought worth taking, given that the CPRS could ultimately appeal to Number Ten.

Given the possibility that departmental officials might try to conceal some facts from the CPRS, one of the qualities required of members of the CPRS was the ability to read between the lines where departments seemed to be obscuring some of the issues or trying to get away with a poorly argued case. Persistence was required in worrying away at the logical weaknesses in a department's argument or keeping up the pressure on it to take action on a difficult problem which it preferred to leave alone. This role of scourge and irritant to departments required a combination of quick-wittedness, confidence, and a thick skin—a combination which not all members of the CPRS possessed. Those of its members who were permanent officials often knew the facts and could detect the flaws in their former colleagues' case, but might be deterred by a sense of 'proper behaviour' from pressing the latter hard. 'Outsiders' might be less inhibited, and could also bring their main career experience, authority, and a 'consultant' network; on the other hand, they could be less adept at Whitehall infighting. In general, the decision factor was probably personality, randomly distributed between insiders and outsiders.

The CPRS was occasionally constrained in pursuing contacts with outside organizations or individuals because of the likely reactions of departments. For example on one occasion Robin Ibbs felt it necessary to cancel a meeting with British Rail because he was worried that the CPRS might be seen to be taking British Rail's side in its mammoth contest with the government. He also insisted on the cancellation of a meeting with John Alderson, the radical and outspoken Chief Constable of Devon and Cornwall, because he feared it would upset the Home Office.

The qualities needed in CPRS members were also useful to a Prime Minister's advisers. When Wilson set up a new policy unit in 1974, many thought it might change the role of the CPRS and possibly even cause its demise. This did not happen, mainly because the two organizations had rather different functions. The official line was that the Policy Unit was concerned with the short term, the CPRS with the medium and longer term. There was something in this distinction, but not much. More important was the fact that where the CPRS worked for Ministers collectively, from time to time taking on specific tasks for the Prime Minister, the Policy Unit worked exclusively and privately for the Prime Minister. In addition, because of its small size the Policy Unit anyway lacked the capacity to do large pieces of work or produce long reports.

It irritated Rothschild that the CPRS was not allowed to see the advice the Policy Unit was giving the Prime Minister but he developed a co-operative and even friendly relationship with Bernard Donoughue.[1] Under Berrill and Ibbs the CPRS continued to have a friendly, although most of the time not an especially close, relationship with both the Labour and Conservative Policy Units. On one or two occasions the CPRS and the Policy Unit worked together. One successful example, during the Callaghan government, was an attempt to write a joint paper for a Cabinet discussion at Chequers on strategy and, in particular, on the generation of economic recovery. After several meetings staff from the two units agreed to differ, and submitted separate papers. Another example, also during the Callaghan government, was a joint paper by the CPRS and the Policy Unit for the Prime Minister on Health Service expenditure. The Prime Minister wanted independent advice about claims made by the Secretary of State for Social Services in a Cabinet paper about the consequences of failing to increase expenditure on the NHS.

Under Thatcher, the CPRS worked closely with the Policy Unit and its first

[1] Bernard Donoughue (now Lord Donoughue) has published his own account of these years based on his inside knowledge as head of the Policy Unit (Donoughue, 1987).

head John Hoskyns; the two units worked together both on questions of the government's strategy in general and in specific policy areas related to a 'supply-side economics' approach. Later, as described in more detail in Chapter 6, members of the CPRS worked intimately with Ferdinand Mount, Hoskyns's successor, on the issue of 'family policy'.

From time to time the CPRS sought the advice of the Policy Unit on such political questions as how to present difficult and controversial recommendations, making use of the head of the Policy Unit's closeness to the Prime Minister and his knowledge of other Ministers' foibles and obsessions. Similarly, members of the Policy Unit could save time by asking the CPRS for information it had already obtained from departments. They could also pick up the CPRS's opinions about what was going on in departments. To this extent there was some reciprocity in the relationship.

Most of the time, however, the two organizations worked separately. The differences in their role and their approach ensured that there was little conflict over demarcation lines. Donoughue's view was that the government needed both organizations. Neither he, nor Hoskyns and Mount, nor their opposite numbers in the CPRS perceived themselves as rivals. It was more a matter of doing a slightly different job for the same firm. During the Thatcher era the Policy Unit was more varied in its size and composition than under her predecessors. Under Hoskyns the unit was very small. A CPRS member who called on Hoskyns and his colleague Norman Strauss in their early days recalled 'the sad sight of . . . them sitting disconsolately in a garret in Number Ten, with only a blackboard, a kettle, and a ropey old telephone not visibly connected to anything useful'. Mount enlarged the unit and included one or two civil servants in the group. As we shall see later, in the end Mrs Thatcher preferred an enlarged Policy Unit to the CPRS. It is worth noting that it was enlarged partly by absorbing two former members of the CPRS.

Under Thatcher, an additional presence in Number Ten was the Prime Minister's Efficiency Unit, initially under Sir Derek Rayner. The CPRS worked closely with the unit, seeing and commenting on the 'scrutinies' which were the main element in its programme (although, as one member commented, 'The CPRS was never as convinced as Rayner that efficiency scrutinies, even with a generous interpretation of their terms of reference, were an adequate substitute for policy analysis'). When Rayner left to return full time to Marks and Spencer, he was replaced as head of the unit by Ibbs.

Rothschild's CPRS had fairly close contacts not only with Conservative Ministers but also political advisers, whether in departments (Mark Schreiber, John Cope) or in the research department. Under Berrill, with Labour in power, contacts were fewer (although the number, and probably the influence, of political advisers had increased). This difference reflected both Rothschild's wide range of connections outside Whitehall and Berrill's caution about being seen to operate on a political as opposed to a bureaucratic network. Neither Ibbs nor Sparrow encouraged the CPRS to build up the kind of political network which had existed in Rothschild's day.

The lack of effective political relationships was undoubtedly a weakness in the later CPRS. Since most members of the CPRS had little direct contact with Ministers, the political adviser could be a valuable source for them of information about a Minister's views. When writing a collective brief, for instance, it was useful to know what line a Minister would take in a Cabinet committee. The CPRS also sometimes used a political adviser to explain to a Minister why the CPRS was advocating a particular course of action, and perhaps also to report back on the Minister's reaction.

Political advisers could be helpful to the CPRS in providing an alternative view of the activities of their department. Sometimes they defended their departments against prying by the CPRS; at other times they were unhappy about the way officials were approaching a problem and were willing to discuss this with someone in the CPRS who might be an ally. There could thus be mutual benefits in communicating and occasionally co-operating. Members of the CPRS and Ministers' political advisers might not always share the same political culture but they often shared scepticism about the Civil Service's willingness to consider radical options. They were also both the object of Civil Service suspicions. Some senior civil servants disliked the potential influence of both sets of young men and women, neither of whom had yet earned it by 'serving their time'.

The extent and the significance of such alliances should not be exaggerated. Many members of the CPRS had little or nothing to do with political advisers of either main party. Most such contacts were with the small minority of CPRS members who were themselves members of the party in power such as William Waldegrave during the Heath administration, and one of us during the Wilson and Callaghan administrations. Adam Ridley, originally a Treasury official, made the transition from member of the Rothschild CPRS to adviser to Heath in Opposition and at the Tory Central Office and, ultimately, to political adviser to two Conservative Chancellors of the Exchequer in the Thatcher administration.

If most CPRS members had little to do with political advisers, there were some political advisers who were actively hostile to the CPRS. Notable amongst these were Francis Cripps and Frances Morrell, advisers to Tony Benn at the Department of Energy; reflecting their Minister's views, they strongly resented the role played by the CPRS in the battles about nuclear reactors in the mid- to late 1970s. Others, such as Brian Abel-Smith, who advised Barbara Castle and David Ennals at the DHSS and then Peter Shore at the Department of the Environment, were critical rather than hostile, on the grounds that the CPRS's advice was often too 'mealy-mouthed' and inconclusive without enough clear proposals for action. Other advisers, whose contacts with the Think Tank were infrequent, were neutral or indifferent towards it.

Generalizations are dangerous in describing a set of relationships between a range of different people over a 12½-year period, but perhaps the most apt description of the relationship would be 'friendly distance'. But it is clear that a body like the CPRS needs reliable understanding of current party politics as well as of the politics of the bureaucracy. In this respect the early CPRS profited from its place, however marginal, in the party political network. The later CPRS was correspondingly weaker.

In its first years the CPRS attracted a good deal of media publicity, in spite of Sir Burke Trend's attempts to ensure that it did not acquire too high a profile. This was partly because it was itself a subject of great interest, and because, unlike other parts of Whitehall, it could be discussed almost wholly in personal terms: Victor Rothschild, the brilliant, arrogant, personally brave, and idiosyncratic scientist turned policy adviser; his relationship with Heath; his young and allegedly brilliant team of analysts. The CPRS also attracted publicity because it did not—at least at first—discourage this. Rothschild, an outsider to the Whitehall club, did not share his fellow Permanent Secretaries' indiscriminate passion for secrecy. If people wanted to write, and to read, about the CPRS, he saw no reason to prevent this. Indeed, in its early days the CPRS not only attracted publicity; it positively courted it.

The most striking case of this was a feature-length article: 'The Brains behind the Throne', which appeared in the *Sunday Times* colour supplement in March 1973. Researched by James Fox, a writer with no specific experience of government, the article was based on extensive interviews with Rothschild and others. It was illustrated with large colour photographs, and was full of references to the brilliant, unconventional, well-connected team who apparently were putting the whole of Whitehall to rights. The article was shown to the CPRS in final draft. Recollections now vary about the precise nature of the CPRS's reaction to the draft. Some recall it as simply alarm at an account full of unconventionally specific and detailed references to personalities and procedures at the heart of government. Others say that it was the inaccuracies in the article to which the CPRS objected, fearing that they might be held responsible.

In any case, it was felt in the CPRS that the article should not be published in that form. The help was enlisted of Donald Maitland, the diplomat then serving as press adviser at Number Ten. He was persuaded to threaten the *Sunday Times* that unless some corrections and amendments were made, the

Sunday Times would be denied access on similar occasions in the future. The article was substantially rewritten, and appeared in a form far more acceptable to the CPRS (Fox, 1973).

It was not, however, generally acceptable to Whitehall at large. It was seen as being simply the most extreme example so far of the inappropriate publicity generated by the CPRS. It was made clear to Rothschild that if he wanted to be treated as a civil servant, he had better behave more like one. He had no ambition to be treated like a civil servant, but he took the hint. He circulated a note within the CPRS: '. . . we have had a fair amount of publicity in recent months and I believe it would be useful for us to lie doggo for a while . . . While everyone is, I think, agreed that it is useful for the public to have a correct impression of what the CPRS does (though not in detail) and what its constitutional position is, it is difficult to guarantee that this correct impression will be put across by the journalists whom . . . we meet.'

In later years the CPRS had little personalized publicity of this kind. The main exceptions to this were an article about its female members entitled 'Who do they think they are . . .? How dare they? Etc., Etc.' (Thomas, 1978) which appeared on the women's page of the *Daily Mail* in April 1978, and a photograph which Berrill permitted *The Times* of the team working on the Review of Overseas Representation—a photograph which was widely reproduced in other newspapers when the report was published. The publicity which attended this study, largely unsought by the CPRS, was far greater than in any other piece of work the CPRS undertook; it is described in Chapter 8. By then publicity was, on the whole, something the CPRS sought to avoid. Even Berrill, during whose regime more CPRS reports were published than earlier or later, took the view that 'all publicity is bad'. Ibbs held this view more strongly still, and enforced it.

Because the later CPRS usually sought to avoid publicity, its relationships with the press were kept to a minimum. It was protected by the Number Ten Press Office, which acted as a gatekeeper and in most cases refused journalists access to information about the CPRS's work and its members. The CPRS, as part of the Cabinet Office, was subject to the extremely restrictive rules which govern public discussion by Office staff of their professional activities. The relevant part of these read:

The work of the [Cabinet] Secretariat and much of the work of the CPRS are essentially confidential . . . It has always been maintained by successive Administrations that disclosure of the process by which Government decisions are reached weakens the collective responsibility of Ministers . . . The first rule, therefore, is that even the existence of particular Cabinet Committees should not be disclosed—still less their composition, terms of reference, etc. . . .

It follows that members of the Secretariat should describe their work in the broadest

terms, referring only to the side of the Office in which they are principally engaged—
e.g. the scientific and technological, defence and overseas, European Communities,
economic or home and legislation side . . . Members of the CPRS should refer to their
work in no more precise terms, and should avoid mentioning areas of work in which it is
not already public knowledge that the CPRS is engaged . . . (quoted in Hennessy,
1986).

However, the names of CPRS members were known, if only because they
were published in the Civil Service List and the more assiduous members of
the press made contact with them direct. And of course many CPRS staff knew
journalists personally. Contacts with them had, however, to be treated with
considerable discretion. As already mentioned, organizations within government containing 'outsiders' are always suspected of being leaky—and often
accused of being so, especially by those (including Ministers) who are in fact
themselves the sources of leaks. There was always the risk that, however
'correct' staff had been in dealings with journalists, acquaintance alone would
give rise to suspicion.

One focus of CPRS contacts with the media was its published reports. When
reports were published, there was a press release and off-the-record briefings
were also sometimes given. However, the CPRS did not hold press conferences
nor did it attempt to handle the press in an active way. It did not manipulate the
timing of releases, give 'exclusives', or respond to adverse press publicity by
defending itself. It is arguable that its scruples in this respect put the CPRS at a
disadvantage on at least some occasions; one former member of the Review of
Overseas Representation team commented that here the CPRS 'certainly
suffered from its gentlemanly, not to say naïve, handling of publicity and the
media'.

Not all CPRS reports were published. A number of those that were not
published, as well as a complete list of all published reports is provided in
Appendix 1. The extent of publication varied substantially at different times.
Less appeared during the early years under Rothschild than in the middle
years under Berrill, which coincided largely with Labour governments. But
less still appeared during its final years. Its report *Education, Training and
Industrial Performance* appeared in May 1980; *Cashless Pay* appeared in June
1981. These were to be its last publications before it was abolished in July
1983. Indeed only one other report, *People and their Families*, was published
under Thatcher.

Policy about publication was never clearly defined nor generally agreed. At
the outset Trend made clear to Rothschild his own strong opposition to
publication. His successors were little more open in this respect. Decisions
about publication were in practice made case by case, depending on the views
of the CPRS and of other interests in Whitehall, and on circumstances. Such

decisions were rarely straightforward and often involved conflict. The CPRS itself was often ambivalent—even during the period when it was advocating greater freedom of information. Publication created extra work: if a report was being prepared for publication rather than internal circulation, every fact had to be even more carefully double-checked and verified; the arguments had to stand up to the most rigorous scrutiny; and the recommendations had to be couched in such a way that they did not raise expectations unduly or cause embarrassment to Ministers if they decided to reject them. For related reasons, the prospect of publication often increased resistance elsewhere in Whitehall to the CPRS tackling a subject in the first place. Publication also meant publicity and the need to handle the media, which were not necessarily going to be friendly. Nor can it be claimed, even by advocates of more open government, that publication necessarily helps to bring about the changes that on rational and political grounds are desirable. Publication gives opponents of change a greater opportunity to organize public opposition, as witness the Review of Overseas Representation.

Conversely, publication can help by providing ammunition for those in favour of changes of the kind advocated in a report. The CPRS report on race relations contained many proposals for which there was only a weak constituency inside Whitehall. It is arguable that publishing this report would have generated enough support among outside interests to ensure that more action was taken on its proposals. Publication could also help by promoting informed public discussion of radical ideas; such discussion can make respectable and even acceptable ideas which at first blush seem outrageous. There was thus a difficult judgement to be made on the desirability of publication. Would it help or hinder progress towards reform? This question could be answered only on an *ad hoc* basis, since each report would have a different audience and offend or impress or boost different groups.

A decision about publication did not depend solely on the likely effect on central government. Nor were all the recommendations of a CPRS report necessarily directed at central government. They might be more relevant to local government, the health service, certain professions, the police, the trade unions, or parts of the private sector. The CPRS study on education and industry was a good example. In any case, the significance of CPRS reports did not lie only in their specific recommendations. The data which they assembled about an issue could be useful to many people outside Whitehall and should therefore be made widely available. A report's analysis of policy problems should be available to a wider public, in the interests of informed discussion and debate. Arguments of this kind were, however, often countered within the CPRS by the fact that the CPRS existed to work for Ministers; Ministers were its principal clients for information, analysis, and recommendations about policy options. The CPRS was not a government-financed research organization producing objective reports for the community at large.

It followed that the CPRS had to consider how far publication and Ministers' interests would be in conflict. The answer was often that some Ministers would stand to lose and others to gain. A further question concerned the balance between short-term government interests and possible longer-term benefits. The latter were often extraordinarily difficult to assess. More generally, the CPRS's own line on publication could be decisively influenced by the attitude of its head. Rothschild and Berrill, despite their differences in other respects, were in general 'publishers'. Ibbs was definitely not. Some of his colleagues felt that in deciding not to publish the results of the CPRS work on nationalized industries in 1982 he gratuitously weakened the CPRS by denying it some legitimate public credit.

The CPRS was not always keen to see its own reports published; among the other Whitehall interests, there was usually at least one keen to prevent publication. Chief among these was the Treasury, always anxious that nothing should be said in public which might either arouse misplaced expectations of some new and costly government initiative, or which might suggest, however dispassionately, that the answer to some problem might be to allocate more resources to trying to solve it. Thus the Treasury was at first uncomfortable with the light shone by the CPRS on selected social problems in the JASP exercise, described in Chapter 6. It initially opposed publication even of the apparently innocuous report 'People and their Families', a mainly descriptive and factual account, on the same general grounds. Publication was in the end agreed at a meeting of a Cabinet committee from which the Treasury Minister concerned was absent. As described in Chapter 6, the DHSS was uneasy about publishing some reports in the JASP series on the ground that these showed that government policies were not having the effects intended.

In these cases resistance to publication originated with departmental civil servants, although their Ministers were prepared to back them up where necessary. On other occasions it was Ministers who gave the lead. Ministers were often understandably reluctant to see publication of CPRS reports critical of their own departments. Thus DHSS Ministers objected in 1978 to the proposal to publish 'Services for young Children with Working Mothers'. They were supported by their officials. But they were overruled by Number Ten, and the report was published. The attitude of the Prime Minister was often decisive in this context, as in so many others. This was particularly true in the Thatcher years; Ibbs's prudent response to a strong signal from 10 Downing Street against publication led, as already mentioned, to a much more restrictive attitude during the CPRS's last years. A little earlier a leaked (and inaccurate) account appeared in *New Society* (June 1979) of the conclusions of a

CPRS study of the Social Science Research Council. The CPRS had envisaged publishing the final report. But when it became known to Berrill, then head of the CPRS, that this story had attracted some not altogether complimentary attention in the Prime Minister's office, he decided that it would be prudent not to publish after all. The sensitivity of the subject-matter and whether the existence of a study had become publicly known were both important factors in determining publication or not. The story of the SSRC study shows that leaks could reduce the likelihood of publication even in not especially sensitive areas.

To summarize, there was no particular logic in publishing the report on the car industry but not that on the computer industry, or in publishing several reports on aspects of social policy but not the earlier report on race relations (large parts of which were in fact leaked to the press some years later). Attitudes on this question became probably slightly more liberal during the 1970s, then more restrictive again in the last years under Mrs Thatcher. The main influence at any time was probably that of the Cabinet Secretary along with the head of the CPRS. There was always a pragmatic choice to be made; if a report were to be published, would the benefits from informing outside constituencies, possible allies against the guardians of established policies, outweigh the disadvantages of more reluctant collaboration on the part of Whitehall, and perhaps of a veto on doing the study at all? Would changes be more likely, and the longer-term influence of the CPRS enhanced, if it adopted a low profile and a gradualist approach, rather than seeming directly to challenge the barons of Whitehall through appeals to the public and the media? Publicity is always a two-edged weapon; there was considerable discussion in the Rothschild CPRS on whether its credibility was damaged by the colour supplement article. In the event, publicity of this kind was probably fairly harmless, doing little long-term damage. Nevertheless, such fears may have influenced Robin Ibbs, outsider though he was, to take an extremely restrictive line on publication.

5

Energy and the Economy: Two Contrasting Areas of Policy

TWO POLICY AREAS in which the CPRS invested, over its lifetime, a great deal of effort were energy and economic management. The impact of the CPRS in each case depended, as always, partly on circumstances and partly on personalities. It also depended on the basic distribution of power and influence in Whitehall. The nature of the CPRS contribution in either area varied over time. There were also some fundamental differences between the two areas and between the role of the CPRS in them. An examination of these differences casts some light both on the CPRS and on the functioning of British government in general. The purpose of this chapter is not to give a comprehensive history of the part played by the CPRS in economic and in energy policy, but to highlight some of the key features of its roles in each.

The main reason for the CPRS's early involvement in energy matters was Victor Rothschild's personal interest. He brought with him, partly derived from his previous job at Shell, not only great understanding of the field but also an extensive network of contacts and personal advisers. Starting with Anthony Fish, of Shell, there was from 1971 a continuous line of CPRS members seconded from one or other of the major oil companies. Throughout his time at the CPRS Rothschild's capacity for lateral thinking and his interest in the subject led to CPRS inquiries, formal and informal, into issues as various as electric cars, the energy-conserving potential of airships, and the generation of methane from farmyard manure.

Far more important was the recognition by Rothschild and some of his staff of the enormous potential significance of energy policy, well before most other people in Whitehall. 'Fuel and power' had been one of the main concerns of governments in the early post-war years, and there had been a separate Ministry from 1942 to 1969 when it became part of the Ministry of Technology. In 1970 'Fuel and Power' was part of the merger which formed the 'giant' Department of Trade and Industry, part of a package of changes that had included the CPRS. The energy divisions were merely a few among the many competing for the attention of a single secretary of state at the DTI; they did not even have their own junior minister. The only energy topic that received much attention was the coal industry. 'High-flying' DTI officials tended to prefer, and to be preferred for, posts elsewhere in the department.

Guided by Rothschild, the CPRS thought this dangerous. It approached the planners at Shell and asked to see the results of their analysis of various scenarios involving substantial increases in the price of oil. It consulted some outside economists (including Ralph Turvey and Michael Posner) about energy supply and pricing policy. It began discussions with the CEGB about the fuel efficiency of different methods of generating electricity, and set up a good working relationship with the National Coal Board, which provided information about its operations.

Apart from Rothschild and Fish (and the latter's successors), none of the CPRS staff who worked on energy matters in the early days had any relevant expertise. But since expertise was also sadly lacking elsewhere in Whitehall, it was not long before the CPRS, plugged into Rothschild's unique network of outside expertise, knew as much about the subject as the departmental officials concerned. However, they could not ignore the officials, particularly after policy disagreements with the CEGB led to a drying-up of information from this source. Thereafter the CPRS relied heavily on information from the DTI.

When the CPRS started serious work on energy, in early 1972, oil was selling at $1.90 a barrel. The price of petrol at the British pumps was 34.5 pence a gallon. The CPRS report on energy policy, presented to incredulous ministers in the summer of 1973, suggested three possible oil-price scenarios for 1985: what it termed EASY ($3.75 per barrel, at 1972 prices), SCARCE ($6 per barrel), and CRISIS ($9 per barrel).

The report itself was in many respects a model for what the CPRS was to do over the next decade, both in presentation and in substance. The style was clear, direct, and jargon-free. Of the report's 65 pages, 30 were mainly statistical annexes. The arguments of the remaining 35 were summarized in a 4-page introduction, followed by a list of recommendations. The report was bound in the striking red covers that were a hallmark of the CPRS's presentations.

The main recommendations in the report were that action in the next two years should assume the possibility of the SCARCE scenario, namely that by 1985 oil could be costing up to $6 per barrel. The major implication of this assumption was that the current policy of shifting from coal-fired to oil-fired power stations should be halted. The situation could be reviewed and followed by more drastic action later if this seemed necessary. There was an extensive list of secondary recommendations. These covered topics such as North Sea oil production (policy towards which should be clarified and should embody a more active approach to licensing); the coal industry (in which new sources should be sought while pit closures concentrated on pits the most expensive in resource, not financial, terms); power stations (where a speedy choice should be made between the two leading types for the next generation of nuclear reactors and research on other types terminated, while the scope for dual coal/oil-fired stations should be investigated); electric vehicles; environmental policy; the tax regime for petroleum products; future Russian demand for, and supplies of, crude oil, and other topics.

The basic theme of the report was simple enough in principle. A national energy policy was needed. Without this, *ad hoc* decisions would be taken, unrelated to decisions in other areas, leading to incoherence and inconsistency at considerable cost to the nation. In this sense the report was a manifestation of the central role of the CPRS. It drew to the attention of Ministers the need for an overall strategy in order to avoid conflicting objectives or the use of inconsistent means to achieve policy goals. It made manifest the CPRS's central role in two other respects. First, it tried to *look ahead*, in this case over a ten-year period. Secondly, it brought together a wide range of material on the likely demand for, and supply of, different types of energy, which it *analysed* in some depth and presented simply and briefly.

The CPRS gave an oral presentation to Ministers of the findings of the report. This caused something of a sensation. Many Ministers simply refused to accept the validity of the SCARCE scenario and accused the CPRS of scaremongering. As a result, most of the report's recommendations were not accepted for implementation. In fact, of course, the CPRS was to prove completely right in principle, even if wrong in practice. The oil price rise came much sooner, and was more drastic, than the report had predicted. Following the Arab–Israeli war of 1973, oil was $11.00 per barrel (equivalent to $9.90 at 1972 prices). It later rose to a peak of $40.40 (equivalent to $19.70); by July 1987 the price was $19.80 ($7.30).

Rothschild and his team were vindicated. Their pessimistic foresight was acknowledged by the rest of Whitehall. This single episode did more to establish the credibility of the CPRS, in its early days, than did any other factor except, possibly, the general support of the Prime Minister. Thus established as knowledgeable and expert in energy matters, the CPRS was to remain active in this field for the next decade. Even after Rothschild himself had gone, the continuing presence among the staff of an expert seconded from one of the oil companies guaranteed that the CPRS would maintain its interests in energy questions—and, more important, its direct access to outside expertise.

One result of the energy crisis was the re-establishment of a separate Department of Energy, set up in 1974. This remained a relatively weak department. Some of its staff had worked in the old Ministry of Fuel and Power, and so knew something about energy issues. Many, however, had come from other parts of the Department of Trade and Industry, the Treasury, and the Foreign and Commonwealth Office. Initially, they knew much less about their department's subject-matter than did the CPRS. Moreover, since departments were naturally more willing to second people whom they felt they could spare, the quality of the new department's staff was distinctly uneven. The CPRS was thus able to play a uniquely direct part in the department's affairs, being regularly represented at meetings of its senior officials and actually briefing them on many issues. CPRS relationships with the department's Ministers varied. The CPRS got on well with the first Minister, Lord Carrington, and equally well with his Labour successor Eric Varley. The same was not true of Varley's successor Tony Benn, as described later in this chapter.

Continuing CPRS work on energy policy towards the end of the Heath government led to a major presentation to Ministers—but, ironically, to Ministers of the Labour government, in March 1974. Reviewing the situation as it seemed likely to develop for the rest of the decade and beyond, the CPRS noted how vulnerable to supply disruption was an energy-intensive economy such as Britain's. It reviewed future demands for energy and the likely comparative costs of the main energy sources—oil, coal, gas, and nuclear generation. It came down heavily in favour of nuclear power, with coal as the next best alternative. Orders for oil-fired power stations were to be cancelled, and none further placed in future.

This emphasis on nuclear power was strongly backed by Rothschild, who argued that the safety problems of nuclear reactors had been exaggerated. (He used to irritate his opponents by claiming that the accident statistics for nuclear installations were in fact better than those for windmills.) The CPRS continued to take this line after Rothschild's departure; its pro-nuclear stance was to be a source of suspicion elsewhere in Whitehall and outside and, ultimately, a source of conflict.

One other recommendation in the March 1974 presentation was that the CPRS's own report on energy conservation should be published. This study had been carried out in the face of considerable scepticism and lack of interest elsewhere in Whitehall, including the Department of Energy. It has to be acknowledged that most members of the CPRS were equally unenthusiastic: the completion of the study and the publication of the report in July 1974 was almost wholly due to the perseverance of one member of the CPRS, Ian Read, seconded from Shell. As usual, however, the report was presented by the CPRS collectively, and the CPRS as a whole took credit for the good reception which it got. The report took a comprehensive look at the main uses of energy,

78

in transportation, electricity generation, industry and the home. It looked as far ahead as the year 2000. Through it ran the same main themes as the CPRS had put to Ministers: Britain's vulnerability to interruptions of supply, the significance of nuclear power, the scale on which energy was currently being wasted. The scope and the recommendations of the report are neatly indicated and summarized by the table which appeared as its frontispiece and is reproduced here.

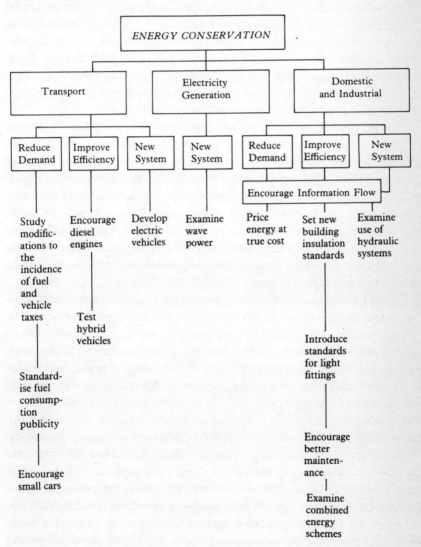

Although it proposed that a study should be made of the scope for harnessing wave power, most of its recommendations related to the use made of energy in the several main fields. In relation to transport, it advocated various measures to reduce petrol consumption including a legal requirement to provide information about fuel consumption over a standard cycle on all new vehicles; encouragement to car manufacturers to improve their position in the small car market and develop more economical engines and more aero-dynamically efficient car bodies; research on problems relating to starting small diesel engines and eliminating the unpleasant smell of diesel fuel; the examination of increases in duty on petrol relative to that on diesel and of the incidence of fuel and vehicle taxes including the possibility of increasing the duty on petrol and introducing a differential tax favouring smaller cars and penalizing larger ones; and finally (another CPRS favourite) research and development batteries for use in electric vehicles.

The report's recommendations in relation to the home and industry covered pricing policy and taxation, insulation, more efficient light fittings, proper ventilation control, and the scope in industry for the greater use of hydraulic systems in place of electric motors. A good deal of emphasis was placed on the need for greater publicity on a number of issues including the true cost of running domestic appliances, the relationship between higher room temper-atures and higher fuel bills, better maintenance of domestic and industrial space heating boilers, and better information on techniques of fuel efficiency.

Few of the proposals were new, but taken as a whole they formed a set of practical, and largely practicable, steps. Despite this, implementation was slow. The Department of Energy, for reasons already given, had little weight in Whitehall, and found it hard to persuade other departments to take energy conservation seriously and to modify their own main programmes accordingly. The latter could often find an ally in the Treasury, rarely likely to accept long-term resource savings as justifying short-term increases in public spending. A notable example of this was the Treasury's negative response to the CPRS proposal to pay improvement grants to householders, towards the costs of insulating their houses. In this case, effective joint action by the CPRS and the Department of Energy won the day; insulation grants have been established policy since.

Other energy topics on which the CPRS later worked were to include the structure of the National Nuclear Corporation, the future of North Sea gas, the licensing and taxation of North Sea oil exploitation (where the CPRS found itself allied with Harold Wilson's adviser Lord Balogh in opposing what both saw as the Foreign Office's propensity to cede too much to foreign govern-ments—in this case, Norway and France—for the sake of some far from certain improvement in diplomatic relations), the Coal Board's ten-year plan, the future of the power plant industry (described in Chapter 7), and the choice of reactor for nuclear power generation. This last issue was to involve the CPRS in a highly publicized row with a leading Labour Minister—the Secretary of State for Energy, Tony Benn. In the summer of 1975 Benn and the energy Minister, Eric Varley, swapped jobs, in a move designed by the Prime Minister to play down the 'socialist' industry policy to which the government had been formally committed since its election victory the year before. As industry Minister Benn had several times found himself on the opposite side of the argument from the CPRS; by the time he moved to Energy he seemed to see the CPRS as a potential enemy rather than an ally (although in fact the CPRS was to support Benn's line on matters as various as the future of the coal industry, the establishment of the British National Oil Corporation, and the need for a tough stance in relation to the oil companies and to challenges by foreign governments concerning the boundaries of Britain's continental shelf). When the CPRS challenged Benn's view on the appropriate choice of nuclear reactor, he took great exception.

As already mentioned, the CPRS's views about the insecurity of oil supplies led logically to support for nuclear power generation. This in itself was a cause for suspicion on the part of those, like Benn himself, who were in general opposed to the nuclear option. The CPRS felt that Benn's views on these matters clouded his judgement on all questions relating to nuclear power, including even the choice between types of nuclear reactors. His championship of the British-built advanced gas-cooled reactor (AGR), rather than the American-built pressurized water reactor (PWR), was seen by the CPRS as an emotional expression of anti-Americanism which took no account of economic reality. The CPRS itself was strongly in favour of the PWR, a position which—for once—it shared with much of the rest of Whitehall, Department of Energy officials, the Central Electricity Generating Board, the South of Scotland Electricity Board, the National Nuclear Corporation.

The argument was protracted even by Whitehall standards. It was not till the following spring that proposals were finally put to Ministers, after prolonged wrangling between the protagonists of the two main options: the CPRS and most of official Whitehall on one side, and Benn, Bruce Millan (Secretary of State for Scotland), and one or two other Ministers on the other. The Prime Minister, James Callaghan, believed that Benn's passionate commitment to the AGR was wrong. He encouraged the CPRS in its anti-AGR line. The CPRS, perhaps emboldened by the strength of its allies, was unusually robust. It provided a strongly worded collective brief, favouring the PWR, for the Cabinet committee which considered the issue. It also engaged in extensive lobbying throughout Whitehall, to ensure that the case of the PWR was fully understood, despite the technicality of the subject-matter. These were the activities resented, and later criticized, by Benn. Even James Callaghan subsequently felt that on this occasion the CPRS had gone rather beyond its proper role (interview with authors).

The final outcome was a compromise, aimed to satisfy both groups. It was accepted that the PWR was the right choice for the longer term, provided that outstanding doubts about its safety could be resolved; design work on it was to proceed, subject to safety clearance. But in the short term, to the relief both of the British industry and of Ministers anxious about growing unemployment, especially in the North-East, two more AGRs were to be built.

The delay in reaching a decision, and the untidy nature of the decision that was made, was due to several causes: limited expertise in the Department of Energy (in what was admittedly a highly complex subject area), conflicting scientific advice, uncertainties about safety and also about the economic and balance of payments implications of either option. There was also the fact that, with the passage of time, the decision ceased to appear urgent, as energy prices soared and the general recession reduced the demand for electricity from whatever source. Given the ultimate cost of a nuclear reactor programme, and the virtual irreversibility of decisions once made, it is perhaps not surprising that there was procrastination. In many ways the most effective contribution the CPRS could have made would have been to press for a rapid decision—as it had itself urged in its 1973 report. Had there been less delay in formulating a nuclear reactor policy, the decision reached might have been different. For example, had the necessary development work on the PWR started earlier, it might have been possible to allay the doubts about its safety. As things were, the decision finally came to be taken in the worst possible circumstances, with the British industry desperately worried about its own future and Labour Ministers, facing the prospect of an election in a year's time, equally worried about the levels of unemployment.

The CPRS continued to play an active part in energy questions throughout the Thatcher years. Rothschild's successors continued his practice of appointing someone on secondment from one of the major oil companies. By the end the oil company place had become virtually monopolized by BP, which provided the last five incumbents in succession. The resident energy expert saw all the relevant Cabinet and Cabinet committee papers, and sat on the relevant interdepartmental committees. The head of the CPRS, briefed by this expert, continued to intervene regularly in Ministerial debates on energy matters.

The CPRS remained wholly 'credible' in energy matters until the end of its existence. But if in the early 1970s this credibility had derived largely from the CPRS's relative expertise in energy matters, a decade later an additional factor was the relative speed with which the CPRS adapted to the new style of policy under the Conservatives. In the energy sector—coal, gas, electricity, nuclear—state ownership and state intervention had long been fundamental; it was not surprising that the parts of government mainly responsible for energy matters found it hard to come to terms with the free-market approach of the new government, including the drive to privatization. Especially while the moderate, ex-Heathite David Howell was the Secretary of State for Energy, the CPRS tended to find itself urging the new Tory line on a reluctant Department of Energy. This happened less often when Howell was replaced by the more hardline Nigel Lawson.

The CPRS was thus active in developing the rationale of the programme to privatize some of the industries with whose control it had been so preoccupied a decade earlier. In early 1982 it was commissioned by the Cabinet to review the 'state monopolies' and to consider the case for returning each of them to private ownership. At about the same time it was asked to look at the long-running issue of electricity pricing policy. Was it true, as alleged by British manufacturing firms consuming large quantities of electricity, that they were disadvantaged compared with their Continental competitors whose governments subsidized electricity prices; and if it was true, should the British government follow suit? A CPRS team was set up, visited British and, unusually, overseas producers and consumers of electricity, and came down firmly in favour of economic pricing—advice which was taken by the government.

Applying the same basic principles, the CPRS also advised against the Department of Energy's cherished project for a 'gas-gathering pipeline' (a government-funded common carrier to link and convey natural gas from the several privately owned North Sea oil fields). In this argument the CPRS and Treasury found themselves allies against the enthusiasms of the Departments of Energy and Trade and Industry, the guardians of the interventionist inheritance from the 1970s. The line-up was the same in the Mossmorran affair: once again CPRS and Treasury opposed the same two departments in resisting the claims of ICI for special taxation treatment which would enable its existing plant for processing North Sea gas to compete effectively against Shell's new plant at Mossmorran. On other energy-related issues such as coal grants, gas exports, depletion policy, and North Sea taxation, the CPRS line reflected what it saw as its role in resisting departmental special pleading which would have deflected government policy from the straight and narrow application of market principles.

In doing this the CPRS—though obviously not alone—appears to have had some impact. 'Ministers listened to us', recalled a former member of the CPRS, 'because Robin Ibbs had acquired such a reputation as a trouble-shooter, because the Treasury was too *parti pris* and because the Department of Energy couldn't deliver the goods.' The situation could hardly have been more different from that in which Rothschild had begun the CPRS's involvement in energy matters, but the justification of the role was one of which he would probably have approved.

Economic Policy

Energy policy was a sector in which the CPRS very early on established itself as a force to be reckoned with. There was at first no relevant policy department to challenge CPRS incursions into its territory, and for some time after 1973 only a new department still finding its feet. On some major energy issues the CPRS was unquestionably right while other people were equally clearly wrong, and its views on energy were in general treated as authoritative.

The area of economic policy was very different. For a start, it was undeniably the province of the Treasury, the most powerful department in Whitehall. The Chancellor of the Exchequer has regular access to the Prime Minister and can normally depend upon the latter's support. Commenting on the struggle between the Treasury and 'spending' departments at the time, in the autumn of 1976, when the IMF was insisting on expenditure cuts as a condition of making a further loan to the UK, Edmund Dell observed that 'there was never at any time any question but that [the Prime Minister] would support the Chancellor of the Exchequer. There was therefore at no time any question but that the Cabinet as a whole would submit to the Chancellor of the Exchequer. The tactical question the Prime Minister had to decide was not *whether* to weigh in behind Denis Healey but *when* to do so' (Dell, April 1980).

The close relationship between the Chancellor and the Prime Minister is both cause and effect of the Treasury's enormous power in Whitehall. This power is reinforced by several other factors. First, and most obviously, the Treasury, like any other department in normal circumstances, commands some deference in dealings on matters for which it is responsible. The same is broadly true of Defence on defence matters, or Transport on transport. But whereas relatively few major policy issues have a defence or a transport dimension, few do *not* have an economic dimension—or cannot plausibly be claimed by the Treasury to have one. It thus in effect has a right of entry into virtually any argument going on in Whitehall, and in consequence is in a state of perpetual readiness to do so. The second and third reasons derive from the Treasury's intrinsic capability: its administrators are unquestionably, as these things are judged in the British Civil Service, the intellectual élite of Whitehall. In addition, they are supported by a specialist élite, in the form of professional economists, of a quality unmatched in other departments, working with the generalists in an integrated way still rare in Whitehall. Fourthly, many aspects of economic policy are shaped wholly outside the collective processes in which the CPRS was acknowledged to have a legitimate part to play. Many issues and much of the general thrust of policy, are settled privately and bilaterally between Chancellor and Prime Minister. Others are settled in the framework of major set-piece events at long intervals—such as the annual Budget or public expenditure round—in which roles are recognized and structured and leave little scope for intervention by newcomers such as the CPRS. Yet others are decided in the course of a continuing process managed by the Treasury, such as intervention in money markets.

The Treasury, variously respected, feared, and hated by the rest of Whitehall, thus controls many of the processes in which it takes part and finds little difficulty in establishing a *locus* for itself in any area in which it is interested. Many Treasury officials never accepted the CPRS claim that it had something additional and distinctive to contribute to the economic policy process; they saw the CPRS as at best redundant, if not impertinent, and at worst as a threat to the fragile consensus on economic policy issues—or to the equally fragile sovereignty maintained by Chancellor and Prime Minister over the great barons in the spending departments.

The CPRS for its part recognized from the start the extent of the Treasury's power and influence, and therefore the desirability of having it as an ally. Conversely, it recognized the difficulty of successfully challenging the Treasury unless there was a difference of opinion between the Chancellor and Prime Minister or, at the very least, doubt in the Prime Minister's mind about the course of action proposed by the Treasury. In many circumstances the CPRS and the Treasury found themselves ranged alongside each other, often in the face of one or more spending departments; there was bound to be some affinity between two organizations occupationally inclined to challenge the unverified assertions and unquestioned assumptions so often emanating from the rest of Whitehall. But there were also bound to be occasions when it was assertions and assumptions by the Treasury which seemed to require challenge. The CPRS often had to argue that economic and financial considerations, important though they were, were not always overriding, and that despite the Treasury's expertise its advice on economic matters was not always above challenge.

The CPRS itself always possessed a fair amount of economic expertise. Victor Rothschild was not an economist, but his deputy, Dick Ross, was. Ross had worked in the Treasury earlier in his career; he thus understood the system and knew some of the key people. Rothschild himself was replaced by an economist, Kenneth Berrill, who had previously been the Chief Economic Adviser in the Treasury. Berrill headed the CPRS for nearly half its life. When Ross left in 1978 he was replaced by a Treasury administrator on secondment, Gordon Downey. Downey was replaced by another Treasury administrator, Alan Bailey. There were always two or three other junior economists in the CPRS; several of these, too, were seconded from the Treasury.

This line-up gave the CPRS an intellectual strength in economic policy matters at least as great as that in any other sector. Some CPRS members felt that economists were, indeed, over-represented in a small unit compared with other specialists; others wondered if the Treasury background of so many CPRS economists inhibited the latter's willingness to challenge their parent department. There is no convincing evidence that this was so.

The CPRS's working relationship with the Treasury embraced both challenge and collaboration. The relationship developed over the life of the CPRS. It was, in any case, not homogeneous. It was affected by personalities, by the state of the economy, by the stage reached in the life cycles of governments, and by the consequently fluctuating relationships between the Treasury and other departments. It also varied between issues.

Much the same was true of the CPRS relationship with Prime Ministers on Treasury matters. Close though Heath was to his Chancellor, Anthony Barber, the CPRS had relatively easy access to 10 Downing Street in those early years. Economic policy was high on the agenda at the meeting between Heath and the CPRS in the summer of 1972, and CPRS advice was a major factor in encouraging the celebrated 'U-turn' in relation to incomes policy in late 1972. Berrill, the only economist to head the CPRS, was on less close terms with the Prime Ministers he served although, as mentioned below, he played a major role in briefing Callaghan at the time of the IMF visit and subsequent Cabinet crisis in 1976. Wilson and Callaghan also looked less than had Heath to the CPRS for advice to counter the Treasury, being able to turn to their Policy Unit, which included several able economists. Mrs Thatcher had even less need of, or desire for, CPRS advice in this area. Not only was the essentially Keynesian Berrill, in charge of the CPRS when the Conservatives took office in May 1979, out of sympathy with the new government's monetarist policies, but Mrs Thatcher also appointed her own personal economic adviser—during the CPRS's lifetime, Professor Alan Walters from Johns Hopkins University in the USA. Robin Ibbs, who replaced Berrill, had strong views about the damaging impact of monetarist measures on his own firm, ICI; but he did not think it was appropriate for him, as head of the CPRS, to press these views on the Prime Minister.

When the CPRS first came on the scene, the Treasury took the line that short-term economic and fiscal policy was not a proper subject for the CPRS. The CPRS challenged this diktat. On fiscal policy it was almost entirely unsuccessful. Rothschild made a determined effort to open up this area for collective discussion; he argued strongly against the traditional exclusion of most Ministers from the process of making the annual 'Budget'. Briefed by a CPRS economist, he suggested that not more than a quarter of so-called 'Budget secrets' had any good claim to be kept secret. He tried to deploy some of the CPRS's developing views, derived from its work on energy, about the case for a fuel tax rather than an annual vehicle excise tax. But although, towards the end of the Callaghan administration, some concessions were made in giving the Cabinet earlier notice of the contents of the Budget, the central citadel remained unstormed. The CPRS was never able to play an overtly active part in matters of fiscal policy.

On public expenditure the position was quite different. Part of the original case for having a CPRS at all, as stated in the 1970 White Paper, was 'to establish the relative priorities to be given to the different sections of [Ministers'] programme' and to 'play an important part in the extended public expenditure survey process'. The CPRS exploited this opening vigorously. From the beginning it played a central role, as significant as that of the Treasury, in the new system for evaluating department spending programmes, Programme Analysis and Review (PAR). As mentioned in Chapter 3, the CPRS was active in helping to choose subjects for PAR, in overseeing progress in the reviews and in commenting on the latter's conclusions. The Treasury argued that only high spending programmes should be 'PARed', and tended to favour conclusions that favoured cut-backs in programme spending. The CPRS, more concerned with effectiveness than with economy, was quite willing to see reviews made of programmes currently consuming relatively low levels of resources, and to support the conclusion that it might be more cost-effective to spend more. The CPRS remained active in PAR throughout the latter's life, including its later days under the Wilson and Callaghan governments when Labour Ministers were unenthusiastic about this un-wanted inheritance from the Conservatives, and when the Treasury was equally unenthusiastic about what it rightly saw as a technique which could not be guaranteed to support the case for lower levels of public expenditure.

More significantly, the CPRS early established its right to contribute to Ministerial thinking about priorities in public spending. Dick Ross took the line which greatly influenced CPRS thinking during its early years, that the Treasury generally knew best about overall targets for public expenditure as a whole. But this did not preclude a great deal of CPRS activity in relation to particular spending programmes, and to discussions of the relative weight to be given to any of them in conditions of growth or of economic stringency. The CPRS saw its role here as deriving directly from its own concern with the government's overall strategy: it insisted, as far as it could, that decisions on which programme to increase, cut, or simply shield from cuts should bear some coherent relationship to the government's general thinking about policy priorities and to any decisions about these already taken. 'Dick Ross and I went round a number of departments', recalled a member of the CPRS in its early days, 'to try to get departments to be more explicit about their priorities, particularly for public expenditure purposes. We hoped to get them to think aloud about these in a way they would never do in front of the Treasury; but for the most part we failed . . .'

The CPRS also inserted position papers of its own into the discussions in the annual PESC round, commenting both on the Treasury's proposals for the level of total expenditure and on the positions of individual spending departments. Personalities were important here; the Treasury Second Permanent Secretary in charge of public expenditure was John Hunt (later Cabinet Secretary). Having taken up this post a month before the CPRS started work, he came to talk to Rothschild about CPRS involvement in public expenditure issues. He said, according to a CPRS member who was present at this discussion, that 'there was little that he did and knew that we would not or should not know'.

The high point of the CPRS involvement in decision-making on public expenditure came in September 1973, when the Cabinet—not for the first or last time—in belatedly trying to control the 'Barber boom' found itself unable to reconcile the totals proposed by the Treasury and aggregated from departmental bids. Hunt was at this moment in the process of taking over as Cabinet Secretary from Sir Burke Trend. When Ministers asked if the CPRS could help them in their dilemma, Hunt and Trend agreed that a CPRS presentation might be valuable. The presentation duly took place in the Cabinet room; material prepared for the CPRS on the basis of Treasury figures was presented by a succession of members of the CPRS. This was one of the earliest high-level applications by the CPRS of a technique long familiar in the private sector, but still even in the 1980s not widespread in Whitehall and in the 1970s virtually unknown: the use of graphics to take decision-makers through some quite complex alternative futures, based on differing assumptions, and to show them in easily comparable form the consequences of the different decisions that they might make. In this case the CPRS advice to Ministers was to ignore the 'siren voices' urging on them some simplistic solutions to the problems of choice (such as cutting the fastest-growing programmes, or cutting all programmes across the boards, or relying on greater efficiency and less waste). Reasoned choices had to be made, said the CPRS, reflecting the government's major objectives. The latter might include, for example, investment-led growth; some rise in standards of living; a reduced rate of inflation; fairness; and others. The right action might include cuts in programmes such as agricultural support, the hospital and school building programmes, minor roads, and the deferment of the third London airport and Channel Tunnel projects. The final pair of slides were a typical Rothschild flourish: two specially commissioned drawings from the *Daily Express* cartoonist Cummings, one of which showed the Cabinet, having failed to accept the subtle guidance of the CPRS, in a state of uproar, while the other showed the tranquillity and good humour which might follow from a better outcome.[1]

---

[1] These were subsequently reproduced in Rothschild's book of reminiscences (Rothschild, 1977).

Even with these sweeteners, the pill was not swallowed. No decisions were taken at the meeting, which was followed by further bilateral discussions between the Treasury and spending departments and a series of somewhat arbitrary cuts in late 1973 and early 1974.

On broader macro-economic policy the role and authority of the CPRS fluctuated during its life, depending—as so often—on personalities and on circumstances. Despite the Treasury's initial view that the CPRS had nothing to contribute here, the first CPRS 'strategy' paper presented to the Heath Cabinet in the summer of 1971 contained a section on economic policy. 'We did this partly by compiling what was known', said a senior CPRS economist, 'and emphasising the uncertainties more than the Treasury might do. We inserted some scepticism about both official and ministerial views.' The CPRS repeated this approach, in subsequent papers, for as long as the strategy meetings continued—that is, until the autumn of 1973. During this period the CPRS thus licensed its own involvement in discussions of economic policy, despite the Treasury's disapproval.

The CPRS was also involved in the discussions that led up to the Heath government's decision to allow sterling to float, in June 1972. Its encouragement to Ministers to break free from the shackles of a fixed exchange rate may well have helped to tilt the balance of their decisions to do so.

During the Heath years the CPRS also established itself as one of the leading actors in Whitehall in the field of prices and incomes policies. Though their approaches varied, both the Conservative and Labour governments agreed on the importance of finding some kind of framework within which to contain wage and price increases. Dick Ross was throughout this period regarded as among the most authoritative experts in Whitehall.

In economic policy-making in general the CPRS played a rather smaller part under Labour than under the Heath government. This was partly due to the discontinuation of strategy meetings, partly—as already mentioned—to the Labour Prime Ministers' possession of their own economic advisers in the Number Ten Policy Unit. However, the CPRS played an active part in the discussions about a possible, more 'socialist', alternative economic strategy, as advocated by Tony Benn in the Cabinet and other left-wing elements outside. At one stage the CPRS, it is thought at the request of the Prime Minister's office, wrote up a paper making a case for and a case against the Benn approach. The case for, one of its authors later recalled, was far more plausible and internally consistent than anything '[Francis] Cripps [Benn's special adviser] managed. We were rather proud of it and the Policy Unit complimented it too.' But in this context in general, as in others, the CPRS followed Dick Ross's lead in broadly supporting the orthodox Treasury line.

Although the role of the CPRS as a whole in economic policy was relatively limited under Labour, Ken Berrill's personal status ensured him, at least, an entrée from time to time. Thus he and Dick Ross privately briefed the Prime Minister during the IMF crisis of 1976. This activity was regarded as so sensitive that even its existence was not revealed to the rest of the CPRS—a concealment which upset the other CPRS economists who believed, understandably though incorrectly, that the CPRS was failing to make its proper contribution to the major issue of the day. Later, towards the end of the Callaghan government, a regular seminar on economic policy was held involving the Prime Minister, the Chancellor of the Exchequer, the permanent head of the Treasury (Sir Douglas Wass), the Governor of the Bank of England, and Kenneth Berrill.

The relative ineffectiveness of the CPRS in macro-economic policy under the Labour government is well illustrated by an episode towards the end of this period. The story began in late 1976. The CPRS had contributed to an exercise entitled the National Recovery Programme. Ministers had decided that they wished to examine ways of regenerating the economy and improving output and performance. In the autumn of 1976, the CPRS and the Prime Minister's Policy Unit had been asked to prepare a joint paper for a meeting of the Cabinet Committee on Economic Strategy. The Policy Unit and the CPRS were unable to agree on the line to take and produced two separate papers. The CPRS paper did not go down well with Ministers. It had made the fatal mistake of omitting any reference to unemployment in its list of recommendations at a time when the jobless total was growing and causing concern among Labour Ministers. Subsequently some members of the CPRS thought this omission should be rectified by carrying out a full-scale study of the economic aspects of unemployment and possible policies to deal with it.

The study received the Prime Minister's blessing and there was no opposition from the Treasury, the Department of Employment, or elsewhere. A CPRS team of four was set up in the autumn of 1977 to do the study. Two of its members were economists. To these were added an outside academic economist as a consultant (Chris Allsopp from the University of Oxford), and a trade union representative (Roger Goulbourne from the Electrical, Electronic, Telecommunications, and Plumbing Trade Union (EETPTU) research department. This was the only occasion that a trade union official was brought in to work with the CPRS.

The usual discussions took place with other departments, including the Department of Employment and the DHSS as well as the Treasury. The CPRS also analysed the many lengthy papers produced by the Manpower Group, an interdepartmental official committee chaired by the Department of Employment, which had been concentrating on what became known as 'special measures' to reduce unemployment. These included various schemes such as job release, which allowed for retirement a year earlier, the job creation and work experience programmes and schemes which subsidized employers to take additional workers. Discussions were held with employers' organizations and the representatives of individual trade unions as well as the TUC.

A draft report was produced around Christmas 1977. It was a forthright Keynesian statement on the need to reflate the economy. It began by suggesting that if nothing was done (i.e. if the policies of the time were continued), unemployment could reach three million by the early mid-1980s. This sentence was removed by the head of the CPRS from the final version on the grounds that it might be thought exaggerated and scaremongering. The report went on to examine the argument that concern about high levels of unemployment was unjustified because unemployment and other benefits protected everyone from the extremes of poverty it caused during the thirties. The report dismissed this argument on the grounds that, for the individual, high levels of long-term unemployment led to low morale, boredom, social isolation, feelings of inadequacy, and material losses. For the nation it led to waste and inefficiency. Nor were increased leisure, more adult education, earlier retirement, and improvements in training opportunities for young people acceptable alternatives to providing people with work, desirable though all of these were in their own right.

The report then analysed the causes of the current unemployment and recommended remedies. The conventional wisdom at the time was to lay increasing stress on the structural causes of unemployment. The report questioned that and went on to argue the significance of cyclical factors. The most important of those was prolonged recession.

The rest of the report fell into two parts: a long section on the macro-economic context and macro-economic measures to deal with unemployment; and a shorter section on 'special measures' both to reduce unemployment in the short term and to ease the lot of the unemployed. In the first part the CPRS argued that there were two pressing arguments in favour of stimulating the UK economy. First, investment would not recover without sustained growth in demand; and the longer the recession the greater the likelihood that when growth did at last occur it would be constrained by structural problems and inflationary pressures. Secondly, the country's competitiveness would become even more of a problem if the exchange rate went on strengthening as seemed likely whilst low growth and North Sea oil combined to produce balance of payments surpluses. Faster growth would relieve this pressure on the exchange rate. In spite of the acknowledged dangers to a growth strategy, the CPRS team was convinced that a judicious mix of tax reductions, resumption of growth in public expenditure, and special counter-cyclical schemes would stimulate demand but could have a substantial reversible element so that the expansion could be controlled. Moreover, North Sea oil provided unusual leeway on the balance of payments although industrial and exchange rate policies would need to keep the current account of the balance of payments within a reasonable distance of balance. Continued co-operation with the trades unions would be needed on pay and increasing productivity. The report acknowledged that this strategy would not solve unemployment quickly. But in spite of the risks the alternative of inaction was, it argued, unacceptable. Inaction would increase the obsolescence of capital stock. It could lead to a rising pound and a further weakening of the ability of British goods and services to compete with foreign substitutes.

The report also advocated the extension and strengthening of certain special measures. Even with a strongly reflationary policy unemployment would remain high in the short term. Whilst subsidies to employment and other micro-economic measures to mitigate the impact of unemployment were little more than palliatives and no substitute for general reflation, the CPRS proposed more action in terms of selective employment measures to underpin the main strategy. It also proposed various measures to help the long-term unemployed, and, finally, the establishment of a review of ways of improving the system of income maintenance for the unemployed.

A report containing recommendations of this kind, though clearly out of place during the Thatcher regime, might have been expected to get at least a sympathetic hearing under a Labour government, even if the strategy proposed were eventually rejected. Even under Labour, however, it was decidedly out of line with current Treasury thinking. Moreover, it failed to enlist the support of Kenneth Berrill, perhaps because he had not been sufficiently involved in its preparation in its earlier stages. Faced with a rather suprising *fait accompli* in the shape of the penultimate draft, he was both uncertain of the merits of the argument of the report and concerned about the possibility of a head-on confrontation with the Treasury. He was probably relieved when, the report having been submitted to the Prime Minister, the latter decided not to circulate it to his Cabinet colleagues.

This episode was only one of many examples of what the CPRS saw as a continuing failure to take decisions about economic policy in a rational way. The point was not that the decisions themselves ought to be in some sense more 'scientific', less 'political', or even that they should have been different in any particular case. But they should be the outcome of a much more logical process, so that they took account of the relevant facts and bore some relationship to Ministers' other decisions.

The most elaborate effort by the CPRS, early in its life, to put across this view was a short report with the somewhat anodyne title 'The Presentation of the Public Expenditure Survey'. This grew partly out of the CPRS's frustration at the September 1973 presentation and its aftermath, although the report was not completed until nearly a year had passed and a new Labour government had come to power. It criticized both the quantity (too much) and the quality (largely uninformative) of the data presented to Ministers being asked to make decisions about resource allocation. It argued that the public expenditure survey did not help Ministers to relate such decisions to their own objectives, nor gave them any guidance on the costs and benefits of constraining—or expanding—private as well as public spending. The survey also appeared to be asking Ministers to analyse, compare, and choose between programmes in their totality, for example 'education' as opposed to 'defence', whereas in fact they needed only to decide on the distribution of marginal increments of additional resources: the question was where an extra £1 million of resources would offer the best value for money, given Ministers' basic aims. The report was not endorsed by the Treasury, and seems to have had little impact either on Ministers' thinking or on the ways in which these matters were handled.

The area of macro-economic policy on which the CPRS did make a substantial contribution was incomes policy. As in many other contexts, the CPRS took a middle-of-the-road view, midway between the *laissez-faire*, market economy views of the right and those on the left who advocated free collective bargaining. But it was an interventionist view, and as such was initially at odds with the non-interventionist stance of the Heath government. The unmentionable option of a statutory incomes policy was first mentioned by the CPRS in a 'strategy' meeting in the summer of 1972. Soon after this the CPRS was actively working on Heath's Stage I Incomes Policy. One of its first contributions was a paper on the incomes policy of the current Nixon administration in the USA which, having at first also rejected such a policy, had subsequently developed one. The first draft of the paper was prepared in Washington by Kate Mortimer, then working at the World Bank but due to join the CPRS in October 1972.

From then on the involvement of the CPRS in this area seems to have been generally welcomed in Whitehall. The Departments of Employment, Industry, and later Prices, as well as the Civil Service Department, all had vested interests with their own client groups putting them under pressure. It was an area where a non-departmental view was valuable. Even the Treasury accepted that there was a role for the CPRS.

This was, however, a highly politicized area of policy. Emotion, ideology, and short-term considerations were usually dominant. During the miners' strike Rothschild suggested that the changed economic situation that resulted from the oil price rise would justify the government in rethinking its resistance to the miners' pay demand. This was a highly unpopular view. To most members of the government the issue was not a matter of changed economic circumstances, but one of principle about who ran the country and the rule of law. The advice was rejected.

When the Wilson government came to power, with a manifesto commitment to avoid a statutory incomes policy, the CPRS prudently lay low for a while. The Pay Board was wound up. However, between the summer of 1974 and the summer of 1975 wages started to rise rapidly. The Treasury pressed for a pay freeze or tight limits on wage increases with statutory powers. This was not acceptable to Ministers. With the help of the Economic Committee of the TUC the 'Social Contract' was devised; this involved voluntary wage restraint in return for action to control prices, various policies to help the low paid, improvements in the social wage, manpower planning, and industrial investment. The CPRS intervened again, trying to encourage Ministers to address themselves to some uncomfortable questions about what would happen next.

In January 1976 the CPRS produced a forty-page paper on the need for a permanent prices and incomes policy. The paper discussed the causes of inflation and the role of incomes policy in controlling it in the longer term; the lessons of past counter-inflation policies in the UK and elsewhere; the characteristics of a continuing counter-inflation policy; and the implications of the next round of counter-inflation policy in the UK. It ended with a number of specific recommendations on the next pay round. These were linked to a general message. Counter-inflation policy should be presented not as simply a temporary device, involving short-term sacrifice to get through a crisis but as a permanent necessity. To put it another way, an incomes policy had to be seen as a vital ingredient in faster-rising real incomes in the medium to longer-term.

In the event, it was the Callaghan government's failure to obtain adequate backing and agreement for a longer-term counter-inflation policy, which eventually contributed to its fall and the return to power of the Conservatives in 1979. The government found it difficult to arrive at an appropriate target for the 1978–9 pay round. If it did not improve on the 1977–8 guidelines it might appear defeatist. On the other hand, if it set too low a figure there was a danger that the whole policy would collapse. That is exactly what happened. The 'winter of discontent' followed, with a government struggling to survive with a parliamentary majority and facing widespread industrial action in the public sector (and being blamed, as a result, for the fact that it was not possible to bury the dead). The Treasury, the CPRS, and the Number Ten Policy Unit had all backed a figure of five per cent. None of them had anticipated the extent of the disaster which resulted.

With Mrs Thatcher's victory in May 1979 the CPRS ceased to work in incomes policy, since the new Prime Minister did not accept the need for such a policy. Nor did she seem to feel much need for advice from the CPRS on economic questions more generally. Alan Walters effectively replaced Berrill, and Ibbs preferred not to intervene in this area at all. More generally, and reflecting Ibbs's line, the CPRS developed the view that there was little scope for it to contribute effectively on macro-economic issues. As one senior CPRS economist said ruefully, 'if you have a Prime Minister who insists on a doctrinaire monetarist approach to macro-economic policy your scope [for intervention] is rather limited.'

This view may well have been mistaken in a narrow analytical sense. A Treasury official reflecting the CPRS's relative inactivity commented later that there were plenty of other changes in priorities in which the CPRS could have been involved—for example, new directions in public expenditure. The CPRS's abdication of a significant role in economic policy was almost certainly a mistake in a wider tactical sense. It was a major factor in the general weakening of the CPRS which paved the way for its eventual abolition. 'If you're excluded from talk about short-term economic policy,' said a CPRS member who served under both Heath and Thatcher, 'you're inhibited from kicking things about as a think tank should.'

The CPRS did, however, continue to make occasional contributions to discussions about public expenditure. It was, ironically, one such contribution whose leaking to the press led to its becoming the focus of a major row and probably the single most important factor in the eventual abolition of the CPRS. The story started during the summer of 1982. In the course of the annual public expenditure round, departments, led by the Treasury and using Treasury figures, took a worried look at forward projections for public spending. It was all too clear from this that spending, so far from falling as the government had publicly promised that it would, was due to go on rising throughout the 1980s—unless some major policy shifts took place. Treasury Ministers asked the CPRS to indicate some options as quickly as possible for such a draft. Nothing was to be considered too radical in principle: the objective was to show to Ministers the kinds of ways in which they might cut public spending by £1 billion by 1990.

The CPRS team, led by Alan Bailey (himself a seconded Treasury official), had no time for elegant or refined analysis, either of the ways in which savings might be made or of their implications. The scale of the cuts required meant that they would have to fall on a limited range of programmes—defence, education, social security, health. After a review lasting only a few days, and a process variously described by some involved in it as 'quick and dirty' and 'back of the envelope', the CPRS produced a short paper outlining the options.

The options were predictably unsurprising given the known ideological position of the dominant group in the Cabinet. They included the cancellation of Trident and the freezing of defence's share of the GNP after 1986; ending state funding of higher education with fees at market rates, a scholarship scheme, and student loans; the introduction of education vouchers for primary and secondary schooling; an increase in the number of pupils per teacher; and ending the index-linking of social security payments, including pensions. The options canvassed also included dismantling the National Health Service and replacing it by a private insurance scheme.

These proposals were first seen by the Cabinet in early September 1982. Ten days later a comprehensive (and broadly accurate) account of them appeared in *The Economist*. The article suggested that the CPRS paper had provoked a major 'wet' versus 'dry' clash amongst Ministers—the first for over a year. It claimed that 'Treasury Ministers were furious when the wets lined up en masse to block discussion of a paper which owed its inspiration to them' (*The Economist*, 1982).

This was followed by articles in the quality Sunday newspapers and the *Guardian*. Inevitably such proposals were greeted with shock and horror. The proposal to dismember the Health Service attracted the most odium. The CPRS was portrayed as a villain behind the scenes providing the necessary preliminary back-up work for the government to dismantle the Welfare State. In fact as far as the Health Service was concerned the CPRS paper had made it clear that this was not an option worth pursuing. International comparisons indicated that privatized systems were more expensive than the NHS in resource terms.

The source of the leak was never discovered. Many people—probably including most Ministers and some senior officials—suspected that the leaker was in the CPRS. Others, including members of the CPRS, felt it more probable that the culprit was in the DHSS, which would certainly have wanted to see such proposals rejected as quickly as possible. The leak was certainly an effective way of achieving this. The Prime Minister immediately made it plain that the government had no intention of pursuing any of the options put forward.

In the CPRS there was consternation. It was clear that suspicion would fall upon it, and that its credibility would be damaged. This was indeed the case. The damage was lasting, and ultimately fatal.

When the text of the CPRS report itself (referred to, but not generally distributed, in public in 1982) was leaked by Peter Shore as part of Labour's 'Secret Manifesto' exercise during the closing days of the 1983 election campaign, Ministers' irritation with the CPRS was increased still further. Here, they feared, was an organization which not merely leaked the highly sensitive papers it wrote on those strategic issues fundamental to its *raison d'être*; it was happy to recycle them or play the same game *again* during an election campaign. It was easy, though not necessarily justified, to conclude that this organization—or indeed perhaps anything like it—was too much of a risk to keep alive.

As so often in such cases, the immediate furore generated by the leak was out of all proportion to its real significance (except, of course, to the CPRS). It is hard to show that it did the government any harm in the longer term, although it certainly embarrassed them in the short term. The Prime Minister privately accused the CPRS of political naïvety. However, despite its repercussions, no one in the Think Tank felt that the brief had been inappropriate for it: the CPRS had been set up to think the unthinkable about major policy questions, and had done so.

It is worth adding a note about the CPRS's relationship, during its lifetime, with the Treasury. To the CPRS the importance of the Treasury was second only to that of the Prime Minister. For reasons given earlier, the Treasury was the one department which the CPRS, like other departments, could never ignore or try to bypass. As already said, the CPRS found itself at different times and in different contexts supporting or opposing the Treasury. In the heyday of PAR the CPRS was with the Treasury in insisting that departments put forward programmes for analysis, against the Treasury in arguing for the inclusion of low-spending programmes—which might have disproportionately large impacts—and, sometimes, in arguing for increases in programme expenditure to bring about a more favourable cost–benefit ratio. The CPRS was frequently at odds with the Treasury over the latter's cautious attempts to modify CPRS proposals which might encourage higher public expenditure. Energy conservation was one example. Race relations was another; as one ex-member of the CPRS commented, 'Lord Scarman would be less well-known today had more heed been taken of the CPRS in this matter.' When the CPRS briefed Callaghan at the time of the IMF negotiations in 1976, it advised that some of the cuts suggested by the Treasury were excessive and could do permanent damage to the social fabric. In putting forward such counter-views the CPRS preferred to operate by stealth rather than risk a head-on confrontation with the Treasury, privately briefing the Prime Minister, directly or through the Cabinet Secretariat, rather than circulating a collective brief—'like Afghan tribesmen', said a senior CPRS member, 'sniping from secret hideouts rather than using heavy armour and frontal attacks'.

In other contexts the CPRS was wholly with the Treasury, for example in many critiques of departments' unyielding defences of existing programmes at existing levels of expenditure. The somewhat esoteric question of what in Eurojargon is known as 'sheepmeat' is one illustration. The Treasury, in common with much of the rest of Whitehall, believed the Foreign Office to be more interested in maintaining good relations with foreigners, especially influential European foreigners such as the French, than in defending British interests, economic and other. At one point the Treasury felt that the FCO had not been tough enough in countering French opposition to British lamb imports. The CPRS had done some work on agricultural policy, producing a 'red book' report on the subject. The Treasury found it useful to draw on CPRS support in advocating a more robust and nationalistic line than was favoured by the Foreign Office.

Particular episodes apart, the relationship fluctuated. One ex-member of the CPRS suggested that the variations in the relationship reflected the constant of the CPRS's own 'centrist' views. The CPRS, by this account, tended to give advice which implicitly pulled both Labour and Conservative governments towards a consensus of the centre of the political spectrum and away from either radical right or radical left. Thus, taking public expenditure as an example, the CPRS opposed the Treasury line under the Thatcher government in urging the case for spending in various areas. Under the previous Labour administration the CPRS had implicitly backed the Treasury in frequently cautioning Ministers on their spending ambitions. Leo Pliatzky, a former Second Secretary in the Treasury, suggested that in general its problem was in having 'to speak with a different voice from the Treasury even when it had no real disagreement with the Treasury line, if it was to have any real credibility with Cabinet.' (Pliatzky, 1985).

Some observers felt that, on the contrary, the CPRS in general took a position too close to that of the Treasury to be useful to Ministers. It was suggested that the personal links between CPRS and Treasury—in the form of Ross, Berrill, and some of the young economists and administrators—inhibited the CPRS from challenging the Treasury as boldly as it challenged other departments. Such views were held not only by Tony Benn, critical of what he saw as the CPRS's adherence to an orthodox Treasury line in its opposition to his 'alternative economic strategy'. Bernard Donoughue, head of the Policy Unit in Number Ten in the Wilson and Callaghan governments, considered that the CPRS might have played a more independent line. A former CPRS member felt that in advising the Prime Minister on economic policy the CPRS did not put enough grit into the machine. However, the same person mentioned the difficulties of second guessing the Treasury; the CPRS simply lacked the resources to do this adequately.

Not everyone in the Treasury shared this view. Treasury officials clearly often saw the CPRS as simply one more opponent—and a dangerously well-placed one, at that—of its reasonable attempts to manage the British economy. This line of thinking was nicely expressed by Leo Pliatzky:

In the eyes of its admirers [*and, he may have been thinking, in its own eyes*] the CPRS stood, perhaps, for a more rational, more dispassionate element in the decision-making process. In practice it had its own human frailties . . . Collaboration with the CPRS was not easy when Victor Rothschild was its head and concerned to assert its influence . . . When the U-turn came midway through Mr. Heath's Government, the CPRS jumped enthusiastically on the big-spending bandwagon. Under the Labour Government, the CPRS still seemed to me at best to contribute little and at worst to render the task of bringing expenditure under control that bit more arduous (Pliatzky, 1985).

These attitudes were reciprocated within the CPRS. The Treasury was resented for its pretensions and for what was seen, in relation to the role which it claimed for itself, as its incompetence. Its claim to be the final arbiter in matters of public sector resource allocation was hotly disputed by the CPRS. As one senior member of the CPRS under Thatcher told us, 'The Treasury's total failure to plan the distribution of national resources in any systematic way was a major justification for the CPRS. In any case, the Treasury is quite unconcerned with the *pattern* of distribution.' Hunt himself was later to make the same point. The Treasury, he said, was primarily concerned with the effect which total spending would have on the domestic economy, and 'tends to be neutral as between particular spending plans' (Hunt, 1983). As one of us has written elsewhere,

The Treasury's concerns are as sectional as the concerns of any other single department. It is easy to assume that economic objectives, or the particular objective of controlling public expenditure, override all other objectives—and indeed are in some sense almost exactly congruent with the overall objectives of the government as a whole. But it is quite misleading to do so.

A second reason for feeling that the Treasury is not the appropriate source of advice on governmental priorities is that it is, quite simply, a finance department. And as such it is, or certainly has been up until now [1985], both temperamentally and organisationally incapable of advising on questions of effectiveness rather than on efficiency, or on trade-offs (which must logically acknowledge the possibility of spending more rather than less on some individual programmes) (Plowden, 1985).

This line of thinking influenced the CPRS attitude to Treasury policies in many sectors. In industrial matters, one CPRS critic thought, the Treasury suffered from 'ivory tower arrogance'. It believed that it could obtain all the information necessary to reach the right answers from within its own resources; its staff failed to get out into the 'real world' and to talk directly to people in private or public sector firms. In relation to the nationalized industries, the Treasury's attitude was felt by the CPRS to be thoroughly unconstructive; its role veered from damaging intervention to apparent lack of concern.

Whatever mutual attitudes and relationships, this chapter has shown that the effectiveness of the CPRS in relation to economic matters varied sharply between issues. The two major variables here seem to have been, as in so many other cases, the degree of 'interdepartmentalism' of the issue and the relative expertise of the CPRS. Like other departments the Treasury could much more easily hold off CPRS challenges to policies which could be seen as its sole responsibility. Fiscal and monetary policies, and the question of the overall level of public expenditure, were such; and in these cases the Chancellor of the Exchequer could usually rely confidently on the support of the Prime Minister. No leader of a government is likely to welcome what his leading colleague will describe as damaging onslaughts on the government's economic strategy and thus on its general credibility. The Chancellor can also always justify claims to be advised by a team whose collective expertise on such matters is hard to match, inside or outside government.

By contrast, the CPRS did have some status on issues such as public expenditure priorities or on incomes policies. The former is essentially interdepartmental in Whitehall; only the Treasury can claim to have any expertise in advising on choices between different departments, and this is a claim which, as already mentioned, many people including the CPRS would regard as unjustified. Incomes policy again is strongly interdepartmental. In addition, this was not a traditional area of Treasury activity in which its expertise was beyond challenge. In both these areas the CPRS was able to establish its own credibility and to play a part.

6

Social Policy

THE FIRST HALF of the 1970s saw the last great expansion of what might loosely be called 'welfare' spending, and perhaps the final phase in the post-war attempt to patch and adjust the ragged blanket of welfare provision so as to cover the whole person of the community, toes as well as nose. The 1980s were to see the development of the philosophy that, whatever the defects of the blanket, it should never have been depended upon in the first place: hands and other parts of the body suppliant ought to warm themselves. The bridge between these viewpoints was the realization that even if the blanket approach was right in principle, the blanket would never be large enough; Britain's poor economic record dictated that some painful choices had to be made as to which parts to keep warm.

The CPRS was involved in the welfare or social policy field from its earliest days, and put a great deal of resources into it in the first seven or eight years of its life. Under the Thatcher government social problems and policies in general were given lower priority, with the particular exception of inner cities, where the CPRS, in its closing phase, scored a resounding and a surprising success.

Soon after the CPRS had begun work, in the early spring of 1971, and before all its staff were in place, it organized a 'trawl' around Whitehall soliciting suggestions for its future work programme. One topic suggested in several quarters was 'interdepartmental aspects of social policy'. The suggestion was recorded and filed and became part of the CPRS's steadily evolving ideas bank.

Meanwhile the CPRS was developing a broad line of analysis which was to be one of the central themes in its activities for the next ten years. It concerned the relationship between patterns of resource distribution and the priorities of the government. A long series of CPRS papers and presentations was to confront successive generations of Ministers with pictures of the ways in which resources were currently distributed, and might on current trends be distributed in the future, among different programmes and—at least implicitly—allocated to identifiable objectives: and then to enquire of

101

Ministers whether the ordering of programmes and objectives corresponded with what they were trying to achieve. For one of the first of these presentations, in the summer of 1972, the CPRS produced an enormous chart showing the national distribution of all productive resources between activities of every kind (industry, defence, public administration). It also presented a separate paper on 'social affairs'. This analysed and discussed the distribution of resources between social programmes, and tentatively argued the need for greater co-ordination within central government and between it and other agencies. 'The social departments', said a member of the CPRS at that time, 'seemed to believe . . . that their programmes could go on growing at what they regarded as a "natural" rate, which just happened to be wildly in excess of the rate of growth of the economy. There was a patriotic assumption either that defence cuts would provide; or that public expenditure would go on growing as a proportion of GNP; or alternatively that somehow Allah would provide.'

A little later, the CPRS suggested that a Ministerial 'strategy group' for social affairs should be set up to discuss these larger questions of priorities. It was to be briefed by the CPRS. This proposal was not resisted by the DHSS or by other departments. The Cabinet Secretary, Sir Burke Trend, was acquiescent if not particularly enthusiastic.

This was the starting-point of what came to be known as the 'Joint Approach to Social Policies', or JASP. The basic aim of JASP was simply a sub-set of the general objectives of the CPRS: to apply analysis (and implicitly 'reason') to the process of working out governmental priorities, to try to ensure that individual developments reflected those priorities, to counteract the fragment-ation of governmental policies among competing agencies, and to contrive a more deliberate relationship between different decisions, taken at different times, about different issues. The aim of JASP was to apply these general principles to 'social' or welfare policies—which might be assumed to share a common objective of modifying the effects of inequitable distribution of resources and opportunities in the community.

The JASP episode fell into three phases. The first comprised the initial 'selling' to Ministers of the general principle that resource constraints now made it necessary to give more thought to questions of priorities in the social field. It took place during the second half of 1972 and early 1973. The second phase (JASP Mark I) perhaps came closest to an attempt to apply an ideal model of rational and co-ordinated policy-making to the untidy processes prevalent within Whitehall; it was an ambitious, schematic, and completely unsuccessful attempt to devise a comprehensive system for doing this. It followed on from the first phase and came to an end late in 1973. The third phase (JASP Mark II) was a much more modest attempt to encourage 'joint' thinking and action in a limited number of specific contexts. In the middle of this last phase, the CPRS, against its own better judgement, found itself once again involved in a second unsuccessful attempt to produce a comprehensive plan. It ran for most of the period the Labour government was in power, petering out towards the end of the Callaghan era.

The first phase culminated in a meeting of the Ministerial strategy group in early 1973. With the help of the management consultants McKinseys, the CPRS submitted to the group not a conventional Civil Service memorandum, but an oral presentation supported with slides. (In a further departure from custom, the meeting was held not during daytime hours in an official committee room, but over and after dinner in the Whitehall flat of one of the Ministers concerned.)

The aim of the CPRS presentation was to persuade Ministers that total public spending on social programmes could not continue to increase at current rates—or, in other words, that the resources available for social programmes would inevitably be quite inadequate to meet all future demands. Some difficult choices would therefore have to be made. These would need to be derived from some set of priorities agreed by Ministers collectively. Agreement on priorities would require a new and more analytical (as opposed to adversarial) approach to policy-making. The CPRS proposed that it should develop such an analytical approach.

Faced with these very general propositions (which as presented did not explicitly challenge the priorities of any individual Minister present), and perhaps relaxed by the informal circumstances, the Ministerial group agreed that the CPRS should do some further work on the subject.

This was the starting-point of the second phase, which might be called 'JASP Mark I'—an application of an 'ideal model' of rationality in policy-making, in an extreme form. Great reliance was placed on the ability of analysts, or planners, to develop a reliable synoptic view of the whole field of social policy, of the relative severity of the various problems perceived there and of the relative quantities of resources currently devoted to each problem. Moreover, it was also assumed that policy-makers, i.e. Ministers, once faced with this battery of facts would be able to read off the appropriate decisions and would be prepared to act accordingly. The aim was to ensure that patterns of resource allocation corresponded more closely to Ministers' priorities, which should in turn reflect a better understanding of where the most urgent problems lay. This understanding was to come largely from an analysis by the CPRS of the needs of different 'client groups' and of the impact of government programmes on each of these.

During this period the Home Secretary, Robert Carr, was given the task of leading a co-ordinated interdepartmental work programme directed at urban problems. There was an echo here of a post, set up by the previous Labour government, of coordinating Minister for social affairs, and held for a while by Richard Crossman, with the major difference that Carr was given no special non-departmental staff to help him in this task. The CPRS, which was invited to join a small group to oversee this programme, took the chance to 'adopt' the Home Secretary as honorary sponsor of its own programme. (How this arrangement would have worked it is hard to say; the Home Secretary had not been able to play much part in developing urban policies, let alone take a close interest in the activities of the CPRS, before the economic and political crisis of the winter of 1973/4 and the fall of the Conservative government in February 1974.)

In the autumn of 1973, the results of the CPRS work were circulated as a paper to Ministers. Though it appeared over the signature of the Home Secretary in his capacity as 'co-ordinator', it was, in fact, largely drafted by the head of the CPRS, Lord Rothschild. The paper proposed that the CPRS should help Ministers think comprehensively about priorities by analysing needs and programmes in terms of 'client groups', and by setting up a continuous monitoring process to be known as the 'Social Audit'. These two approaches together would help Ministers to identify which programmes were under- or over-resourced in relation to Ministerial priorities, and so to decide where to increase or to cut expenditure. The whole proposal was couched in the assertive, 'scientific' prose, admitting of little uncertainty or possibility of compromise, which was characteristic of Lord Rothschild.

It was probably the style of the paper, as much as its extremely ambitious content, which made its proposals unacceptable. Ministers, presumably briefed by their departments, declined to endorse them. The CPRS was instructed to go away and talk to departmental officials, and to come back with something much more modest. These talks revealed widespread scepticism within Whitehall about the value of the approach, combined with the fear that it would lead to a great deal of additional work for departments. DHSS officials in particular, who had themselves been trying to develop joint approaches involving some of their own programmes and some of other departments', were unhappy at the swamping or possible frustration of their own earlier more modest activities in the 'comprehensive' exercise. They also resented what they saw as a CPRS attempt to take over some of their responsibilities by insisting that these be discussed collectively. The CPRS, faced with the prospect that the whole initiative would founder, went back to the drawing-board.

This was the start of 'JASP Mark II', an enterprise far more successful, at least in the short term. The CPRS took the realistic view that departments were now suspicious of its attempts to collectivize decision-making in 'their' policy areas, and that they would not accept the case for a joint approach across the board; the approach would have to be developed 'with the grain', in specific contexts where departments saw some benefit to themselves. In style, Mark II was to be far more incremental and consensual, and much less grandiose; there was no longer any pretence of a comprehensive approach to problems and policies. The CPRS team determined to pick a series of specific issues to which a joint approach seemed likely to be relevant, to study them in some detail, and to draw up proposals for action in each case.

JASP Mark II was also much more political in that the CPRS accepted the need for allies and for stratagems. In particular, the CPRS sought to work closely with the Cabinet Secretariat under its new head, Sir John Hunt. Hunt was as sceptical as any other Permanent Secretary about the value or practicability of the comprehensive approach of JASP Mark I. But he was conscious of what he later called 'the hole in the centre' of government (see Chapter 2). Hunt was sensitive to Prime Ministerial demands on the Cabinet Secretariat for advice on the substance of policy, as opposed to its traditional products of neutral briefs and minutes of meetings, and was eager for the Secretariat to be capable of providing this. He saw the CPRS, in JASP as in other contexts, as a valuable resource for this purpose. His own previous experience as the senior Treasury official responsible for managing the public expenditure process had left him dissatisfied with its mechanistic bilateral nature. He was also a friend, as well as a colleague, of the permanent head of the DHSS, Sir Philip Rogers, and approved of his efforts to encourage interdepartmental working. All this led Hunt to welcome the CPRS's attempt to develop 'strategic' thinking in the social welfare field. He agreed to convene and to chair a new committee of Permanent Secretaries, to oversee develop- ments and encourage progress in JASP, and to underpin the group of Ministers already set up by the CPRS. His support was invaluable and probably essential.

The nature and pace of the programme was not greatly affected by the general election of February 1974 and the replacement of the Conservatives by a Labour government under Harold Wilson. The CPRS as a whole found itself temporarily in the doldrums; the new administration had no experience of the CPRS and regarded it initially as a Conservative inheritance which might have to be abolished. It therefore had little work to do. CPRS members working on JASP were thus fortunate in having a continuous activity. Probably the most important aspect of the change of administration was the arrival at the DHSS of Mrs Barbara Castle, an implacable promoter of her departmental interests with a strong commitment to truly 'socialist' policies in welfare as in other fields. An almost equally important arrival at the DHSS with Mrs Castle was her distinguished policy adviser, Professor Brian Abel-Smith of the London School of Economics. Neither a career bureaucrat nor a politician, but a genuine expert with his own well-developed views about what should—and could—be done, he was an ideal intermediary for the CPRS team in its attempts to develop policies which would take account of political and bureaucratic realities yet which would not be unduly constrained by either.

A similar change connected with the arrival of the Labour government was the creation in 10 Downing Street of Bernard Donoughue's 'Prime Minister's Policy Unit'. One member of the unit was David Piachaud, seconded from the London School of Economics, a leading academic expert on social security. He, too, was a valuable link between the JASP team and the politicians.

Another change of some importance for JASP was the departure of Rothschild in the middle of 1974 and his replacement by Berrill. Berrill had no close personal interest in or knowledge of the social welfare field. More important, he obviously did not share Rothschild's commitment to the ambitious yet simplistic approach which had been so badly received in Whitehall the previous year. The Ministerial group set up by the Conservatives had been dissolved and not replaced, and there was thus no political pressure from above for results. The JASP team were thus left free to develop their programme in the way that they thought best.

The way they thought best included a great deal of outside consultation. One of the best features of the Rothschild regime had been the free and, by conventional Whitehall standards, indiscreet use made by the CPRS of outside experts of all kinds. Following this tradition the JASP team virtually co-opted Professor David Donnison, then director of the Centre for Environmental Studies. It also tried to develop a link with the Centre for Studies in Social Policy, a small research institute newly set up and funded by Rowntree. But the attempt to plug the CSSP into JASP as a permanent consultant on a retainer basis failed, largely owing to the Centre's lack of any spare capacity which could be used in this role.

Throughout the lifetime of JASP, the task for the CPRS was to preserve the legitimacy of a programme of activities which involved departments in a great deal of work which, left to themselves, they would not have done. The CPRS also had to overcome the suspicions, on the part of officials and of Ministers, of possible takeover bids for 'their' areas of responsibility and the perennial unease of the Treasury—which grew steadily stronger over time—at enquiries which threatened to excite demands for additional expenditure. If anything, the Treasury regarded Ministers, as a source of such demands, as more of a threat than outside interests and pressure groups.

The first main item in the new work programme was one of some interest to all departments but which threatened none in particular. In effect, its aim was to apply to decisions involving resources of all kinds in the social affairs field the principle which for some years had guided public expenditure decisions—

that demands on resources ought to be looked at in relation to resources as a whole and to other likely demands, over a period of time. The 'early warning system' for social affairs, devised by the CPRS in association with departments, was a modified version of a technique which the CPRS had tried—unsuccessfully—to apply right across the field of policy a couple of years before. Its aim was simple: to look forward six months and to identify issues coming up which would call for decisions, or at least discussion, by Ministers. The hope was that if Ministers could see each issue in even this limited context, this would help them to think more systematically about the relative significance of each and about appropriate action.

During the course of 1974 each department produced its own list of issues and events: expected report of a Royal Commission, second reading of a major Bill, decision on a pay claim. These were grouped by the CPRS under various broad headings and the whole thing, known as 'the forward look', was circulated to all departments.

Meanwhile, the CPRS was trying to put together the programme of discrete studies already mentioned. Choosing subjects for study was a long and painful process; departments were reluctant to see studies led by the CPRS intruding on to their territory, or to agree to studies which might threaten cherished policies. The list of justifications offered for not choosing particular subjects was long: that the subject had already been so exhaustively studied that nothing more remained to be said or done (under-fives), that it could be better approached in other ways (the 'social' impact of housing policies), that it was unsuitable for collective discussion (this was the Treasury view on the interaction of taxation and social security policies), that it was not worth doing (school-leavers). The Department of Education and Science was particularly sceptical about the likely value of activities of the kind suggested; the Treasury was, as ever, uneasy lest discussion of needs, and of how to meet them more effectively, might excite spending Ministers into a collective demand for higher public expenditure which the Chancellor would be unable to contain.

However, throughout the long series of bilateral talks between the CPRS and departments during 1974 a small group of topics emerged for which special studies seemed not only potentially useful but politically feasible. To help the process of consultation each department was asked to nominate one person to act as permanent link with the CPRS. These departmental representatives were also brought together from time to time in an informal interdepartmental group chaired by the CPRS. This was specifically a 'group', not a conventional interdepartmental 'committee'; it met, not in the customary surroundings of one of the committee rooms in the Cabinet Office, but in the Civil Service College, Belgrave Road. The aim was to create a group consisting of individuals engaged in a joint activity with common objectives, rather than representatives defending sectional interests. Indeed, departments were specifically asked by the CPRS to treat the group as, in effect, advisory to the CPRS; their advice and information was essential but the CPRS would take full responsibility for the papers which it produced on the basis of the group's discussions. The departments involved, and thus represented on the group, included the Central Statistical Office, Welsh and Scottish Offices, Lord Chancellor's Office, Home Office, Departments of Employment, Environment, Health and Social Security. This approach worked well; it ensured that the CPRS was fully aware of departments' views on proposals discussed in the group but avoided the sterile wrangling over detailed issues and points of drafting which are so typical of interdepartmental activities in Whitehall.

The proposals discussed and broadly agreed by the group included the setting up of a 'strategic' group of Ministers to discuss social policies and problems; continuing the 'forward look' exercise already mentioned; some interdepartmental work on 'financial poverty' and in particular on the interaction of long-term cash benefits and shorter-term means-tested benefits; the working relationship between Whitehall departments and local authorities with particular reference to the ways in which these relationships affected the possibility of developing coherent 'packages' of services adequately related to the needs of prospective 'clients'; the 'social' aspects of housing policy; a study of a specific client group—preferably the disabled, which would make it possible to build on work already being done by an interdepartmental committee chaired by Mr Alfred Morris, a junior Minister at the DHSS; a longer-term study, perhaps future policy towards women at work or the family.

The main activity involving 'social' departments generally, and probably the most resource intensive element in the whole package, was the better preparation, dissemination, and use of 'social' statistics. This was in effect all that remained, though greatly modified, of the data-based approach of JASP Mark I. With the enthusiastic support of the Central Statistical Office it was agreed that a new 'Social Group' should be set up in the CSO, to oversee a Whitehall-wide campaign to produce better statistical information about social policies and problems, and to present this to Ministers in forms which they could understand and, hopefully, use. A valuable ally here was Anthony Crosland, then Secretary of State for the Environment. He had argued that Ministers faced with decisions about changes in social policies ought to have some idea of their distributional consequences: which groups in the population would gain, or lose? The CPRS and CSO adopted this suggestion, and suggested that departments putting forward new expenditure proposals in the social field should attach to them a summary of their likely distributional effect, particularly on different income groups. The work was to be supported by an effort to improve the dissemination, presentation, and use of statistical material.

These proposals, in the form of a draft report for Ministers, were discussed by the committee of Permanent Secretaries under John Hunt in the spring of 1975. Some Permanent Secretaries were still expressing disquiet at the whole project, fearing—as ever—that in identifying unmet needs and proposing new approaches to deal with these, JASP might provoke appetite among spending Ministers and, if the document became public, pressures from outside interests. These feelings were reinforced when, in May, a long article in the *Times Educational Supplement* gave a comprehensive and fairly accurate account of the draft report, but went on to argue that the main aim of the whole project was to find new ways of cutting social expenditure, especially on education, that an 'inner Cabinet' of senior Ministers would be 'ganging up' and forcing unpopular decisions on individual spending Ministers; and that the whole activity (in ways undefined) would diminish the authority of Parliament (*Times Educational Supplement*, 1975). Even Sir John Hunt was affected by his colleagues' reservations. He insisted that the working title be changed from 'A Joint Approach to Social Policy' to 'A Joint Framework for Social Policies', to make it clear that the main purpose was to provide a better framework for Ministerial decision-taking in relation to client groups rather than to promote CPRS policies as such. Some members of the CPRS thought this was also a subtle way of lowering the profile of the exercise, since JFSP— unlike JASP—was an acronym impossible to pronounce. However, Hunt urged the CPRS not to pay too much heed to the doubts of departments nor to their suggestions for further dilution of the report's language.

In fact, the programme had already acquired enough momentum to carry it forward. In May the report was discussed in the new Cabinet committee chaired by the Prime Minister. Barbara Castle, who through an oversight sent her Minister of State, David Owen, in her stead, described the meeting in her diary:

I was annoyed to find this morning had been pre-empted by a meeting of a Cabinet Committee on Joint Approach to Social Policies. Glancing at my papers, I couldn't even remember what it was all about, so I sent David in my place. He told me afterwards that I clearly should have gone: the PM was in the chair, all the top Ministers were there and they discussed the CPRS paper on a 'joint framework for social policies'. I had forgotten all about it. The pressure of hand-to-mouth work is so great these days that anything more profound one has read some weeks ago gets totally submerged. Since this new committee is part of Tony Crosland's bid for better 'social monitoring' (which is all right in itself, except that it is part of his continuing attacks on my expenditure) I would have liked to be there. There has certainly been no more 'wasteful expenditure' than in the housing field, and I am glad to learn that one of the short-term studies which CPRS proposes is on the social aspects of housing policy—as long as 'social aspects' does not rule out a study of cost-effectiveness. I learn that the CPRS paper is to be published, that the PM is to preside over a ministerial group on strategy, that social monitoring is to be carried out by a 'social group' of senior statisticians in the Central Statistical Office, that the group of Permanent Secretaries is to process all this, and that the first strategic ministerial meeting is to be held at Chequers soon. I certainly must not miss any more of these meetings. Harold must have felt aggrieved that I was not there (Castle, 1980).

The report was published in July. At one point it was intended that it should be launched at a press conference by the Prime Minister; this was at the height of the government's attempt to sell to the trade unions the concept of the 'social wage', that is to persuade them to acknowledge the money value of the many welfare benefits received by their members and to accept these in lieu of higher pay increases. The JASP report, with its emphasis on trying to increase the real value of services to those who needed them most, looked like a useful instrument in this campaign. However, in the event discussions of the social wage became bogged down and the press conference was postponed. Rather than allow the JASP report to miss the tide of interest which, it was hoped, had been generated by the earlier press stories it was thought best to launch it on its own without further delay.

Thus published, the report constituted quite a forthright statement of the incoherence of social policies, and of the need to relate patterns of resource allocation to some explicit views about priorities in social welfare. Though published under a Labour government, its origins in the 'resource allocation' paper put to Conservative Ministers three years earlier were reflected in its emphasis on the need to reduce growth in welfare expenditure and to 'cut back on some plans in the social field, as elsewhere'. But in going on to argue that this called for clear thinking about priorities, it added that this would be necessary whatever the public expenditure situation. Drawing on painful experience, and accurately anticipating the major obstacle to any collective venture of this kind, the report stated as its 'key assumption' the need for departments and Ministers to be 'prepared to make some adjustments, whether in priorities, policies, administrative practices, or public expenditure allocation'. It went on to propose the several separate pieces of work already mentioned.

It is worth noting that the publication of the basic JASP report set a precedent for the rest of the JASP programme, which contrasted markedly with the rest of the CPRS's work, still more so with the practices of the rest of Whitehall, then or later. The only major piece of JASP work not published was the report of the Treasury-led group on financial poverty. The result of publication was an interaction between the JASP teams and the outside world that was as valuable as it was undamaging. The CPRS allowed itself some quite blunt language in its report; Ministers came to accept that these were public property, and did not object. Meanwhile the CPRS received a steady stream of comments—not always complimentary—from academics, the media, pressure groups, and politicians.

The work programme thus launched ran for about two years from autumn 1975 to late 1977. At a purely administrative level, the interdepartmental group chaired by the CPRS met every few months to review progress on the various elements in the work programme, to agree on future activities, and to consider what might be said to the rather rarer meetings of Sir John Hunt's group of Permanent Secretaries and the 'strategic' group of Ministers. This last, initially chaired by the Prime Minister, was soon taken over by Mrs Shirley Williams (Secretary of State for Prices and Consumer Protection). The group on financial poverty, chaired by the Treasury, met regularly. Its main contribution was to draw together in reasonably concise and readable form a great deal of information about the various groups who comprised 'the poor', the nature of their situations, the impact on them of the current 'anti-poverty' programmes, and the scope for helping them by selective improvements in social security benefits. The originality of the group lay in the fact that it was set up not to deal with an urgent specific problem, nor even to process a specific measure (such as a draft Bill), but to survey the whole of a wide field, to analyse the nature and interrelationships of the various problems discovered there, and to think about the most effective combinations of solutions to deal with these. By the restrictive standards of interdepartmental committees, it was an untrammelled and creative body.

A group was set up to look at relations between central government and local authorities, despite the Department of the Environment's objections that this would cut across the work being done by the Layfield Committee on Local Government finance. Most untypically for Whitehall, this group consisted of civil servants plus four local authority officials (a director of education, two chief executives, and a director of social services). It also included a Treasury official who, again untypically, accompanied members of the group on some of their visits to local authorities. In one midlands county, the introduction of the Treasury man provoked a spontaneous round of applause from the local authority representatives who rightly recognized the unique nature of this visitation.

A great deal of work was done by the Central Statistical Office, with the help of departmental statisticians, both in assembling the data needed in the several studies and also in two activities which were, in effect, statistical ends in themselves: planning and producing periodic statistical digests related to social affairs, and devising ways of implementing the Crosland proposal about the

distributional effects of new policies. The digests took specific topics, such as the geographical distribution of the poor, or population change; the current situation and recent trends were shown in diagram form, supported by a fairly neutral commentary. Originally these 'Social Briefs' were classified and were circulated only within Whitehall. Later versions were publicly available.

All this work continued, at different speeds, throughout 1976. The interdepartmental group met every two or three months to review progress and to discuss the conclusions of the different studies as they emerged.

Sir John Hunt's group and the Ministerial 'strategy' group met more rarely. The first of the working groups to produce a full-scale report was the poverty group; its report went to Ministers but, unusually for a JASP report, was not published.

The next report, which was later published, was produced by the group on central/local government relations. The report was completed, submitted to Ministers, and in 1977 published, on working relationships between central government and local authorities. It began with the assumption that joint approaches at local authority level could be greatly helped or hindered by the actions and attitudes of central government. It concluded that there were 'real defects' in the central/local relationship. Whitehall departments—the contrast was made with the Scottish Office—acted 'for most purposes in isolation from each other, and conduct their relationships with local authorities accordingly'. The relationship was also greatly confused by uncertainty about the respective responsibilities of central and local government. The report recommended that central departments should act more corporately, should desist from heavy-handed intervention in the detail of local authority services, and should get to know local authorities, and their problems, better.

A major product of the statistical side of JASP was another report, also published in 1977, on social policies and demographic change. This simple but elegant piece of analysis was based on projections till the end of the century of the size of the various main age-groups in the population. It spelled out the implications of these projections for demand for the main social services and thus for the cost of these services.

The even and moderate tenor of the programme, which had only recently got off the ground, was abruptly disturbed when, in late 1975, the CPRS found itself unexpectedly commissioned by Ministers to carry out what it had long since concluded was impossible—a comprehensive review of spending on social programmes leading to better-informed decisions about priorities across the board. This commission originated with a Cabinet discussion of the need for a review of the social services akin to the annual defence review, with the implicit hope that such a review would give 'social' professionals, especially the doctors, the chance to articulate their demands for resources as cogently as the military seemed to do. It seems fairly clear that this was, in effect, a counter-attack mounted by Barbara Castle on what she saw as the threat to her own programmes represented by the Department of Education and Science and by Anthony Crosland at the DOE.

For the CPRS the commission was doubly unwelcome—first, because it would create a great deal of work on top of the JASP activities, and secondly, because it was in effect a throw-back to an approach which all concerned had rejected. It was uncomfortably reminiscent of the earlier Rothschild paper with its assertion that clear decisions on spending priorities could be read off from a picture of the amount of resources already allocated to each of a list of 'client groups'. However, it was agreed that the review of social spending or 'ROSS', as it half-jokingly became known, should at least be handled by the institutions already concerned with JASP. This ensured that the creature would not develop an independent life of its own since everybody concerned would be personally aware of the continuing demands of JASP. The CPRS concluded that ROSS should aim to be comprehensive only in taking a sweeping glance at the public expenditure figures and that it should then, with as much of a contribution as possible from Ministers themselves, try to focus on some limited topics for more detailed work—the approach already under way in JASP.

With a great deal of help from the Treasury and the CSO the CPRS assembled some statistical time series showing expenditure on the main social programmes, at constant prices, backwards to 1952 and forwards to 1980 (the end of the PESC period). Using figures for other countries derived from OECD and elsewhere, and with the advice of an academic expert, the CPRS then produced some international comparisons showing levels of expenditure on selected major programmes, corrected for the 'purchasing power' of each country; in a series of bilateral discussions with Ministers and their officials the CPRS then tried to tempt the former to indicate their own views of high and low priorities among needs or programmes.

The responses included, from Anthony Crosland, a reply as thoughtful as it is rare in Ministerial thinking about expenditure priorities—an attempt, starting with the assertion that current priorities were not right, to look right across the board of government spending and to indicate which programmes (including some of his own) were receiving too much and which too little (Crosland, 1982). Other Ministers were much less thoughtful and forthcoming and, in one or two cases, openly indignant that Mr Crosland should have suggested that some of their programmes deserved lower than top priority.

The outcome of this work took the form of a CPRS 'presentation' to Ministers—a device by now well established in the private sector but almost unknown in Whitehall, where the preferred mode of putting complex options to Ministers is to summarize the situation in two pages of typescript supported by bulky factual annexes, the whole thing being introduced to his colleagues by the Minister responsible who may, or may not, be personally familiar with the subject-matter. As Barbara Castle noted:

The 'Think Tank' was due to give a presentation of its 'synoptic' view of social policy as the first stage of its 'fundamental review' . . . Harold was in the chair . . . It turned out to be quite illuminating. Ken Berrill introduced a succession of his younger experts, who proceeded to show slides which effectively illustrated some of the things I have been arguing in PESC, e.g. the relative advantage education had enjoyed over the years in public expenditure, despite the move of demographic factors in favour of the health and personal social services . . . The international comparisons . . . showed our expenditure on the social services to be below the European average . . . (Castle, 1980).

The CPRS went on to argue that these aggregate figures did no more than indicate where further investigation might be worth while. It might be helpful to look also at the relationship between supply of services and the need for them, the fit between services provided and consumers' preferences, the important role of local authorities in all this and the sharply rising cost of manpower.

The presentation itself was well received. In Susan Crosland's biography of her husband she describes his reaction to the accompanying paper which was circulated just before the presentation. Describing her Sunday morning ritual of taking a long bath and being interrupted by Tony with comments on his red box reading, she wrote:

His third visit concerned a file he'd just come to in the red box. 'It's a really excellent paper produced by the CPRS discussing policy.'
'I can never remember what these initials stand for.'
'Why should you? It's the Think Tank. The paper is about the effect of the social services on one another. Says several times this approach was put forward by the Secretary of State for Environment. It's what my Chequers letter was about. The paper is an excellent beginning. The Civil Servants wouldn't have done it without a political push' (Crosland, 1982).

But it proved hard to translate Ministers' approval of this broad-brush approach into departmental agreement to do anything in particular. The senior Ministers concerned were so reluctant to discuss the CPRS proposals for the next stage that the task was given to a group of junior Ministers. In the face of departmental prevarication and haggling over the details and terms of reference of individual follow-up studies, the CPRS finally secured agreement that the (independent) National Consumer Council should be commissioned to do some work on housing provision and clients' preferences, and that it might initiate some work on regional variations in service standards and needs.

However, no progress was made on a proposed study, to be led by the Department of Employment, on trends in social service manpower.

Part of the problem here was the by now extreme sensitivity of the Treasury to any activity which might increase, not so much pressure for higher expenditure, as resistance to the cuts which the desperate economic situation was thought to require. It was now 1976, and the International Monetary Fund had demanded sweeping cuts in British public spending. From then and until the CPRS was abolished first the economic and then the political climate became increasingly difficult from the point of view of the expansion of the. social services. Barbara Castle commented on ROSS that 'for some incomprehensible reason the CPRS review was labelled "Confidential" and not published by the Government' (Castle, 1980). In fact, nothing could be easier to understand than reluctance to publish semi-official, and all too well-authenticated, comparisons showing Britain near the bottom of the international spending league on social services.

In the event, little work had been done on the ROSS studies when a series of decisions was taken which effectively brought an end to the work of the CPRS not only on ROSS but also on JASP, and its involvement in the interdepartmental aspects of social policy. These decisions were in fact initiated by the CPRS itself.

In January 1977 the CPRS had a collective two-day meeting at the Civil Service College, Sunningdale. This was the second such annual meeting, organized at the insistence of some of the middle-ranking members of the CPRS and acquiesced to rather reluctantly by Kenneth Berrill. The aim was for the CPRS itself to have a 'strategic' discussion of its objectives and priorities, as the basis for planning its own work programme. The JASP team put to the meeting the proposition that the time might now have come to run down JASP and to turn the CPRS manpower to other uses. Some six people were now spending substantial amounts of their time on JASP activities. The arguments for pulling out were that JASP had now, over time, absorbed more CPRS man-hours than probably any other CPRS study, that it no longer seemed to arouse a proportionate degree of Ministerial interest (which suggested that for the CPRS the opportunity costs were high, given its constant need for its clients' approval), that it was no longer making much impact on the real world, and that the CPRS was in any case an analytical and not an executive body. The CPRS, including Berrill, accepted this judgement.

The effect of that decision was that JASP's life-support system was formally shut off. The CPRS-led interdepartmental group ceased to meet; so did the Ministerial group and Sir John Hunt's group of Permanent Secretaries. No further work was commissioned under the JASP umbrella. Work still in the pipeline continued to appear during 1977 and 1978. The last report whose origins lay in the JASP approach was 'People and their Families'. This broadly factual survey of families' needs for social services was published as late as 1980 and emerged despite the familiar protests of the Treasury that publication would encourage those pressing for increases in public spending. The Central Statistical Office continued to produce for Ministers short factual notes on current social issues, until the radical rethinking of government statistical services and manpower cuts under Mrs Thatcher brought all such 'luxuries' to an abrupt end.

JASP as an ideal lasted much longer. Indeed, the clearer it became during the late 1970s that public spending on social problems was having little impact on those problems, the stronger seemed to be the case for systematic thinking about priorities and for better co-ordinated action. Academics and others periodically called for a return to the JASP approach, or for a new—or more effective—JASP. Unfortunately the difficulties, formidable even when public spending was growing, of co-ordinating the thinking and the actions of different agencies, proved in a period of cut-backs to be politically and managerially almost insuperable.

However, the CPRS did not of course lose all interest in 'social' issues. It continued to work on these during the closing year or so of the Labour government. The PAR process, though itself on its last legs, still caught up some such issues, for example maternity provision. The CPRS itself launched a major study of alcohol and its effect on society—almost a model example of an issue which was everybody's business and yet nobody's. As the report itself noted, 'In central government sixteen departments have direct major interests in alcohol production, sale, and the consequences of its consumption'. The number of vested interests involved constituted a powerful reason for not disturbing the status quo. Despite a great deal of lobbying by the alcohol-producing interests, the CPRS report, completed in May 1979, concluded that the trends in alcohol misuse justified government concern. The government should make clear this concern in its public attitudes and should commit itself to countering the rise in the consumption of alcohol and to reducing alcohol-related disabilities.

This was clearly not a message which Ministers wished to hear immediately before a general election. If it was true, as the report said, that 'Going out for a drink' was the main social activity outside the home, it would be hard to think of a set of conclusions less likely to attract practical politicians. The report was not published. After the election, the proposal to publish it was raised again. The DHSS argued that this was unnecessary, since they would publish something of their own. They did, but it was a very different kind of document. 'Drinking Sensibly', published on Christmas Eve 1981, stated that alcohol problems were a matter of personal responsibility, and that people who got into difficulties should look after themselves (HMSO, 1981).

Although the CPRS report was never officially published, its existence became public knowledge owing to an indiscreet aside to the DHSS press officer. Many demands were made that it should be published; echoes of its conclusions occasionally appeared in the press. It is a sad reflection on British official habits that when, finally, the full text of the report became available this was not in Britain but in Sweden; it appeared with a foreword in English, published by a Stockholm University research project, 'Studies in Swedish Alcohol Policies'. The CPRS report was commended by the Swedish team as 'an important contribution to discussion . . . of considerable interest to all those . . . who take an interest in the issue of advertisement of alcohol . . . should be discussed in an international perspective . . . (Stockholm University, 1980).

Another study done about the same time was a report on vandalism. This had been a concern of Callaghan's who had found middle-aged and older tenants on council estates in different parts of the country complaining bitterly about it. The report set out ways that might reduce it. It stressed, however, that much vandalism was petty destructiveness rather than anything more serious. Moreover, the right way to deal with it was not by punitive action but by various preventive measures. These covered improvements in both the physical design and management of estates and what the report called 'diversionary' measures, that is encouraging other leisure activities. The report, published in September 1978, was aimed at various professional groups, including housing managers, architects, the police, and teachers as well as parents. After the report was published the Home Office ran a one-day conference to discuss its findings with representatives of all the relevant agencies. This was an unusually positive response.

A rather different kind of project during this period harked back to one of the CPRS's earliest interests, applied research and development. The CPRS reviewed government departments' research on the social services and social policy and the operation of the Social Science Research Council. Criticisms of the SSRC later led to Sir Keith Joseph, as Secretary of State for Education and Science, commissioning a report on it from Lord Rothschild; at this stage the CPRS conclusion was that if government departments wanted more 'policy-relevant' research they should improve their own internal arrangements. Indeed it was unpopular in Whitehall because its criticisms were largely directed at departments rather than at the SSRC.

Unlike Rothschild's original study of R. & D., this one was not published, perhaps partly because of the hostility of departments, especially the Department of Education and Science, to its conclusions. Another possible reason for its non-publication was a leak in *New Society* which caught the attention of the Prime Minister (*New Society*, 1979). The study thus acquired an unexpected political salience which may have reinforced Berrill's apparent unease with it and his feeling that the less that was made of it the better.

During the 1970s the CPRS produced one other major report on a complex and thoroughly 'interdepartmental' issue which, had it been acted on, could have prevented a great deal of pain and fury in the years that followed. From an analytical point of view, this report was one of the CPRS's clearest successes. From a political point of view, it was an almost total failure. Its subject was race relations. In the early 1970s race relations was already seen by many as a serious problem area, though much less clearly than was to be seen by many more after the Brixton and Toxteth riots of 1981. The starting-point of this piece of work was the replacement in late 1972 of Peter Carey by John Burgh, a Civil Service Deputy Secretary who had worked in several economic departments and most recently as Deputy Chairman at the Community Relations Commission, the government-funded group set up to promote good practice and better relationships in the race relations field. The CRC was highly dissatisfied with the Home Office, the department nominally responsible for race relations policies, and wholly responsible for immigration policies, which were inevitably closely connected. Within the CPRS the Home Office's reputation did not stand high; it was felt to be among the most conservative and the least analytical of Whitehall departments. Burgh had little difficulty in persuading his new colleagues and, ultimately, Rothschild, that race relations policy was a good subject for a CPRS review. There were, manifestly, many unsolved problems in the race relations field: although the Home Office was theoretically in the lead, this was a classic interdepartmental set of issues since responsibilities for actually taking action were scattered round all the departments of Whitehall. This fact made it an ideal area for CPRS work.

The CPRS seized its chance when, early in 1973, immigration was discussed at Cabinet. The Prime Minister was recorded as saying that the government ought to consider how to deal with the social problems to which immigration gave rise. When Rothschild had one of his regular meetings with Heath shortly afterwards, he mentioned the CPRS interest in race relations. Heath agreed that a CPRS study should be made, provided that the Home Secretary was content.

Neither the Home Secretary, the amiable Robert Carr, or his officials were in fact very content with the CPRS intrusion into their territory, possibly because their basic philosophy seemed to be that the problems were so complex that they were best left alone.[1] The Home Office, which already had

---

[1] Later during the review, a senior Home Office official commended to the CPRS a speech made in the House of Lords by Lord Goodman which, he said, set out well the case for taking no additional powers to deal with racial discrimination. Lord Goodman had said, among other things: '. . . If we look around, we see that coloured people seem to be settling down perfectly happily in large sections of London. I motor through London and see numbers of them in one place, and fewer numbers in another. Nowhere does one seem to see any imminent collision or conflict at this moment' (House of Lords, 1973).

responsibility for the Community Development Programme and for Section 11 Grants (specific grants to local authorities with a high proportion of Commonwealth immigrants to support extra staff in schools, for example, to respond to ethnic minority needs), subsequently made some rather half-hearted attempts to claim for itself a central co-ordinating role in dealing with race relations and urban deprivation. This arrangement was in fact made some months later, though it never had any practical importance. For the moment Rothschild, with the Prime Minister's backing, was unstoppable. By the middle of March the terms of reference had been agreed for a CPRS study of race relations. Because the subject had so many facets, the CPRS team was relatively large—five, plus an independent expert on employment practices, Tom Rees, who was drafted in for the study. Visits were made to Birmingham, Bradford, Ealing, Lambeth, Liverpool, and Slough, and members of the team had direct contacts with a range of interests—including representatives of ethnic minorities—many of whom were quite unknown to the Home Office.

The study was completed in the short time of four months. Preparing a final draft took some time and the report was presented to Conservative Ministers only in January 1974. It was extremely pessimistic, both about the problems identified and about what it saw as the feeble nature of the government's response to these. The report began bluntly:

There are uncomfortable parallels between the situation of Britain's coloured population and that of the Catholics in Northern Ireland. For fifty years British governments condoned discrimination and deprivation in Ulster, and in the end Ulster blew up in their face.

We believe that not only for reasons of social justice but also to preserve social stability and order in the longer-term more should be done to deal with the problems of race relations in this country (Phillips, 1977).

The report went on to discuss what would later be called 'institutional racism' in employment, education, housing, and the police. It expressed particular concern about 'alienated young West Indians', and about the absence of any strong lead from government in improving race relations either generally or in government's own institutions. It suggested that the Civil Service Department should keep records of black and ethnic minority employees and should set targets for their recruitment and promotion; the Department of Education and Science should promote special arrangements for children from ethnic minorities; the Department of the Environment should commit itself to ensuring that local housing authorities should keep records of coloured people on their lists of those housed and unhoused. Firms tendering for government contracts should be required to demonstrate that they had taken effective action to introduce equal opportunity policies in their own organizations. Established government contractors should be regularly surveyed to check on their practices. The report acknowledged that some of these proposals could be expensive to implement but insisted that the cost of doing nothing could be much higher.

This report would have been hard for any government to digest at any time. In fact the timing could hardly have been worse. When Ministers saw it, they were at the height of the crisis caused by their confrontation with the miners, which was to bring the government down within a month. No decisions were taken.

With the new Labour government in power, the CPRS dusted off the report, made some minor factual and presentational changes, and submitted it to a different set of Ministers the following spring. There was a momentary hiccup when an over-zealous member of the Cabinet Secretariat claimed that the report was covered by the convention against showing Ministers of one party advice which had been submitted to another. The CPRS replied that the report was a basic account of a problem which Labour Ministers would certainly want to know about and that provided it were presented to them under a different covering note then the convention would have been observed. The Cabinet Secretary accepted this view.

However, Labour Ministers after the first election of 1974, with only a small overall majority, were in no position to make bold decisions on any topic as uncongenial as race relations. There were no votes to be won, and only the prospect of spending more money. The report had anticipated the likely merging of the two main race relations groups, the Race Relations Board and the Community Relations Commission. The new Commission for Racial Equality started work in June 1977. But Ministers, advised by the Home Office, preferred to side-step the report's more controversial proposals and the general line that central government should now give a firm lead to action against racial discrimination. The report was remitted to a Cabinet Office committee of officials, chaired by the Home Office, on immigration and race relations, and in this unsympathetic milieu it slowly faded away. The government's White Paper on racial discrimination, published in September 1975, was a lukewarm affair. It declared, for example, that 'it would be an unacceptable burden to require all (government) contractors to supply as a matter of form full particulars of their employment policies' (Home Office, 1975).

The report was never officially published. Extracts appeared in the *Guardian* in October 1977. But as by that time the report was in many respects out of date, although its main message remained as relevant as ever, this leak caused very little stir. The CPRS 'social policy' team was by then busy with other projects.

Despite the abandonment of JASP, the last two years of the Labour government were a relatively creative period for the CPRS in the social policy area. As one member of the CPRS put it, 'at the micro-level JASP was still operating'—particularly through the CPRS's involvement in various inter-departmental committees concerned with social policy. There was still quite a lot of relevant expertise in the unit, and Berrill's lack of interest in social issues left his staff relatively free to pursue topics as they thought fit. However, it became increasingly clear that there was no longer a 'client' for this kind of work. The Labour government, said one CPRS member, was 'only just hanging on, interested only in survival. It had no interest in long-term strategic thinking.' Moreover, the economic backcloth of rising oil prices, low industrial output, and loss of international competitiveness did not help. By the end of this period the Social Contract had collapsed and the 'Winter of Discontent' had set in.

At the height of the CPRS work on JASP, which coincided with its Review of the Social Services, as many as six of its members spent a substantial part of their time working on social policy. After the Conservatives were returned to power in 1979 there was a dramatic reduction in this commitment of time and effort. It soon became clear that the new government did not give high priority to social policy; so for the CPRS there was little profit in working on it. Yet to abandon it entirely would have been to neglect a central responsibility of government. Some activity in this area seemed desirable. When the Conservatives came into office two or three CPRS staff whose interests and expertise lay in the social policy field sought to continue some work on it.

Another factor in the decline of the CPRS's work in this area was the big reduction in the number of social statisticians working in the Central Statistical Office. The CPRS had previously co-operated extensively with the CSO in the production of Social Briefs and had backed the CSO's efforts to improve the social data on which well-informed policies could be constructed. However, just as the CPRS felt under pressure to shift the emphasis of its work, so did the CSO; and in the CSO this was compounded by Civil Service cuts in the number of statisticians and the Government Statistical Service.

When Robin Ibbs took over from Ken Berrill the move away from social policy was accelerated. Unlike industrial policy this was not an area with which Ibbs was familiar. By nature somewhat cautious, he understandably preferred to concentrate at first on fields in which he felt personally confident, notably industrial policy. He wanted to establish his own and the CPRS's credibility in the Prime Minister's eyes; this led him away from social policy in particular, and in general to focus on policy areas in which he knew Mrs Thatcher was interested and in which he felt sure of his own and his staff's competence. Under Ibbs the CPRS work on social policy tended to be not on the central issues but on those aspects which had an interface with industrial and employment policy, for example labour mobility. Towards the end of his premiership Callaghan had asked for a CPRS analysis of the constraints on industrial efficiency. This was watered down to a study of labour mobility; in the event, the report went to Thatcher not Callaghan. It seems, however, to have been 'lost' in Number Ten and was not widely circulated. However, some time later the subject was raised again and the CPRS did another study— seemingly with little reference to the first, which reveals one of the weaknesses of an organization with a constant turnover of staff. The origins of the second study lay in the concern of the Chancellor, Sir Geoffrey Howe, at lack of mobility in the work-force. The conventional wisdom among Conservative Ministers was that this was largely caused by wages councils and trade union restrictive practices. The matter was discussed in a Ministerial committee chaired by the Chancellor. This committee was, in theory, concerned with government strategy in the medium and longer term. Its task was to focus in particular on the strategic theme of actions to improve the supply side and to allow the economy to operate more freely. In practice, it became a committee which looked at issues not covered elsewhere. The supporting official committee was chaired by Berrill and then Ibbs. The CPRS picked up a number of remits from it and to some extent used it as a means of getting commissions for work which it wanted to do. Like the equivalent committee in the early months of the Heath government, the later committee eventually faded away. But meanwhile it commissioned the CPRS to examine labour mobility (as well as a number of other matters).

The study tried to evaluate all the schemes the Department of Employment and the MSC had introduced to facilitate mobility; it focused on how to move people to jobs rather than jobs to people. It also tried to draw Ministers' attention to the costs of labour mobility. Loss of the support of family and community could for example lead to greater demands on the social services. The CPRS consulted firms that had relocated about how they had achieved the move. It also talked to Whitehall departments, and to a lesser extent to the trades unions. Its report made a number of recommendations in the employment area. It also suggested that the new exchange scheme in public housing needed to apply to the housing associations too. The study's consideration of housing policies was, however, somewhat hampered by an edict from John Stanley, the Minister of Housing, to DOE officials not to talk to the CPRS staff concerned. Those recommendations that concerned the Department of Employment were in fact implemented; those that concerned the DOE were not.

There are two or three further examples in the areas of education and training of studies relating social to industrial and employment policy. One of the few reports to be published by the CPRS after the Conservatives were elected in 1979 was one on education and training for industrial needs. Like some earlier reports in the JASP series, this contained a disclaimer on the inside cover, which says 'This report by the Central Policy Review Staff is being published as a contribution to public discussion. Publication does not imply that the Government are committed to all aspects of the analysis nor to all the conclusions and recommendations contained in the report.'

The report was a thorough and well-informed contribution to the debate. It came up with some practical suggestions for tackling the rigidity, conservatism, and slowness to respond on the part of both industry and the educational system that it had identified. It also managed to incorporate some of the government's philosophy about the importance of gearing the educational and training systems more closely to the needs of industrial performance. Some of its recommendations were hardly likely to endear the CPRS to traditional educationalists or to the DES. That, however, is no criticism of the report. In suggesting alternative approaches to those traditionally taken, it was playing the role the CPRS was set up to perform.

Its work on this report placed the CPRS in a good position to undertake further work on training. The opportunity to do so arose somewhat later in the context of concern about youth unemployment. Sir Geoffrey Howe had for some time been worried about this, and had asked for a paper from his own officials in the Treasury. This had *inter alia* examined and rejected the idea of a new National Service in the community for young people. The Chancellor was still uneasy about the volume and direction of the spending involved and suggested to the Prime Minister that the CPRS should be asked to do a study. The Department of Employment, at the time under James Prior, was regarded as unsound on these matters by the PM and the Chancellor. In Howe's view the CPRS seemed likely to be more objective and possibly more imaginative. In any case he wished to be convinced that the MSC, an agency of the Department of Employment, was spending wisely the £1 billion allocated to deal with the problem. The Prime Minister agreed to a CPRS study and the work was done in the winter of 1980/1.

The study team used the methods that the CPRS had traditionally employed, working inside Whitehall and obtaining grass-roots views outside. It investigated the conflicts between the Departments of Education and Employment and went round the country talking to organizers and participants in Youth Opportunity Programme schemes in the big cities. The team concluded that because training was so under-valued a major new initiative was required; it endorsed the criticism of the Youth Opportunities Programme made by many educational commentators, that the training element in the scheme was not strong enough. It proposed a new scheme: all sixteen-year-old school-leavers not continuing in full-time education were to have a year's compulsory training. Compulsion was to be achieved by legislation rather than by the withdrawal of benefit to those refusing to attend. The report went to a Cabinet committee. It was rejected because of the recommendation that the scheme should be compulsory. The DES opposed the recommendations on the grounds that it would be difficult to provide extra resources for Further Education Colleges and that if there were to be a further year of compulsory education or training at the age of sixteen it should be in schools.

It was probably an error on the part of the CPRS to make a firm proposal for compulsion rather than putting it forward as one option among others. Closer contacts with Ministers might have made it easier to anticipate opposition. Certainly there was no evidence that the scheme was rejected on resource grounds. However, its rejection does not necessarily mean that it was a failure. Many of the ideas in the CPRS report were soon picked up and developed by the MSC, and eventually presented as the Youth Training Scheme, without compulsory participation by young people, and as the Community Programme (see Manpower Services Commission, 1981).

Government concern about unemployment led the CPRS into other work on the fringes of social, industrial, and regional policy. The Prime Minister herself indicated her apprehension about the high levels of unemployment in Merseyside. The CPRS took up the challenge and produced a report on the region, which, using powerful language, described its plight. It suggested the need for a strategy for the area to stop a further downward spiral and the possibility of inner city disturbances. Its proposals included encouraging tourism to compensate for the decline in older industries. However, the report received a poor hearing from Ministers. It was dismissed as an example of how intelligent people could waste their time and as demonstrating that the CPRS was overstaffed. There were jokes about the 'Costa del Scouse'.

This was the first CPRS paper for Ministers which Ibbs had presented. He was shattered by the reaction. The experience probably reinforced his view that he should avoid subjects which he personally had not mastered. Certainly he was at pains afterwards to steer clear of social policy issues. The event also reinforced his belief that the CPRS should not give advice outside the mainstream of the Prime Minister's concerns. However, the CPRS was to be vindicated. Within a couple of months of the Ministerial discussion of the Merseyside report, inner city Liverpool was being hit by serious rioting. The main author of the report, Quentin Thompson (on secondment to the CPRS from the GLC) was then seconded for a few weeks to work with Michael Heseltine, the Secretary of State for the Environment, to draw up an action programme for Merseyside.

Finally, on the interface between social and industrial policy the CPRS instigated a study on higher education and industry. By the time the study was under way the CPRS, now headed by John Sparrow, had only a few more months of life left. This was not a happy episode. There were serious conflicts within the CPRS team on the approach to be adopted, and an ideological division on the question of academic freedom versus industrial and economic relevance in higher education. The group had difficulty in reaching any agreed conclusions, an illustration of the problems caused by lack of leadership in the CPRS at the time. A report was, however, completed after the CPRS abolition had been announced, and was sent to the DES. When the CPRS was abolished one of its authors, Michael Elliot, was invited to join the DES as an adviser. As a consequence he was able to push some of the report's recommendations from within the department. The report was to some extent reflected in the Green Paper on higher education published the following year.

In largely ignoring social policy issues during the Thatcher period the CPRS was following a lead set by the Prime Minister's own advisers in 10 Downing Street. One exception to this general rule was Ferdinand Mount, head of the Policy Unit between 1982 and 1983. He was personally extremely interested in the impact of government policies on the family; encouraged by one or two members of the CPRS, he invited the CPRS to help him in investigating these issues.

In principle, this was exactly the kind of cross-departmental activity in which the CPRS ought to have played a leading role in shaping policy. In practice, the CPRS's contribution was largely administrative. An *ad hoc* 'Family Policy Group' of Ministers, chaired by the Prime Minister, was set up. Sparrow was a member of this group; officials in attendance included Mount, a member of the CPRS (Gordon Wasserman), and the Cabinet Secretary Robert Armstrong. An early meeting of this committee, in the summer of 1982, considered a paper written by Mount: he asked Ministers during the summer holidays to draft papers, which were to be personal, not departmental, contributions, suggesting ways of strengthening the family. These were to be the basis of a political initiative, in the form of a new 'family policy' in time for the next general election.

The Ministerial papers, when available, contained a mixture of proposals, thoughtful as well as eccentric. One suggestion which received some publicity was that children should be trained in the use of pocket money. An official working group, chaired by Wasserman, tried to distil and filter the Ministerial suggestions and to weave them into a coherent programme. This was done in the face of considerable scepticism among some members of the CPRS revealing, as one observer later commented, how far the CPRS had drifted from understanding the outlook of the government for which it was, in theory, working. None the less, and although the Family Policy Group was disbanded immediately after the 1983 election, the episode showed that the CPRS was still quite capable of collaborating effectively with the Prime Minister's Policy Unit.

Although the CPRS played a mainly secretarial role in the Family Policy Group, it was in principle free to make policy proposals of its own. One, accepted after a long struggle with the main 'service' departments, was for study of the impact of professionalism on the family. The aim of the study was to examine how far the work of the 'caring' professions supported and strengthened the family or how far it undermined it. It was typical that departments tried to get their own client-professionals excluded. The DHSS, for example, tried hard to secure the exclusion of doctors. In the event, the CPRS was wound up before the study could be done.

There was one report dealing with penal policy. This had been started whilst the Labour government was still in office; it focused on the problem of persistent petty offenders and on ways of finding alternatives to prison for them. The context was the continuing rise and escalating cost of the prison population. The report came up with some practical suggestions for alternatives, many of which required action by the DHSS. The CPRS's recommendations were accepted, although it appears that little was done to implement them.

Early in 1980 it was suggested within the CPRS that a study should be initiated on the police, and in particular on value for money. However, Ken Berrill was nervous about further potential conflict with the Home Office. Home Office officials had frequently been annoyed by the CPRS's interventions on a number of subjects. These included race relations, immigration policy, aspects of penal policy, data protection, and international agreements on broadcasting frequencies. The CPRS had been highly critical of the Home Office's failure to take the initiative in many areas. Furthermore, a report on value for money in the police force was also likely to be critical of the police. Given Mrs Thatcher's known views on police, Ken Berrill was also anxious to avoid a confrontation with the Prime Minister. Therefore the study never got off the ground.

The CPRS did participate in some of the interdepartmental work on social policy that went on. For example Hilary Land, an academic social scientist with considerable expertise on the family and taxation, represented the CPRS on a committee chaired by the Inland Revenue on the taxation of husbands and wives. The ethos of a particular department was likely to affect the line which it took in a committee of this kind. In this case the DHSS was basically against the employment of women with children and the Department of Employment for it. The role of the CPRS in such discussions was to try to elucidate, and to discuss, the underlying basic principles of the tax system. Were women, for example, still treated as dependants? Should this continue in the light of changed circumstances?

Some work done by the CPRS reflected its long-standing preoccupation with the prevention of ill health. The intention was to embody the results in a Social Topic note. However, these were phased out before the work could be completed. One by-product was a CPRS intervention on the introduction of compulsory seat-belts. Norman Fowler, then the Minister of Transport, had been opposing legislation. The CPRS stressed the great reduction in serious injuries from car accidents that would result from legislation and the consequently high savings of around £200 million.

Perhaps the biggest commitment the CPRS made to work on social policy in the Ibbs/Sparrow era was a major study on pensions. The study arose from a shopping list of ideas submitted to the Prime Minister in the Summer of 1982. Mrs Thatcher agreed to the study being done. The issue had been raised in terms of long-term public expenditure and how the 'pensions burden' could be reduced. Essentially the work was divided into two areas: the state pension scheme; and occupational pensions and the need for them to become more 'portable'. Both parts of the study were couched in favour of the Thatcher government's interests: the first with respect to reducing public expenditure; the second with respect to improving labour mobility amongst certain occupational groups. The study also met the requirement that some CPRS work should focus on the long term. In fact its time perspective, which involved considering a pensions policy for the twenty-first century was unusually long-term. It started with four premises: the state pension scheme cost too much; it did not focus enough on the genuine poor; there was too little scope in the pensions system as a whole for the individual to look after himself; and that the system of occupational pensions was rigid and inflexible and acted as a disincentive to career change.

The work which was done and its eventual outcome well illustrated two important principles which guided proposals for change put forward by the CPRS if they were to have any immediate effect. The first was the value of having either the Treasury or the spending departments on your side. With both opposed, the prospects of proposals for change being accepted were greatly reduced. The second was the importance of timing. The pensions study fell down on both principles even though in rational terms its analysis was convincing and John Sparrow believed that the reports that resulted had great merit. The first paper on state pensions focused on the inadequacies of the Earnings Related Scheme, including its cost and the fact that it benefited the better off. The paper proposed that the scheme should be phased out and the basic pension raised to buy off some of the key hostile reaction. The DHSS disliked the proposal because it saw it as breaking the 'pensions consensus' which had been established so painfully in the past. The Treasury disliked it because it would cost money initially, a good example of the Treasury's inability to concede the desirability of spending money in order to save later. The second paper made recommendations on how to develop personal pensions schemes as a credible alternative particularly for more mobile employees unsuited to the form of compulsory final salary company schemes.

The work was completed in the Spring of 1983. Soon after, the two reports went to Number Ten; and after an appropriate interval Sparrow went to see Mrs Thatcher to get her reaction. He returned visibly shaken by the response. The problem was simple. Mrs Thatcher was contemplating going to the country in the near future, although the CPRS could not have known this. Most people were predicting an autumn election and she saw the report as an electoral liability. Sparrow was directed to recover the report from departments to ensure that all copies were destroyed. The second paper on portable personal pensions seemed to have been given no consideration at all.

On the face of it this was not a great success story for the CPRS. After the election, when the CPRS had been abolished, some of the ideas in the pensions papers re-emerged in the Fowler Social Security Reviews. Any suggestion of direct CPRS influence must, however, be qualified. Others with influence were also sceptical about the earnings related scheme, including the right-wing Centre for Policy Studies and the Number Ten Policy Unit, and the former was responsible for putting portable pensions irreversibly on to the political agenda through a major initiative launched in April 1983. Perhaps the most that can be said is that the CPRS contributed to 'breaking the mould', a role that it played in a number of other areas and one which should not be dismissed too lightly.

7

Industrial Policy

THE CPRS TOOK an interest in industrial policy issues throughout its existence. In its later years industrial studies made up the bulk of its work programme. This was partly because of the intrinsic importance of the subject to any British government at any time; partly because industrial issues were, characteristically, ones where Ministers' hearts prevailed over their heads (that is, where short-run political arguments almost always won against longer-run economic ones); partly because, like other policy areas in which Whitehall found itself actively involved in the 1970s, this was one in which it had little first-hand experience or relevant expertise. In the department or departments variously entitled Trade, Trade and Industry, or Industry through the period, most policy jobs—as in other departments—were held by generalist officials. Their career moves might well take them from active involvement in the affairs of a sector of manufacturing industry to a post concerned with tourism or the recondite formulae of the General Agreement on Tariffs and Trade. Most of the Ministers who presided over the department during the 1960s and 1970s—Maudling, Erroll, Heath, Jay, Crosland, Mason, Noble, Davies, Short, Benn, Varley, Joseph—were technically no better qualified. Of the long procession of politicians who passed through the post—conventionally regarded as but a stepping-stone to higher things—during this period only one, John Davies, had first-hand knowledge of the private sector of industry; and his political career foundered for want of parliamentary skills. Through an unfortunate mixture of bad management and bad luck the breakneck pace of Ministerial turnover at the industry department continued throughout the 1980s. By 1986 Joseph, Mrs Thatcher's first appointment, had been followed by Jenkin, Parkinson, Tebbit, Brittan, and Channon.

By comparison, the CPRS was relatively strong in commercial and industrial expertise. From the beginning its members included a few with private sector backgrounds, notably those seconded from the oil industry (although in fact most of their time in the CPRS was devoted to specifically energy-related

129

problems, rather than to those of industry in general). A few CPRS members had worked for management consultants, and one or two more in general management positions in manufacturing industry.

Apart from the CPRS's own industrial expertise, from the beginning two other aspects of its style of working gave it a distinctive edge over departments which, at least on paper, might have seemed equally competent. The first was the Rothschild technique of seeking outside experts, with specific skills and experience which few civil servants could match. Harold Lever, Arnold Weinstock, and Hugh Parker of McKinseys were only a few of the more prestigious 'consultants' used quite regularly by the CPRS at different times during Rothschild's period as its head. Rothschild's own connections gave him easy access to the City, as did Kenneth Berrill's rather different background. Robin Ibbs himself was seconded from one of the most successful British firms, ICI, and the last head of the CPRS, John Sparrow, from the merchant bank Morgan Grenfell.

The second CPRS technique, equally open to departments but much less practised by them, was that of actually getting out into the field and talking to people in industry. Although unsystematic personal impressions can sometimes be misleading, these first-hand contacts undoubtedly gave the CPRS members a 'feel' for particular situations that their departmental colleagues all too often lacked. One problem here was that the relative prestige of the CPRS, combined with outsiders' accurate perception that the CPRS was potentially an important channel of communication with the very top of government, resulted in CPRS contacts being mainly with managing directors and chairmen of companies or their most senior management colleagues. CPRS members commented subsequently that they might have acquired a more accurate and honest picture of the current situation in a firm from middle management or from the trade unions.

Several of the earliest CPRS interventions in industrial policy related to the all-too-familiar type of case where governments found themselves, for a variety of reasons—good and bad, economic and social, domestic and international— expensively supporting activities which on strictly commercial criteria should have been allowed to decline without further government intervention. Early in its life the CPRS intervened, via a collective brief, in the Heath Cabinet's discussion of whether or not to save Upper Clyde Shipbuilders. Ministers' decision, against the CPRS's advice, to save this lamest of lame ducks was the straw in the wind pointing to the gale which before long was to blow the government's industrial strategy entirely inside out. A decade later, the CPRS was involved in the Thatcher government's discussion of the future of the Invergordon Smelter. The smelter, which had been losing money for some years, was sited North of Inverness in a marginal constituency held by a junior

Minister, and there was a strong likelihood that the employment and political issues as against those of industrial policy would dominate. Robin Ibbs was asked by the Prime Minister to report on the matter. With some involvement from the Treasury, Ibbs analysed the problems associated with both retaining and closing the smelter. The decision was finally taken by a Cabinet committee to close it. The junior Minister concerned lost his seat in the 1983 election.

One of the very first CPRS reports was on a topic which had for some time interested Rothschild personally: the future of the Anglo-French Concorde project. This had been inherited by a theoretically non-interventionist Tory government from a Labour administration which itself, on inheriting the project from its Tory predecessors, had tried to pull out of it. Rothschild commissioned Mark Schreiber, then working as a political adviser to Lord Jellicoe, to trace back the history of the project before the CPRS started work on the problem. In a typical Rothschild gesture he sent Schreiber a bottle of Château-Lafite '45 to thank him for his labour.

The CPRS report on Concorde opened with a characteristic Rothschild flourish. 'Concorde is a commercial disaster.' But then recognizing that the point of non-return had long been passed, the CPRS recommended trying to maximize the return on this truly disastrous investment by completing it as rapidly, and marketing the product as aggressively, as possible. To press home the point about marketing, Rothschild commissioned a specially produced Concorde tie from Marks and Spencer to accompany the report for each member of the Cabinet. A comparable headscarf was produced for Mrs Thatcher, then Secretary of State for Education.

The Concorde study was shortly followed by a study of government policy towards the computer industry and, in particular, towards the single surviving UK manufacturer of mainframe computers, ICL. ICL was in effect a government creation, formed in July 1968 as the result of a merger between ICT and the business and scientific computer interests of English Electric. It was a classic product of government intervention in the brief age of the 'white hot technological revolution', reflecting the strongly held belief that the United Kingdom must have its own independent computer manufacturing industry. Under the Labour government ICL had been kept alive both by direct financial assistance through massive cash 'research grants' and by a highly restrictive purchasing policy on the part of central government and agencies—such as the National Health Service—controlled by central government. By 1971 ICL's share of the central government market had risen to 90 per cent; it also took a comfortable majority of orders from local authorities and from public corporations.

The Conservative government had dissolved the Ministry of Technology but had inherited its officials and an only slightly modified version of its policies towards the computer industry. Some Conservatives were uncomfortable with this continuing degree of intervention in industry. In the case of computers, their doubts were reinforced by the objections of many parts of government, for example the Ministry of Defence, at having to buy British when British was by no means obviously the best; users' resentment at having ICL hardware forced on them mingled with their anxiety that if ICL were to fail they would be left with an enormously expensive task converting to, say, IBM equipment. But even hard-nosed Conservatives who might have been willing to see market forces play unconstrained on 'traditional' and perhaps dying industries, such as shipbuilding, were uneasy at the thought of abandoning a modern industry which, it was argued, contained within itself the seeds of the second industrial revolution. The 'buy ICL' view was strongly expressed by DTI. The 'buy the best—even if foreign' counter-view was expressed on the users' behalf by the Civil Service Department, responsible for government purchasing policy. The two arguments met at hardly any point. It was a classic case for involving an uncommitted third party such as the CPRS.

The CPRS team set up to deal with this project exemplified Rothschild's insistence on the value of experts and his ability to summon them. The core of the team was two 'lay' CPRS members. To these were added Sir Brian Flowers (now Lord Flowers), a distinguished physicist, who was then chairman of the Science Research Council and had recently been chairman of the Computer Board for Universities and Research Councils; James Joll, a finance expert from the staff of Rothschild's bank; and a senior member of the staff of Government Communications Headquarters at Cheltenham, an organization at the time unknown though later notorious, and then as now a major purchaser and user of information systems. The willingness of the uncommitted laymen on the team to ask fundamental questions about policy, allied to the different types of technical expertise brought by the outside expert members, gave the team a cutting edge which the Department of Trade and Industry could not match.

The CPRS report on ICL illustrated well the role of the policy analyst as constructive critic. It was critical, in dismissing the central case either for favouring the indigenous manufacturer of computer hardware at the expense of the indigenous user, or for trying to preserve the indigenous manufacturer regardless of cost—which had in effect been official policy. It was constructive, in acknowledging that, none the less, Ministers might want to continue supporting ICL, and in going on to suggest ways of doing so that would be more effective and less costly than the existing policy. It concluded with recommendations for improving central government's own organization for computing matters.

The approach that underlay these proposals differed in several ways from that of the department. First, the CPRS looked critically at people. Civil servants in Whitehall were neither qualified nor eager to make judgements about the capability of private sector managers, even when in charge of firms receiving large-scale support from government. The CPRS team, by contrast, did not shrink from some trenchant comments on the top management at ICL, and the importance of improving it if ICL were to continue to be a chosen instrument of the government.

Secondly, the CPRS insisted that if ICL were to continue to receive government support, it must be far more accountable than in the past for the ways in which the money was spent and for the results that were obtained; 'monitoring' the implementation of policy, even in the 1980s not an automatic part of the process, was here an integral part of the package proposed to a sceptical industry department. Thirdly, the CPRS paid particular attention to alternative means of providing necessary support. Applying the expertise of James Joll to a question which, once again, civil servants were ill equipped to answer, the CPRS looked at ICL as a quoted investment opportunity which, for all the government's interest in it, was critically dependent on its continuing credibility in the market-place; the method proposed was government underwriting of a new ICL issue of convertible loan stock, to be taken up by existing shareholders in proportion to their current shareholdings.

It has to be acknowledged that for ICL the respite was only temporary. It was a cause for concern on several occasions during the 1970s. In 1980/1 it was firmly back on the Cabinet agenda. Nobody in the Department of Industry or even in the CPRS then recalled the CPRS's earlier report on the firm. At the instigation of one of the original team still working in Whitehall, the report was retrieved from the archives, dusted off, and reread. ICL was shored up with a loan guarantee proposal and a new Managing Director and Chairman put in to try to improve its performance. By 1987 its position was a good deal stronger.

The major theme of industrial policy in the early 1970s was selective intervention. Much of the official rhetoric was in terms of the need for tough decisions—to let go those industries whose day—at least in Britain—was done, and to concentrate attention and report on those where we seemed to have some kind of long-run comparative advantage. The difficulties in implementing this kind of policy were twofold. First, allowing any industry to decline led to confrontation with well-organized sectional interests, and particularly with representatives of areas of high unemployment. Secondly, it was much harder than anticipated to draw up a convincing list of industries which could be said to have some kind of future. The computer study had revealed both dilemmas. Was computer hardware an example of a sector in which Britain's competitive position was so weak that there was no point in trying to remain in it? Or was it, on the other hand, precisely the kind of infant industry of the future that justified massive government support during the difficult years of struggle to acquire the necessary market share? In the computer study the CPRS had given its own answer, but had failed to define any general principles, still less to secure a general agreement on these.

In its early years, the CPRS did, however, make two attempts to define some general principles. One was theoretical, one was empirical. The theoretical attempt was a project called 'Growth and Declining Industries'. This was one of the earliest CPRS studies, beginning in April 1971. Its aim was to identify industries which might be said to contain within themselves the seeds of long-term growth or decline. The government, in devising its industrial strategy, would thus have some basis for deciding which industries and firms should be supported and which it would be realistic to abandon.

By the autumn of 1972, after a great deal of consultation with academic and commercial experts and with government departments, the broad conclusions of the analysis were fairly clear. The medium-term prospects for much of British engineering industry were distinctly poor; employment levels in this sector were likely to fail, with serious results for parts of the country in which they were concentrated. The structure of the British economy was likely to go on changing rapidly. There could be problems in relation to redeployment of labour, regional imbalances, and the need for retraining. Looking at the government's economic, industrial, and manpower policies, the CPRS concluded, in effect, that their objectives were probably in conflict with each other but that they were too inadequately defined to tell.

But this was as far as the study was to go. The CPRS had reviewed, briefly, the whole field of industrial or micro-economic policy. It had concluded that there was no overall strategy and that there were many problem-areas in which government action was possible and probably necessary. In the absence of any guidelines from Ministers about their objectives the CPRS found it impossible to indicate the kind of action which should be taken even in relation to declining industries. Was it to let certain regions decline even faster, to encourage labour mobility and retraining away from old industries and skills, to channel large-scale investment towards 'new' industries? Had the considerable amount of money which had been spent on regional support achieved anything? This issue became the subject of a separate CPRS study, and was returned to by the CPRS from time to time later.

Although the CPRS analysts found it easy enough to identify a selection of industries in which Britain's ability to compete was manifestly declining, they were defeated by the task of singling out a matching group with equal prospects of growth. Reliance on outside advisers did not help; merchant banks and others consulted came up with the kind of lists of short-run investment opportunities that they might have offered a client with a few hundred thousand pounds to spare—sports goods, for example.

134

A more empirical approach to the same general questions was an attempt to analyse the experience of post-war Japan. Were there any lessons to be learned for the management of British economic and industrial policy? In the later 1970s this kind of question was to become commonplace. The CPRS was ahead of its time in organizing a weekend 'think-in' at the Civil Service College in September 1972, bringing together selected experts on Japanese industrial policy, including the Japanese director of the Japan Trade Centre, and British officials. They discussed such questions as 'What are the factors which have enabled Japan to be so successful in her post-war recovery, and does the United Kingdom have any lessons to learn from this?' At his request, though doubtless prompted by Rothschild, a summary of the conclusions of this meeting was sent to the Prime Minister. One conclusion reached by the CPRS was that more still needed to be known about the Japanese experience.

But the gap between Japanese and British practice and institutions seemed, at the time, too wide to bridge and this initiative was gradually allowed to run down. The attempt to persuade Ministers, who had already backed down when confronted in the autumn of 1971 with the problems of Upper Clyde Shipbuilders, to be more rigorous in selecting sectors or firms for assistance or abandonment, was politically far too hard. But it has to be acknowledged that in trying, however briefly, to think systematically about these issues the CPRS was ahead of its time. A decade later experts in the industrial countries of the West were still asking themselves the same questions about the relationships between Japanese governmental and commercial institutions.

Much the same problems were confronted in microcosm in the case of the motor car industry. This was an example of an industry in which Britain had long been established, and whose growth prospects world-wide seemed assured. It was unquestionably a twentieth-century industry in the sense that, say, coal-mining or shipbuilding were not, whose abandonment seemed certain to lead to increased localized unemployment and an increased trade deficit. Yet it was a painful example of an industry where major British firms were being kept alive only by massive continuing government support. By the early 1970s the British car industry was dominated by American multinational producers: Ford, General Motors, Chrysler. The only large British-owned producer was British Leyland, which by 1975 accounted for only 31 per cent of British car registrations and 48 per cent of car output. British Leyland found it hard to compete with the multinationals, and its continuing revenue problems exacerbated its problems of under-investment. By mid-1974, following the oil price rise and the three-day week of 1973–4, BL was in an acute cash crisis. In December the Labour government guaranteed £50 million of working capital and set up an inquiry, led by Sir Don Ryder, to investigate the company's longer-term prospects and needs. The Ryder Report, produced in a mere four months, recommended that the government should, in effect, 'rescue' BL through a programme of loans and equity finance totalling over £1 billion (a figure which was to have doubled within eight years) (Department of Industry, 1975).

At the same time as the appointment of the Ryder team, the CPRS was asked by Ministers to carry out a wider-ranging study of the British car industry as a whole. This request originated with a Cabinet committee chaired by the Prime Minister, an interesting and unusual example of a major CPRS study arising from a Ministerial initiative. The CPRS reported to Ministers in October 1975; the report was published a month later.

The car industry study was one of the most thorough and, ultimately, most influential pieces of work ever done by the CPRS. The approach used was novel and effective. A small CPRS team of three planned the study, drew up terms of reference for its conduct, and then subcontracted all the detailed legwork to a firm of commercial consultants. McKinseys, who had worked with motor manufacturers all over Europe and North America, were chosen by competitive tender.

This joint team produced a detailed and devastating report. Drawing a series of comparisons which subsequently became part of the conventional wisdom about British uncompetitiveness, the report showed conclusively that—if the motor industry were any guide—the problems of British industry could not be blamed on under-capitalization, poor production design, or lack of modern technology. The Ford Escort production lines at Dagenham and Cologne, the report showed, were nearly identical and were producing identical cars to identical specifications. But the productivity of Cologne was far higher than that of Dagenham. Similar disturbing comparisons could be made between Vauxhall and Opel. As the report bleakly summarized one of its most important findings, 'On average, the man-hours required in Britain to assemble the same, or a similar, car are almost double those required on the Continent. The implications for the British car industry are extremely serious.' One member of the CPRS team commented that he could understand the high sales of British newspapers when he looked at the stationary production lines in a British car factory, with the workers engrossed in the *Sun* or *Daily Mirror*.

The conclusions reached by the CPRS and McKinseys from these comparisons were that the prospects for the British car industry were bleak, facing increasingly aggressive competition not only from Western but also from Eastern Europe and, above all, from the Far East. There were 'too many manufacturers with too many models, too many plants, too much capacity and too much manpower'—a judgement almost identical to one made 30 years earlier, when an official inquiry into the post-war prospects of the motor industry had concluded that its export prospects were gravely affected by its division 'into too many, often small-scale units, each producing too many models' (Barnett, 1986). Labour relations and product quality were both poor. The government, which now owned half the industry, had a responsibility to give a lead, in changing attitudes throughout the industry, rationalizing plants and assembly capacity, and stabilizing the domestic market.

A discrete problem within this generally unsatisfactory situation was presented by Chrysler (UK), the unsuccessful subsidiary of a by then unsuccessful US manufacturer. The Chrysler story went back 15 years. In 1960 the British-owned Rootes group had yielded to a mixture of pressure and financial incentives from the then Conservative government and had built a large new car-manufacturing plant not where manufacturing logic would have indicated, next to its existing operations in Coventry, but 150 miles away at Linwood, near Glasgow. At the time this was hailed as a great success for the long-standing policy, followed by all governments, of trying to drive jobs away from the congested Midlands and South, towards the areas of higher unemployment in the North. But during the next few years Rootes's financial difficulties—compounded by this far-from-ideal location—drove it by several stages into the arms of Chrysler, the smallest of the large American producers, which at the time was avidly buying into the European car industry. In 1967 the Labour government gave Chrysler permission under exchange control legislation to take control of Rootes. The government took a 15 per cent shareholding through the Industrial Reorganisation Corporation.

By the end of 1974 it was known that Chrysler (UK), as the old Rootes group had now become, was in financial trouble. During the next year, Chrysler's troubles worsened. So, too, did its increasingly public insistence that, unless government aid were forthcoming, it would have to close down. This was also the strong view of officials and Ministers in the DTI.

Unlike the Ryder report, the CPRS study of the car industry reviewed all the foreign-owned producers, including Chrysler, as well as British Leyland. On Chrysler its conclusion was, in effect, that if the government was serious in its wish to keep BL afloat at vast public expense, there was no sense in simultaneously supporting one of BL's foreign-owned competitors. There was excess productive capacity in Britain; under almost any foreseeable scenario the right outcome would be for Chrysler to close down.

The report went to Ministers in early October 1975. They were evidently impressed by its main conclusions, including the withdrawal of support from Chrysler. The government announced that the report would be published (HC Deb. 1 December 1975, col. 395). However, the government was subjected to enormous pressure both in relation to the report as a whole and its particular proposals on Chrysler. The trade unions at first simply refused to accept the general tenor of the report or its analysis of the British car industry's weaknesses. At one of several presentations of the report to senior trade union leaders the latter's comment was 'Diabolical!' The unions appeared to believe that many of the figures in the report, and especially the productivity comparisons between Britain and Germany, had been fabricated in order to put British workers out of a job or, at least, to justify holding down their wages.

The debate about Chrysler was much more intense, and much more public. In brief, Chrysler's increasingly insistent threats that, unless it received government help, it must close, became the focus of a well-orchestrated campaign of lobbying whose motive power was the trade unions and, inside government, the Scottish Ministers. Ken Berrill was involved in the early internal discussions which concluded that Chrysler was no longer viable and should be allowed to close down. But despite these conclusions, vigorously supported by the Trade and Industry Minister, Eric Varley, the option of saving Chrysler was kept alive by the Scottish Ministers until, quite unexpectedly, their case was successfully taken up in Cabinet by Harold Lever, then Chancellor of the Duchy of Lancaster.

The outcome was a government agreement to make a massive loss subsidy, plus guaranteed loans. This deal was announced on 16 December, the same day that the CPRS report was, belatedly, published (HC Deb. 16 December 1975). It was widely claimed that this timing was deliberate: had the report been published earlier it might have helped to sway informed opinion against the Chrysler rescue to which the government was by then committed.

The government's decision to rescue Chrysler effectively made nonsense of the CPRS recommendations and thus, by definition, of the attempt to devise a strategy for the motor industry. As the historian of government industrial policy and the motor industry remarks, 'For a brief period during 1975–76 the British government had a coherent, well-reasoned policy for the motor industry. It came and went in the blink of an eye' (Wilks, 1984). It was 'stifled at birth by the Chrysler rescue, sacrificed to job preservation and the Scottish vote,' was the verdict some ten years later of the principal author of the CPRS report (Hawkins, 1985). This was not an unfair comment. But it would be less than fair to the CPRS if it was taken to imply that the report had no impact at all. It is undeniable that informed analysis of British industrial problems was profoundly affected by the report. In relation to the car industry critics would never again be able to argue, as the unions in particular had done, that the basic problem was under-investment, and that if only management would bring plant and equipment up to the standards of that in, say, Germany, British industry would be fully competitive in world markets. In relation to other industries, this argument would need to be sustained by demonstrable facts, rather than simply asserted as a self-evident truth. The devastating comparisons between British and German Ford became part of the 'conventional wisdom' in discussion of British industrial productivity, and the model for similar comparisons in future.

It is arguable that some of the trade unions' objections to the car industry report could have been overcome had the CPRS invested more effort in consulting the unions. It is certain that more could have been done. More was done, a year later, in relation to the power plant study. The CPRS was instructed by Ministers in May 1976 to review the prospects of the UK power plant manufacturing industry. It was to examine 'urgently . . . the problems arising from the mismatch between plant manufacturing capacity (particularly for turbo-generator and power station boilers) and prospective orders'. It was to make an interim report within six weeks and a final report by the end of October.

To carry out the report the CPRS co-opted two engineers from the Programmes Analysis Unit,[1] and also hired the consultants Booz-Allen and Hamilton. The conclusions of the study—presented to Ministers at the end of October—were that the UK needed a power plant industry, that there was 'substantial over-capacity' in the industry, that the government should help the industry by accelerating and stabilizing the power plant ordering programme, and that the industry should help itself by 'rationalizing' i.e. by mergers. In particular, the turbine-generator firm C. A. Parsons should merge with its more profitable rival GEC.

CPRS representatives spent a great deal of time discussing this and other options with the firms affected, unions as well as management. Broad agreement was gained for the conclusion that mergers were needed in the industry if it were to survive. Ministers were, at first, inclined to accept this. But in the end they were deflected by vociferous protests in Parliament and by a vigorous lobbying campaign on behalf of the smaller firm, Parsons, masterminded by one of the geniuses of modern British public relations, Will Camp. The Secretary of State for Energy, Tony Benn, was in any case doubtful about the role of GEC in this area, which further reduced the likelihood that the two firms would be merged. In the end Drax B was awarded to Parsons in July 1977.

CPRS interventions in industrial policy, as in the case of ICL and the motor industry, and the line taken in each case, reflected the anxieties of a group of economically literate, well-informed, and relatively disinterested analysts about policies which over time seemed to have built up an irresistible momentum, but which ran largely counter to the kind of principles which government spokesmen were prepared to defend in public. In both cases the

---

[1] The Programmes Analysis Unit was an in-house consultancy to the Department of Industry and the UK Atomic Energy Authority providing analysis and assessments to assist in decision-making in the long-term planning of projects. It was dissolved in 1977.

CPRS realized that Ministers might be unwilling to adopt the 'tough' policy, but could not persuade them to acknowledge the full implications of the 'soft' policies actually followed. It proved particularly hard to get agreement on a clear definition of the terms on which the government would continue to support such non-economic industries and the circumstances in which support would be discontinued. There was, in short, no strategy. The difficulty of defining terms and circumstances was increased by the lack of expertise of departmental officials. The Department of Trade and Industry was short on what might be termed 'analytical propensity'. As the leader of the car industry study later commented, 'To the outsider it may seem strange that this study was not initiated or carried out by the Department of Industry . . . However, the role of sponsor and monitor of an industrial sector is not normally seen by the generalist civil servant as including an analytical study of that sector with a view to devising a strategy for it, even though such a study could be carried out by a joint team with management consultants . . .' (Hawkins, 1985).

A more general point was the reluctance of departments at either Ministerial or official level to take a firm line with 'their' client industries or firms. Departmental structures inevitably reflected past events and policies shaped by those events; they helped to keep alive policies and attitudes when the rationale for them had diminished. As with ICL or the motor industry, the CPRS felt that departments were too often over-protective of firms and industries which they sponsored; it could often be in a firm's longer-term interest to have to compete internationally, and in the national interest if a proven American missile or computer were purchased rather than a less satisfactory British alternative. It was a major problem to create new attitudes and to launch new policies through existing organizational frameworks. The first Thatcher government tried to provide clearer guidance on effective purchasing by issuing guidelines about public purchasing policy, including buyer/supplier relationships and investment appraisal. The CPRS contributed to preparing this guidance.

Two other episodes illustrate both the problems and the kind of contribution which a body like the CPRS can make. The aerospace industry raised many of the same problems as computers. By the mid-1970s decisions were looming about the next generation of long-haul aircraft. In Britain, there was a major user interest in the form of British Airways. In this case as in others, British Airways wanted to buy from Boeing. There was a major producer interest in the form of British Aerospace and Rolls-Royce (who constructed the engines) but whose interests diverged sharply in that British Aerospace naturally wanted to sell their airframes to British users, while Rolls-Royce seemed to see more secure long-term prospects in collaboration with Boeing so as to produce American airframes for British engines. There was a powerful

US competitor in the form of Boeing itself, but a beguiling alternative in the prospect of collaboration with European manufacturers, with whom British Aerospace felt more nearly on equal terms. This diversity of interests was reflected by a diversity of views among Whitehall departments. The Department of Trade was the 'sponsor' for British Airways, the Department of Industry for the airframe and aero-engine manufacturers. The Foreign and Commonwealth Office was alternately swayed by the economic arguments in favour of collaboration with Boeing and the EEC arguments in favour of the European connection. The Treasury had a close interest in the outcome, even if uncertain as to what it wanted this to be (see Dell, April 1980).

The CPRS was thus an obvious candidate for honest broker. Kenneth Berrill was at the time chairing an interdepartmental group of officials advising the Prime Minister, James Callaghan, on economic matters. The aerospace issue came up in the group and was, in effect, taken over by Berrill and the CPRS. Berrill himself had good contacts with Rolls-Royce and with British Aerospace, less good with British Airways. He saw the CPRS role in this matter not as advocating a particular outcome but as helping the Prime Minister to elicit an outcome which made reasonable sense from all points of view. Berrill himself, in his role as Prime Ministerial adviser rather than chairman of an official Cabinet committee, accompanied Callaghan to the United States to talk to Boeing.

The final outcome was that British Aerospace went into partnership with the French on the Airbus project, that Rolls-Royce collaborated with Boeing, while British Airways purchasing policy was left unchanged and consequently led to the choice of Boeing aircraft. One CPRS member commented that the CPRS involvement had done little to affect the substance of the outcome, but certainly helped to speed it up. Callaghan himself commented that in this affair there was no single powerful Minister capable of acting as a political co-ordinator, and that in consequence the value to him of the CPRS and Berrill, playing an analytical and administrative role, had been considerable. The CPRS returned to the subject in the last year of its life when its head, by then John Sparrow, once again found himself chairing an interdepartmental committee on the subject.

The CPRS was not concerned only with manufacturing industry in the accepted sense. For example, in the early 1970s, under Rothschild, the CPRS did some work on agriculture. Pursuing a favourite line of Rothschild's, the CPRS investigated the question of the case for an 'agricultural strategy' analogous to the strategy for energy which it had advocated in another study. The question was looked at in a European context: was it possible to devise a comprehensive system of taxation, subsidies, and other instruments which would encourage, in different parts of the EEC, local types of agriculture most suited to local conditions—including, of course, in Britain? Despite Roths-child's enthusiasm, this project got nowhere—'one of the least successful of all CPRS studies', commented a member of the CPRS team. This failure was probably due to the opposition of the Ministry of Agriculture and the National Farmers Union, the fact that the study had made only little progress by the time negotiations for British entry began, and the intrinsic difficulty of the subject. The CPRS continued to take a sporadic interest in agricultural matters after Britain's entry into the EEC, often siding with the Ministry of Agriculture and the Treasury, against both the French and the Foreign Office, in denouncing the protectionist EEC sheepmeat regime. This change of orientation towards agriculture was a general one. Once Britain was in the EEC there was less need to take a tough line with MAFF, recalled a member of the CPRS, 'since they then started fighting the EEC who would have given farmers more than MAFF would ever have done'.

Another major 'non-manufacturing' study reflected, like the work on agriculture, the view quite strongly held in the CPRS that governments paid too much attention to the 'metal-bashing' industries in comparison with other commercial activities at which the British were probably more competent. In early 1972 the CPRS embarked on a project known as 'The future of London as an international financial centre'. Its aim was to identify the constraints on the continuing development of the City, and to suggest any government action needed to remove these. The study tried to envisage the changing framework within which the City would be operating, including the consequences of Britain's entry to the EEC.

The small CPRS team working on this study soon found itself short of the necessary resources to conduct an inquiry of this kind. The job was subcontracted to the Inter-Bank Research Organisation, a wholly owned subsidiary of the clearing banks, which agreed that IBRO's services should be provided free of charge. The IBRO team was led by James Robertson, who a few years before had been a member of Lady Sharp's group of ex-officials advising Mr Heath.

IBRO's report was completed towards the end of 1972 and submitted to the CPRS. Its main conclusions were that an interdepartmental 'task force' should be set up in Whitehall, to devise a strategy to guide City and government; that the Department of Trade and Industry should be given the task of putting together a coherent framework of regulations; and that a new body should be created in the City to represent its interests to government, to the EEC, and to public opinion.

The study was greeted with a great deal of suspicion in City circles, above all by the Bank of England; the Bank, wary of any investigation which might threaten its own established position as guardian of the City and as intermediary between it and government, was reluctant to allow its officials even to talk to the IBRO team, a fact which was noted in the final report. Rothschild showed the report to several City contacts, including his son Jacob. They did not like it, and said so. It was unfortunate that, following a brief 'leak' about the report in the *Daily Mail*, the CPRS, without consulting the clearing banks, unattributably briefed the economics correspondent of *The Times*, Peter Jay, so as to get a more accurate version on the record. The result was an extensive apparent 'scoop' for *The Times*, to the fury of the clearing banks, which had not been consulted and had not had the chance to consider whether or not the report should be published (Jay, 1972).

The report was in fact published six months later, in June 1973, amid grumbles from the clearing banks that their hand had been forced. It attracted some favourable press comment. The principle of the project had been welcomed by *The Times*. 'It marks one of the first attempts ever to examine the future of the City objectively' (Morison, 1972). The report itself was commended. 'The central proposals, the setting up of a Whitehall task force and of a single City representative body, are urgent' (*Guardian*, 1973). But the report had little impact. The Bank of England was as unhappy with it as before. Rothschild had never had much confidence in it. The oil price crisis was at its height. Robertson himself was about to move on to another job. In all the circumstances it is not surprising that the report and all its conclusions were quietly shelved.

Early CPRS attempts to anticipate future industrial developments had achieved little. The 'growth and declining industries' project was too ambitious, both conceptually and in its coverage, while the pioneering work on comparative Japanese approaches was abandoned largely because of the difficulty of actually applying any of the likely lessons in practice. Much later in the life of the CPRS, more narrowly defined 'modernization' projects made more progress. This was partly due to the unexpected acquisition by the CPRS in 1976 of a new post with a new 'outsider' to fill it—the Government Chief Scientist.

The creation of this post was itself an indirect and delayed result of Rothschild's own 1971 report on applied research and development. (It had in fact been agreed in principle some years earlier by Sir William Armstrong that the CPRS was the right place for the Chief Scientific Adviser, but in practice he was apparently reluctant to endorse it for fear that too much power might be concentrated in the CPRS.) Rothschild later said that one of the purposes of his report had been to try, 'in the most modest of ways', to change what he saw as the Civil Service's discrimination against those with professional qualifications; he instanced scientists, engineers, accountants, and lawyers. Perhaps, he added, 'it had a very minor success in that, for example, the

143

Ministry of Agriculture and the Department of Health now have Chief Scientists in relatively senior positions.' (Letter to authors). These posts were subsequently abolished.

At Cabinet level, responsibility for the 'science' input into thinking had rested since 1976 with the government's Chief Scientific Adviser, Sir Alan Cottrell. He had been supported by a small group of science officers in the Cabinet Secretariat. This arrangement had not worked very well. Others, and not the Chief Scientific Adviser, had decided what was or was not 'science'; in a classic Whitehall pattern the technical expert had found himself largely excluded from mainstream policy-making and limited to commenting mainly on technical issues. Many micro-economic or industrial topics were considered by the Cabinet without the benefit of any commentary by technically qualified analysts. Like the rest of the Cabinet Secretariat the scientific staff did little forward thinking; they responded to events and to initiatives coming forward from departments.

Cottrell's retirement in 1976 offered the chance to make a change. It was proposed that the scientific staff should be merged with the economic and industrial secretariat, that the post of Chief Scientific Adviser should be abolished, that a new interdepartmental committee of Chief Scientists and Permanent Secretaries should be set up and that an advisory committee of distinguished outsiders should be established to 'advise Ministers and publish reports' on applied R. & D. and its support, on the development and application of technology, and on the scope for international collaboration. It was also proposed that a new post, of 'Chief Scientist', should be created in the CPRS. As the government later explained it, the Chief Scientist would

work together with the other professional staff (scientists and non-scientists) in the Unit. As is usual in the CPRS, the issues studied will be worked upon by small teams of staff members and the scientifically qualified members will operate in a number of separate teams together with other professionals. That is to say, they will remain completely integrated into the work of the Unit and not be a separate sub-unit within the whole . . . The scientific role of the CPRS will not be primarily one of co-ordination but rather that of asking the fundamental or innovatory question and of undertaking certain studies or projects which are best conducted or led from the centre (Lord Privy Seal, 1976).

This formula, largely drafted by Berrill and Hunt, was designed partly to appease some members of the CPRS who felt strongly that the acquisition of the Chief Scientist was a mistake and a piece of opportunistic empire-building by Berrill. Berrill, who took a pragmatic view of the need for the CPRS to respond to the wishes of Ministers and to work closely with senior officials, was very willing to accommodate Hunt by finding room for the Chief Scientist; he also thought the status of the CPRS would be enhanced by thus acquiring a new senior member with some quasi-executive responsibilities for scientific matters. Some of his colleagues disagreed. They felt that a Chief Scientist, part of whose task was to act for the government on scientific issues, could not act as a truly independent commentator. Moreover, giving him a specified subject-area of his own would be a departure from the traditional 'corporate' approach of the CPRS whereby any of its members could in principle be involved in any of its activities, whatever their content.

Despite these doubts, the post was created. The CPRS acquired the Chief Scientist in the person of Professor John Ashworth, a biologist from Essex University. Ashworth was a well-known scientist and a self-confident and extrovert entrepreneur. He found his responsibilities extremely ill-defined and his own freedom to determine the content of his job correspondingly great. Despite the wording of the official statement quoted above, the CPRS did not acquire a larger number of scientifically qualified staff. Its impact in scientific matters was increased mainly by the activities of the new Advisory Committee on Applied Research and Development (ACARD). Views among members of the CPRS at the time differ as to which of ACARD and of the CPRS was tail, and which was dog. ACARD seems, some of the time, to have prompted the CPRS to take an interest in specific topics. It also discussed topics suggested to it by the CPRS, was briefed by the CPRS, and took CPRS drafts as the basis of its own reports. The prefaces to ACARD reports usually thanked the CPRS for its contribution. Since these were invariably published, the CPRS thus found an ostensibly independent ally in the advice which it was giving, internally, to Ministers and a channel for trying to enlist outside support for the same causes. ACARD, on which the Chief Scientist sat, was also, in effect, a standing group of publicly acknowledged specialist consultants whose advice was easily available to the CPRS. ACARD could advise on strategy; it suggested focusing on micro-electronics before the other topic favoured with the CPRS, biotechnology, as being more timely and important. It would also advise on technical detail and could provide valuable ammunition to use against the Treasury, the DES, or the research councils. ACARD reports dealt both with fairly narrow technical issues (e.g. computer aided design and manufacture (ACARD, 1980)) and general issues tackled from a technical viewpoint (technological change (ACARD, 1980) and industrial innovation (ACARD, 1979)). The Treasury at first questioned ACARD's right to concern itself with the latter group but was defeated.

The combination of Ashworth and ACARD was particularly effective in relation to one topic, micro-electronics. Following discussions between Ashworth and ACARD the latter set up a working party in January 1978 to look at developments in the micro-electronics field, especially semiconductors (or 'chips'), and the implications of these for industrial technology and for

British industries. The group had already started work when it became known that the BBC's 'Horizon' programme was working on the same topic. At Ashworth's suggestion the screening of the programme was delayed slightly, to shorten the gap between it and the ACARD report. The programme 'The Chips are Down', first broadcast in March 1978, was recorded by Ashworth; the recording was shown both to Ministers, including the Prime Minister James Callaghan, and to members of the Cabinet Secretariat. The result was to engender an interest on Callaghan's part which stayed with him for the rest of his premiership, and which provided powerful backing for the CPRS's continuing work on the subject. The parallel ACARD report, 'The Applications of Semiconductor Technology', was published in September 1978. It subsequently ran to four editions.

ACARD also prompted the interest taken by the CPRS in 'space' and related industrial and commercial activities, for example satellites, telecommunications, broadcasting. Several departments were interested in parts of this area: the Home Office, Trade, Industry, and the Foreign Office. But because 'space' was not seen as a policy area in its own right, no single department had a leading responsibility for it; the parts concerned of the Department of Industry played only a minor role, and although Industry scientists were conscious of the need to develop a coherent space policy, they lacked the weight needed to convey their views to their own Ministers.

There was thus a classic role for the CPRS, in the double sense of both pulling together separated bits of the Whitehall machine and of putting a topic on to the Ministerial agenda. A CPRS-led 'space' group was set up, and produced an internal report in June 1980. This report led, among other things, to much closer working relationships between British Aerospace and Marconi and ultimately to the establishment of a Ministerial post in the Department of Industry with specific responsibility for space-related activities. If space was a neglected topic because there was no 'lead' department, another topic on which the CPRS intervened was neglected because, in effect, the wrong department was in the lead. The topic, of apparently minor technical interest, was the allocation of radio frequencies. Radio regulation, for mainly historical reasons to do with security and broadcasting, was the responsibility of the Home Office. When the so-called World Administrative Radio Conference was due to be held in 1979, it was therefore left to the Home Office to advise on the British government's 'line' and to brief our representatives accordingly. The Foreign and Commonwealth Office at first paid little attention to this, despite its international implications and the importance of ensuring that Britain's interests were safeguarded, at a time of increasing pressure from both developed and developing countries for access to the finite resources of the radio spectrum. The CPRS felt strongly that the Home Office was not coping effectively with this issue and, indeed, did not understand its importance. They alerted the FCO, which subsequently moved into the lead position on the conference, to the apparent chagrin of the Home Office officials.

In its work on micro-electronics the achievement of the CPRS was, in effect, to get the subject taken seriously by other people in Whitehall; the natural scepticism of civil servants had been reinforced by memories of earlier premature enthusiasm about the possible impact of computers. In this context it was almost certainly valuable that in the CPRS technically qualified people were working on an equal footing with generalist administrators, and thus at only one remove from Ministers. Since they were in the CPRS on only very short secondment their first-hand knowledge of developments in industry was fully up to date. By contrast, scientists in departments such as Trade and Industry, however great their personal expertise, felt that they were unable to get their ideas through to Ministers since they had to communicate with the latter through generalist administrators—whose relevant knowledge was often both incomplete and out of date.

In the case of information technology (IT), the CPRS succeeded in solving a problem which dogs all new interdepartmental initiatives in Whitehall. In whatever terms an issue may be defined, and the case for action on it recommended, that perception has to be filtered, and that action taken, by existing government departments none of which are likely to see the problem in the round; all of them, in considering whether action is necessary at all and if so what form it should take, are likely to react in ways most likely to advance—or least likely to harm—their own interests. The result, all too often, is that even when some inquiry or piece of research has succeeded in defining an issue in the round, at the implementation stage it falls back into the hands of the several departments concerned, whose ill-co-ordinated responses are unlikely to add up to any kind of sensible policy. In the IT case, the problem was made much worse by the change of government in 1979. A Prime Minister with an intense interest in new technology was replaced by one at first indifferent to it. Perhaps more serious, a government with an ambitiously interventionist approach to industry was replaced by one with exactly the opposite philosophy; the arch-exponent of non-interventionism, Sir Keith Joseph, became the industry Minister. The CPRS can take some credit for helping Department of Industry officials to persuade Joseph not to dismantle the IT programme, and for helping to persuade Mrs Thatcher of the programme's value—aided by the reassuring report of management consultants whom the CPRS, again, had been instrumental in appointing to review the programme.

More important, the CPRS, having taken the lead in putting IT on the government's agenda, succeeded in establishing a successor-body to take over

147

this role. The Cabinet Office had proposed a conventional interdepartmental committee to co-ordinate the several interests involved. Such a committee was set up and ran for a year, with considerable input from the CPRS. In theory, the CPRS could have continued in the lead, using the committee simply as a clearing-house, but in practice the CPRS concluded that it should bow out, rather as it had done with JASP. There were several reasons for this. First, the fiction had to be preserved that the government did not have, in its Labour predecessor's sense, an 'industrial policy'; the work of the IT Unit, commented a former member of the CPRS, was 'such an anomalous interventionist industrial activity that it looked better done outside the CPRS, of which people might have been suspicious'. Secondly, a great deal of detailed executive work still had to be done, at what would have been high opportunity cost to the CPRS. Thirdly, for security reasons it seemed necessary to create a specialist unit.

The final outcome was the establishment in the Cabinet Office of a new free-standing Information Technology Unit, on the lines of the existing European Unit which had originally been set up to implement Mr Edward Heath's commitment to take Britain into the EEC. Adrian Norman, the CPRS expert on Information Technology, was transferred to the unit, which was headed by a senior civil servant from the Treasury. Whilst the outcome was what the CPRS had originally proposed, it took two years to achieve. It required the backing of the Prime Minister, the Secretary to the Cabinet, and the head of the CPRS, all of whom changed over this period. As a member of the CPRS put it, 'it was extremely difficult to get all three balls in their hole at the same time'.

When Ashworth left the CPRS in 1981, to become Vice-Chancellor of Salford University, he was replaced by Robin Nicholson, a Fellow of the Royal Society and former Professor of Metallurgy at Manchester University, then working as managing director of the private firm INCO Europe Ltd. Nicholson consolidated the position established by Ashworth—to such effect that, when the CPRS was abolished in 1983, the government Chief Scientist and his team of eight people were kept on as an apparently permanent central unit, playing a more interventionist and generally more effective role than any of the pre-CPRS Chief Scientific Advisers. The key to the survival of the CPRS Scientific Group was ACARD, which was an ally and protector of the Chief Scientist, when he was under attack. It acted as a protective pressure group for the CPRS's work on scientific policy. The stature ACARD achieved through its publications helped to give it the status it needed to support the work of the CPRS scientists.

One other major industrial topic, which took up a great deal of CPRS time at different stages, raised many of the issues just discussed, but in a totally different institutional framework. This was the vexed question of governmental relationships with the nationalized industries. Again, this was a highly appropriate topic for the CPRS because the resources and costs involved were enormous, the subjects contentious, and the main points of view apparently irreconcilable. On the one hand, the major argument for public ownership of activities such as railways, steel, gas, or airways was that these were either so important to public welfare or so incapable of operating according to normal commercial criteria that they had to be owned by, and managed on behalf of, the state. On the other hand was the principle that if these organizations were to have management good enough to run them efficiently, the management must be left alone to get on with the job and not be continually harassed and deflected by Whitehall. In this debate the instinctive interventionism of the CPRS was balanced by its almost equally strong belief that departmental officials themselves had little knowledge or understanding of management or commerce. In this respect it was hard to choose between the DTI and the Treasury. CPRS thinking on the subject, as on others, also reflected its exasperation at the distortion by Ministers on political grounds of otherwise 'rational' decisions. A milder version of this view was that although it was perfectly legitimate for Ministers to act in this way, they too rarely thought through the consequences of such action, and too often subsequently regretted it.

The first CPRS project on relations between the government and the nationalized industries was started in early 1972. In the style characteristic of the early CPRS the members of the project team had a great many contacts with interests outside Whitehall, including most obviously the industries themselves. They talked to most of the chairmen and many Board members. As a CPRS view on the subject developed, it came strongly to reflect the chairmen's opinion that their relationship with Whitehall was most unsatisfactory, and that Whitehall understood neither the activities of the industries nor the consequences of governmental intervention in them.

When the project was already fairly advanced Lord Rothschild persuaded the Prime Minister to set up a special 'strategy group' of Ministers on nationalized industries. The members of this included the Chancellor of the Exchequer and three or four other senior Ministers. The group met for the first time in July 1972. The only item on the agenda was a typically idiosyncratic paper largely drafted by Lord Rothschild. This urged Ministers to take a more analytical view of the role of the nationalized industries and a more statesmanlike attitude in the face of the short-run pressures on themselves to intervene in the management of the industries. The paper was circulated to members of the strategy group under cover of a note from the Prime Minister. Rothschild was nervous about the reception of this paper by departmental officials. At one stage he envisaged proposing to Ministers that they should not allow themselves to be briefed for the discussion by their departments, but was persuaded that this would be both provocative and completely un-productive. He compromised by warning the Prime Minister that depart-mental briefing was likely to be hostile, not least because officials objected to their Ministers being encouraged to think.

Departmental briefing was indeed hostile, partly in response to the abrasive tone of Rothschild's paper but, more fundamentally, because of the proposals in it. Perhaps the most basic of these was the suggestion for some kind of institutional barrier to be erected between government and the nationalized industries—a kind of holding company, which could itself be subject to a certain amount of Ministerial intervention but which could hold Ministers off at arm's length from the industries themselves. The upshot of the strategy group meeting, held at 10 Downing Street over the large part of a day including lunch, was an extremely unspecific invitation to the CPRS to give more thought to ways of encouraging the government to disengage itself from the day-to-day activities of the nationalized industries.

Following this rather lukewarm lead, the CPRS worked away during the summer. In the autumn the strategy group met again, and considered another much more detailed CPRS paper. This elaborated the CPRS view that the government should plan 'strategically' for the nationalized industries and should not intervene on 'tactical' matters, that clear ground rules should be drawn up—and published—to define the working relationship, and that some kind of holding company should be interposed between industries and departments.

Ministers, even though as always briefed by their departments, broadly approved this approach. The CPRS line seemed to have prevailed. This was an illusion. As in most such Whitehall confrontations, the real battle began only at the point where Ministers, having completed their part of the discussion, yielded the field to their officials. In the words of one of the CPRS team, 'Ministers handed back the responsibility for action to their senior officials, who insisted that Ministers would never be able to act in the ways that had been proposed. Officials were totally pessimistic and cynical.'

By this time the nationalized industries were being increasingly indiscrimi-nately used as an instrument of the government's counter-inflation policy. Their pricing and pay policies were the subject of more, not less, Ministerial intervention. Against this background the CPRS proposal to publish a White Paper redefining the relationship between the government and the industries was rejected by Ministers as unacceptable in principle. But when, as a compromise, the CPRS suggested drawing up some ground rules to regulate the relationship within the framework of current policy, it proved impossible to reach agreement with the departments concerned, including the Treasury, on the details. The whole exercise ran gradually into the sand. This was one of many cases, commented a CPRS member, where the CPRS devoted too little time and energy to the massive task of follow-up. 'Though our solution was on the right lines, neither officials nor Ministers were likely to accept it while the government had no long-term industrial policy nor underlying development plan.'

The CPRS did not return to the issue during the lifetime of the Heath government, nor in the Wilson government that followed it. However, during the period under Callaghan when the 1978 White Paper on Nationalised Industries was being prepared, the CPRS commented on the drafts and was able to influence the outcome.

In the last phase of the CPRS's existence under the Thatcher administration nationalized industries once again became the subject of a major CPRS inquiry. It is characteristic of the circular nature of the governmental processes that this latter project once again covered much of the same ground as the first one. However, the work done on nationalized industries by the CPRS under Robin Ibbs, in 1981/2, was one of the CPRS's final successes.

There were several ironies in the situation. First, that in 1981, unlike 1973, the CPRS was trying to devise ways of *increasing* Ministerial control of nationalized industries. Secondly, that their very success led to heated disagreements within the CPRS about how much attention the CPRS should continue to give to the subject. Thirdly, that had the CPRS capitalized on its success in this area by publishing the results of its work, it might have been strong enough to resist its eventual abolition in 1983.

The episode began with a commission from the Prime Minister. In the winter of 1980/1 Mrs Thatcher expressed extreme dissatisfaction both with the performance of the nationalized industries and with the increase in their demands for cash. These were one of the main factors which drove the public sector borrowing requirement far above the limit set for it in the Chancellor's medium-term financial strategy announced in March 1980. Lacking confidence in the ability of the Treasury or of sponsoring departments to produce an effective solution, Mrs Thatcher invited Robin Ibbs, in April 1981, to study and report on the industries' relationships with government. Though the terms of reference were vague, the task was clear: to find ways of controlling the industries and of limiting their demands for finance without at the same time increasing the degree of governmental intervention in their management—which Mrs Thatcher's administration was, in fact, pledged to reduce.

Ibbs's response to this brief was to become one of the largest projects ever managed by the CPRS. Within the CPRS, a 'Nationalised Industries Review Staff' was set up. With half a dozen members, mostly seconded from outside Whitehall, and mostly working mainly on nationalized industry topics, this team became virtually a 'CPRS within the CPRS'. It developed its own secretariat and its own programme of weekly meetings (immediately after the CPRS's traditional Monday morning meeting).

Asked to report by the summer recess, the team did so before the end of July. It recommended that more clearly defined strategic objectives should be set for each industry, as a basis for more rigorous monitoring of its performance. It proposed much smaller and higher-calibre boards for the industries with a majority of non-executive directors appointed from outside the industries concerned. Finally, the report was critical of the general capacity of Whitehall civil servants to perform even their existing role in relation to the industries, let alone the more interventionist one now envisaged. The CPRS therefore proposed the establishment of 'Business Groups' headed by someone from the private sector in each department to help officials to prepare their industries' strategies and to monitor their implementation.

There is more than an echo here of the earlier Rothschild report. The difference in the later case was that the study had been commissioned by the Prime Minister, who was anxious to see some changes made without delay. Mrs Thatcher thought the report excellent, and said so. In its general disdain for Whitehall, and given its proposals for replacing existing procedures, it was certain to put civil servants' backs up. It did so. Hardly had it been read in Downing Street than a leaked and highly tendentious account appeared in *The Economist*. This was a classic piece of rubbishing in *The Economist*'s anonymous style headed 'Think Tank's Damp Squib'. It read, in part:

The report's main proposal . . . is unlikely to find favour with either the Prime Minister or Cabinet . . . [The Business Group proposal is] not an idea guaranteed to appeal to any Tory just now. The Chairmen of the industries do not know whether to laugh or cry . . .'

In fact the Chairmen, perhaps characteristically, had not been shown the report and were not to see it until late autumn. Left with only a hazy idea that the CPRS had found them wanting, they were in no mood to act as the allies the CPRS badly needed in the battle against departments. At the Department of Trade and Industry, Sir Peter Carey, an experienced Whitehall campaigner with the added advantage of having himself served in the CPRS, was determined to resist changes which would not only have altered his department's traditional semi-interventionist attitude towards the industries, but which would also have handed over a large part of its task to the Business Groups. Although the arguments within Whitehall were fairly evenly balanced, in public they appeared one-sided. As in the aftermath of the Review of Overseas Representation (see Chapter 8), the CPRS felt unable to use the same weapons as its opponents, who therefore made much of the running in the media. The reason for this seems to be that Ibbs's general aversion to publicity of any kind was reinforced by his reluctance to reveal anything more of a report which was so critical of the competence of Civil Service colleagues. The report was not published and was never to be. The result was that Whitehall was, in effect, playing on home ground. Whilst some outsiders were brought in at senior level, the Business Groups in the form originally intended did not materialize.

For the CPRS, however, the outcome was rather better than a defeat, or even a draw. A long and circumstantial account of the whole battle was published in *The Economist* in March 1982. This was written by the paper's political editor, Simon Jenkins, himself a part-time member of the British Rail Board. Like the earlier stories, and building on the suspicions which those stories had themselves created among the Chairmen, it gave the strong impression that they were hostile to the conclusion of the CPRS report (*The Economist*, 1982). This was by now more nearly true than it had been earlier. However, when the Secretary of State for Industry came to speak in the Budget debate a week later, he was able to say that the government—'helped by the consideration given by the CPRS'—was aiming to put its relationship with the nationalized industries on a more satisfactory basis (HC Deb. 15 March 1982). First, the government intended to discuss and agree with the industries their strategic objectives. Second, the government would be talking to Chairmen about ways of slimming down their Boards and making them more effective. Third, the government intended to introduce new arrangements 'so that nationalised industries' performance and plans could be more systematically addressed'. He did not add that these arrangements included a new Ministerial committee on the nationalized industries, amongst other things to oversee the implementation of the report's recommendations, to be serviced by the CPRS, or that Ibbs's nationalized industries team was to be kept in being to perform this task.

For a year it acted as the secretariat to the Nationalised Industries Committee. The team was to last almost to the end of the CPRS's life. Its work seems to have satisfied the Prime Minister and, while he was there, Ibbs himself. But in doing so it ran up against the same difficulties as had faced the JASP team five years earlier. Was it right for the CPRS to invest such a high proportion of its resources in a single subject area, and to concern itself so closely with implementation rather than doing analysis? Some members of the CPRS, including members of the nationalized industries review staff itself, felt that the focus of the staff's work was misplaced in both respects (as well as requiring expertise lacking in the CPRS, for example for examining the detail of the industries' accounts). At one stage Ibbs suggested 'hiving off' the NIRS. This was successfully resisted on the grounds that, apart from the Chief

Scientist and his assistant, it would leave only four or five people available for all other business. But 'Ibbs in effect disbanded the CPRS by putting so much effort into nationalized industries work', commented an ex-member later. 'He seemed to be intent on running down the other side of the CPRS.' When Sparrow replaced Ibbs in the spring of 1982, this imbalance was to some extent corrected.

Although Simon Jenkins's *Economist* article had suggested that the Nationalised Industries Report's proposals represented a fairly mouse-like outcome, the CPRS was quite satisfied with the result. It is true that departments' monitoring practices remained patchy, while the Treasury—especially after the disappearance of the CPRS in 1983—never abandoned its tendency to treat the nationalized industries as though they were government departments, whose financial policies were wholly dependent on Treasury goodwill. But there had been some progress. Norman Payne, Chairman of the British Airports Authority, told an Oxford seminar in 1983 that he had recently held his first ever meeting with the Secretary of State for Trade to discuss his industry's strategy and objectives. The three-year statement of objectives for British Rail by the Secretary of State for Transport in October 1983 was hailed by British Rail as the first statement of its kind since nationalization thirty-five years before (Fowler, 1987). The publication by the Post Office some three or four years later of its strategic objectives was another longer-term outcome of this work. It seems reasonable to suggest that the greater focus by the government on agreeing strategic objectives with the industries was in some part due to the CPRS. However, not long after the CPRS completed its work in this area, the government's policy changed. Henceforth the emphasis was not on controlling the nationalized industries but on privatizing them.

During the 12½ years the CPRS operated, the governments it served varied quite considerably in how interventionist they wished to be in this area of policy. To some extent, thinking in the CPRS reflected the ideology of the government of the day. Thus in the later period of the Heath government and under Labour in the seventies the CPRS advocated rather greater intervention than under Thatcher in the eighties. However, in the last period many of its staff found it difficult totally to accept the free-market orientation of the government and tried to pull it back towards the centre. One free-marketeer in the CPRS thought this resulted in too much fudging of the issues. It would have been better, he thought, had the CPRS been more direct in expressing its opposition, driving home the logic of its argument. It was being 'wishy-washy', as we shall see later, that Mrs Thatcher most disliked.

8

The Review of Overseas Representation

OF ALL THE projects undertaken by the CPRS, that which caused the most problems was unquestionably the Review of Overseas Representation. Undertaken at the suggestion of the CPRS itself, but with the approval of the Foreign Secretary and the Prime Minister, the study took up a sizeable proportion of CPRS staff time for eighteen months. It resulted in a report of over 400 pages—the largest CPRS report ever. It was the subject of controversy, in private and in public, even before it was published—and considerably more so after publication.

The focus of a debate in the House of Lords, of investigation in a Select Committee, of literally hundreds of column-inches of newsprint, it did more to publicize the CPRS than any other single episode—but not in terms that the CPRS would have chosen. It was condemned by Edward Heath—the creator of the CPRS—and by many others, not only on the grounds of its conclusions but as a study entirely inappropriate for the CPRS. Berrill, head of the CPRS at the time and also leader of the study team, later described the project as an 'own goal'. Other commentators, however, saw the whole episode as classically illustrating two features of established British institutions: their total incapacity to accept radical critiques, and their misplaced energy and agility in mobilizing opposition to such critiques. When researching this book nearly a decade later, we found no other issue that excited such varied reactions among outside observers and ex-members of the CPRS alike.

The story begins with the two serving members of the Foreign Office who, in 1975, were on secondment to the CPRS. John Guinness was a member of the banking branch of this well-known family. Clever, rich, and no respecter of persons or institutions, he had been a diplomat since starting his career. He had served in the British Mission to the United Nations and, most recently, in Ottawa. In this last post in particular he had been struck by the apparently excessive size and the underemployment of its able staff. This had started him thinking about the nature, scale, and appropriateness of UK representation overseas.

He found support for this line of thought from his Foreign Office colleague in the CPRS, Marrack ('Mig') Goulding. Goulding was possibly more committed to diplomacy as a career; he returned to the FCO after his period in the CPRS, served with distinction as Ambassador in Angola, and left the FCO only in 1985 to become the Under-Secretary responsible for the peace-keeping forces at the United Nations in New York. Guinness never returned to the FCO; he transferred to the Home Civil Service and left the CPRS for the Department of Energy.

There had recently been two inquiries into the United Kingdom's representation overseas, led by Sir Val Duncan (1969) and by Lord Plowden (1964). Neither, however, had asked the kind of fundamental questions that Guinness and Goulding came to think necessary. They began to float, inside the CPRS, the proposition that there should be another inquiry.

In the early autumn of 1975 Jim Callaghan had been Foreign Secretary for eighteen months. His Permanent Secretary was Sir Thomas Brimelow, a diplomat of strongly liberal tendencies, who probably uniquely amongst those who have held his position was a member of the Fabian Society. He was, however, due to retire very soon and within the CPRS thought unlikely to favour a review of the kind the CPRS was contemplating. By then it was also known that his replacement would be Sir Michael Palliser. Palliser had been our Ambassador to the EEC, one of the two or three most important Foreign Office posts abroad. In this post Palliser had had a great deal of contact with other Departments (indeed many of his staff in Brussels had come from other departments), and with the overseas policy-making process beyond the FCO. His time in Brussels thus reinforced his earlier experience, as the Foreign Office Private Secretary in Number Ten, of dealing with a number of other departments. Palliser was believed to be concerned about some aspects of the co-ordination of overseas policies and about the respective roles of the Foreign Office and other departments in this context. He was also known to believe in a high quality but smaller diplomatic service.

The change-over of Permanent Secretaries thus seemed the right time for the CPRS to propose a study, although no one knew what view the Foreign Secretary might take. Mig Goulding with the help of one of us (Tessa Blackstone) drafted a short paper. This argued that Britain's role in the world had changed substantially in the last twenty years but that the nature of Britain's representation overseas had not been adjusted to match. Changes cited included the decline of Britain's share of world trade, in Britain's defence role (including the withdrawal of troops from East of Suez), in its share of total OECD Gross Domestic Product and of GDP per head, and in its share of official aid and private direct investment in developing countries. The paper noted that our overseas representation should not necessarily be reduced in direct proportion to the decline in our role in the world. Referring to the recommendations of the Duncan Committee, it suggested that a middle-ranking country such as Britain did not have world-wide interests; these were instead concentrated on those parts of the world on which its security and prosperity most directly depended. The current distribution of our overseas representation did not, it argued, reflect these interests.

The paper also asked whether even in those countries where there were substantial British interests the work could be done with fewer people at less cost. In every case Britain had more staff in France, Germany, Italy, and Japan than those countries had in Britain. It was also suggested that the administrative and other back-up services might be unduly lavish in British Embassies. An eye-catching comparison was that between the eleven official cars at the British Embassy in Paris and the one official car at the French Embassy in London. The paper concluded by recommending an inquiry—but an internal inquiry rather than one reporting publicly, as had Plowden and Duncan. The paper did *not* suggest that the CPRS should undertake the study.

Meanwhile the FCO had been subjected to a certain amount of a public criticism in the press and Parliament about the style and nature of its operations. In September 1975 the Bonn correspondent of the *Financial Times* wrote that it was

sobering to learn that no fewer than 500 people provide Britain's diplomatic representation in West Germany. Although Germany has re-established itself as one of the most powerful countries in Europe, diplomats will admit privately that such a massive presence is unnecessary and is symbolic of the overmanning and of superfluous activity in the Foreign Office at home and across the world . . . [The British] foreign service is overstaffed across the board and is suffering from a surfeit of officers at counsellor level. Unlike the British Army or the American foreign service, the British foreign service has developed no tradition of 'promoting out' those who have not reached a certain rank by a certain age. As a result the post-war base of the pyramid is now trying unhappily to feel like the peak in a profession whose natural law is increasingly that of Professor Parkinson (Colchester, 1975).

A cruder critique on similar lines appeared in the *Daily Express* a month later. Written under a pseudonym by someone claiming to have spent 30 years in the Foreign Office, it noted that,

Diplomacy has changed. Yet this change has not been reflected in the activities, composition and expense of overseas missions . . . A government really bent on economy might well start by looking into its foreign representation. Let a beginning be made with the information and commercial work and then let the fatty tissue of traditional diplomacy be surgically removed. In comparison with other exercises in national economy, this would be the kindest cut of all (Stuart, 1975).

At around the same time a House of Commons Committee revealed that the Property Services Agency had spent £380,000 on the residence of the relatively junior ambassadorial post at the OECD in Paris (House of Commons, 1975). This produced hostile comments in many newspapers. On top of this press criticism a number of backbench MPs from both sides had been tabling hostile questions about the diplomatic service. Led by two Conservatives, Christopher Tugendhat and Norman Lamont, they had concentrated on the scale and cost of the diplomatic service but had also touched on the wide range of tax-free allowances received by members of the service, a subject which Norman Lamont was to take up again later.

These press stories and parliamentary activities were not in themselves greatly significant or novel. But they helped to create a climate in which the Foreign Secretary might be well disposed towards the proposal of an inquiry with the FCO. Late in 1975 the CPRS proposal—previously discussed with the Cabinet Secretary Sir John Hunt and with the Civil Service Department, responsible for all central government manpower—reached the Foreign Secretary. He agreed that an inquiry should be set up. But he widened the scale of the inquiry in two ways. First, he suggested that it should also consider ways of improving interdepartmental co-ordination and resolving interdepartmental conflicts on overseas issues. He thus led the inquiry to focus not only on the work of the diplomatic service abroad but also on Whitehall. Secondly, he proposed that the review should embrace the overseas work of the BBC and the British Council. Moreover, and of much greater significance for the CPRS, he asked the CPRS itself to undertake the inquiry. This request was wholly unexpected. The terms of reference, worked out by the Cabinet Office, the CSD, the FCO, and the CPRS were carefully phrased and comprehensive. The study was

to review the nature and extent of our overseas interests and requirements and in the light of that review to make recommendation on the most suitable, effective and economic means of representing and promoting those interests both at home and overseas. The review will embrace all aspects of the work of overseas representation, including political, economic, commercial, consular and immigration work, defence matters, overseas aid and cultural and information activities, whether these tasks are performed by members of Her Majesty's Diplomatic Service, by members of the Home Civil Service, by members of the Armed Forces or by other agencies financially supported by Her Majesty's Government.

From then on overseas representation was simply a term of art to describe the work of the review. Clearly it went far beyond what might conventionally be understood by this term. Indeed the only aspect of the overseas policy-making work of the government and its administration that was excluded from the review were the terms and conditions of work of the diplomatic service and their allowances. Berrill accepted the task and the terms of reference. Initially hesitant about the inclusion of the BBC and the British Council, he finally agreed, on the grounds that the wishes of Ministers were paramount. For the many who later felt that the review was an unfortunate episode for the CPRS, this was seen as a misjudgement, which contributed to the difficulties later. Some of them felt that Berrill ought not to have accepted the commission on any terms.

Before Callaghan had time to announce the inquiry, the first of many leaks occurred in what was to turn into a long saga of leaks. On 29 December 1975 the *Daily Mail* published a front-page article under the headline 'Too many men in Jim's army—Think Tank report angers the FO'. In lurid language it claimed:

A secret report by the Whitehall Think-Tank claims that up to one in three of the 12,000 Foreign Office diplomats could be fired with little or no effect on its efficiency. The report accuses the FO mandarins of perpetuating an elitist cadre, lavishing perks and privileges on its staff on a scale unknown elsewhere. They are also said to be acting and spending money as if it were still the heyday of the British Raj, instead of the humdrum regime of Foreign Secretary Mr. James Callaghan. The Whitehall investigators uncovered scores of examples to prove that, except for America and Russia, our diplomatic service is probably the most overloaded and expensive in the world (Greig, 1975).

The article alleged 'a major row between the Foreign Office and Downing Street about manning levels—and the shock waves are still rippling out'. This row, it said, would probably stop a more comprehensive study of Foreign Office staff levels.

In response to this the Number Ten Press Office issued an on-the-record statement the same day. This stated that some preliminary work had been done by the CPRS not just on the diplomatic service but on the whole of the British overseas effort, that the purpose of the work was concentrating the effort rather than cutting it, and that the conclusion from the initial study was that a more detailed inquiry was needed. There had been no report submitted and no row. All the major newspapers reported on this the following day. The diplomatic correspondents were briefed by the Foreign Office to the effect that it was the only department which had reduced its numbers since 1965 (about which *The Times* said it was 'particularly pained'—Spanier, 1975), and that its representation abroad was very much in line with that of France and Germany, when the different methods of undertaking export promotion were taken into account. The general tenor of the press comments favoured an inquiry. Two weeks later Callaghan announced that a major review of Britain's overseas representation would be undertaken, and that the CPRS had been asked to undertake it (HC Deb. 14 January 1976).

The first task for the CPRS was to construct a team to work on the review. Berrill himself took the lead. The rest of the team consisted of the authors of the original paper and of David Young, a tough no-nonsense Yorkshireman, who was an Assistant Secretary on secondment from the Ministry of Defence; Kate Mortimer, a long-time member of the CPRS, an economist who had previously worked at the World Bank in Washington; and John Odling-Smee, another economist from the London School of Economics, who had earlier been an adviser to Dr Busia, the Prime Minister of Ghana. The team was later joined for a short period by Tony Hurrell, an Under-Secretary from the Overseas Development Ministry, though he left the CPRS before the study was completed. Unusually for the CPRS the names of the team were later made public.

Meanwhile, on the other side of Downing Street the Foreign Office was putting together a review team too. Its task was to co-ordinate the collection of information and evidence from the Foreign Office for the CPRS, to help organize a programme of CPRS visits to posts round the world, and to comment on drafts produced. The unit was headed by Sir Andrew Stark, a Foreign Office Deputy Secretary close to retirement, whose last job had been as Ambassador to Denmark. He had a small supporting staff. This was in principle a useful organizational device, and relationships between the CPRS team and the FCO Unit were in general friendly. But some of the team saw some truth in the title bestowed by the press, the 'Anti-Tank Unit', in that they suspected that Stark was himself a source of anti-CPRS briefing to the press.

The first decision the CPRS made was to divide the study into two stages. The first was concerned with analysing objectives. It looked at the UK's interests overseas, the policies employed to promote them, and the requirements which these policies generated for overseas representation. The second stage, it was decided, would look at the actual mechanics of overseas representation in depth. In other words, it would examine the most suitable and effective *means* of meeting the requirements identified in the first stage. The second decision was to seek the views of as wide a range of 'users' of the system and informed commentators as possible. These ranged from ex-Prime Ministers to exporters large and small, from journalists to experts on aid to developing countries. Written and oral evidence was sought and obtained from a wide range of individuals and organizations. The third decision, strongly urged by the Foreign Office, was to undertake the extensive programme of visits to British posts abroad.

The first six months of the study was largely spent in amassing evidence about Britain's overseas interests. Documentary evidence was produced by the Foreign Office and the many home departments involved in overseas policies. Many senior officials in all these departments were interviewed about their perception of British interests. By June 1976 an interim report on the first stage was ready to go to Ministers. There was never any intention that it should be published. It was hoped that it would provide Ministers with some idea of the way the CPRS was thinking. Ministers in turn could then provide a 'steer' for the second stage. In this respect the CPRS was to be disappointed. Ministers were not particularly interested in reading an *interim* report of 140 pages. They preferred to wait until the final version was complete. The situation was not helped by the fact that Wilson had resigned; Callaghan had replaced him as Prime Minister. Crosland, who had replaced Callaghan as Foreign Secretary, was still reading himself into the job.

The CPRS therefore got on with the second stage without guidance from Ministers. Most of the analysis in the interim report was incorporated into the final report. A hectic programme of foreign visits then took place in the late summer and autumn of 1976. The team had identified the major functions to be undertaken in pursuit of our overseas interests. These included foreign policy, economic, political, defence, education and cultural work; aid; external broadcasting; the control of entry to the UK; consular work; administration. The performance of these functions was supported overseas by additional activities such as entertainment; the management of property; administration; and security. One member of the team with support from one other took the lead on each of these functions, although the final report was a team effort. The form of the report was nevertheless shaped by this functional approach. The posts to be visited abroad were also selected to ensure that there would be adequate coverage of each function in a wide range of countries including the USA, Japan, France, and Germany as well as Burma, Bolivia, and the Gambia. For these visits the team subdivided, usually into groups of three. In this way it undertook seven trips, each covering a group of three or four countries to different parts of the world.

In each of the embassies, high commissions, and consulates visited, the CPRS members began with a discussion with the head of the post. They followed this with a meeting with all the staff at which they explained the coverage and approach of the review. The rest of the visit was spent in interviews with staff in all the sections and a round-up meeting with the head of post at the end. Where possible the CPRS team also met the ambassadors and other officials of what it called the 'analogue countries'. These were France, Germany, Italy, Japan, Australia, and Canada; comparisons were made with the nature and scale of their effort in each of the countries visited. In every post the CPRS visitors were provided with all of the facilities and information they needed. In most, it was clearly accepted that, since the CPRS had been asked to undertake a radical review, its questions would be liable to challenge some basic objectives and assumptions. The character of the ambassador—whether open-minded and intellectually searching, or simply self-confident about the value of his work—was important in influencing his staff to respond readily and frankly to this kind of questioning. There were, however, exceptions. In some posts—again often following an ambassadorial lead—staff objected to the CPRS's mode of questioning; they let it be shown that they resented any suggestion that some of their work should be given a lower priority or might be done more efficiently or more effectively elsewhere.

Most notable amongst these exceptions was the Embassy in Paris. Here the ambassador, Sir Nicholas Henderson, did not conceal his personal hostility to the CPRS and the review. He was reported by one of his colleagues as saying that the team 'were only concerned to find evidence to confirm their existing prejudices which were based on a "class-war attitude" ' (Donaldson, 1984). He was strongly supported by his wife. (Foreign Office wives, under the aegis of the Diplomatic Wives Association, gave evidence elsewhere—quite often conservative and defensive in tone.)

The CPRS team had expected that their visits would arouse a certain amount of understandable defensiveness and resentment, but Henderson's response was exceptionally hostile. Some of the contrasts were striking. In Teheran, for example, an excellent rapport was easily established, helped no doubt by the open-minded and intellectually searching character of the ambassador himself, Sir Anthony Parsons. Many of the same questions were raised in Teheran as in Paris. They simply got a different kind of hearing.

Unfortunately the Paris episode could not simply be dismissed as an unlucky but isolated incident. It soured the relationship with the diplomatic service generally and, more than any other event, led to the propaganda campaign that was mounted against the CPRS and its investigation.

Henderson, a senior figure in a position of considerable influence, wasted little time in giving vent to his feelings of distaste for what the CPRS was doing and the way it was going about it. Stories got around that the CPRS had suggested the Ambassador to France should live in a villa in suburban Neuilly and take the metro to the Quai D'Orsay. The CPRS had in fact asked whether it was still appropriate to house the Ambassador in an eighteenth-century palace, and whether the Embassy needed such a large fleet of official cars in a city with one of the best transport systems in Europe. As the psychology of rumour got to work, each story became more lavishly embroidered than the next. The CPRS began to appear as a group of hard-left *apparatchiks* mainly concerned with getting at the external trappings and so-called privileges of the diplomatic service. The cumulative effect was devastating. Callaghan himself was later to say that the report had been 'destroyed by a former ambassador' (interview with authors).

Having completed its overseas visits the team continued its examination of the roles of the various Whitehall departments. It also tried out on officials in London some of the ideas it had formulated abroad. Departments consulted included the Home Office, the Department of Trade, the British Council, the Department of Employment, the Ministry of Defence, the Department of Education and Science, the Treasury, and the Overseas Development Ministry, as well as the Foreign Office. The CPRS also looked at the work of specialist quangos such as the Export Credits Guarantee Department, the Inter-University Council (responsible for interchange between countries in higher education), the Central Office of Information, and the Property Services Agency. In most places the CPRS met staff as well as management. Many non-governmental organizations, with an interest in overseas represent-ation, submitted oral and written evidence to the CPRS as well as having more informal discussions. These ranged from the Bank of England and the British Overseas Trade Board to voluntary bodies representing immigrants. If the ability to take an independent non-departmental view in such inquiries is an important criterion, the CPRS was undoubtedly right for such a review.

Because the CPRS had consulted widely, some leaks were always likely. It was, however, not until the writing-up stage had been reached that they turned into a steady flow. Their sources were obscure. But a number of journalists have since claimed that the Foreign Office was the main source. Whilst the leaks were along the right lines, they usually gave an exaggerated version of what the CPRS was proposing—perhaps because the leakers wished to discredit the CPRS and any radical proposals by suggesting others likely to be perceived as unrealistic or plain silly. After a few of these, in February 1977, Sir John Hunt, having consulted Berrill, the head of the Home Civil Service Sir Douglas Allen, and Sir Michael Palliser asked the press secretary at 10 Downing Street unattributably to brief the press, with the aim of scotching some of the wilder rumours. If such a briefing was given, it had little impact. The scare stories continued, and multiplied.

Thus a front-page story in the *Guardian* on 25 April 1977 was headlined 'Think Tank suggests an end to the FO'. The paper's respected columnist, Peter Jenkins, apparently writing from Washington, reported that the review would recommend the abolition of the Foreign Office. Foreign policy would be co-ordinated from the Cabinet Office. 'This notion', wrote Jenkins 'is regarded by the professionals as so far-fetched—and so unlikely to be accepted by the Cabinet—that there is growing belief that the report will be toned down before it reaches the Foreign Secretary.' One high source in the diplomatic service was then quoted as saying, 'The report will very likely be absurd.' The 'chief villains' were said to be the women members of the team, Kate Mortimer and Tessa Blackstone, the latter known in the Foreign Office as 'the dark-eyed evil genius'. The professionals were, it said, asking how the system could possibly work if the diplomatic service were abolished. How, for example, would expertise in speaking difficult languages or specialist knowledge about certain parts of the world be maintained? And what would happen to the Foreign Office's superb communications network? Finally, it suggested that the recommendations and conclusions were likely to be redrafted by Sir Kenneth Berrill 'in a less extreme form' (Jenkins, 1977).

Unsurprisingly, the story was picked up by a number of the other papers and embroidered on in a variety of ways. Other articles commented on the relative youth and inexperience of the team. *The Times* noted that 'the chief complaint about the Berrill team is that unlike its predecessors that produced the Plowden and Duncan reports, it is staffed by people with little personal knowledge of the foreign service' (Hennessy, 1977). And the *Daily Telegraph* pointed out that the team had 'earned the sour soubriquet of the Young Butterflies' (Conyers, 1977).

The report was completed and submitted to Ministers in June 1977. It was sent to the Prime Minister and the Foreign Secretary. The latter in turn sent it to each Cabinet Minister with a direct interest in its recommendations. He attached a draft statement he intended to make to the House which he saw as giving a first indication of the government's attitude towards it. The CPRS objected to the terms of the draft statement, and in particular to what it saw as implying that some of the CPRS's analysis reflected prejudice rather than judgement. Berrill protested about the draft and defended his team and their recommendations. The statement was subsequently amended.

As published at the beginning of August, the report contained twenty-one chapters and over 400 recommendations. Some of the recommendations related to the relative importance and effectiveness of the fourteen main functions or areas of work identified in the review. In general the report argued that the amount of work done was not justified and should be reduced. The reasons for this varied. In some cases the effectiveness of the functions was overestimated, and there was not sufficient return on the resources committed. Examples were information work overseas and diplomatic entertainment. In other areas insufficient account had been taken of Britain's declining role in the world. For example, too much effort was being put into the collection of political and economic information, which was not needed by policy-makers in London, and in trying to influence foreign governments with little prospect of success.

In some cases the government was undertaking work that could be done by others. This included broadcasting to countries in Western Europe in their own languages, the provision of consular services for tourists and British residents in Western and Southern Europe, and British Council work in promoting and funding educational and cultural exchanges between the UK and other developed countries. In other areas there was scope for greater selectivity. The best example of this was export promotion, where the report recommended concentrating more on particularly promising markets or products, plus the Soviet bloc. Finally, there were cases such as aid administration, where the policies of the time of distributing the cake in many tiny pieces led to a wasteful use of resources and high overhead costs. The report recommended reducing the number of small bilateral aid programmes, and trying to make multilateral programmes work better.

Other recommendations were concerned with the way the functions were being performed rather than with their relative importance. Some procedures were unnecessarily complicated or ineffective. Examples included immigration procedures and the way posts were administered. In some areas there was duplication or unclear definition of roles; the report proposed, for example, the amalgamation of various agencies administering educational aid and the development of a system of lead departments in Whitehall for the collection and analysis of economic information about other countries. In many areas work was being done to an unjustifiably high standard; over-qualified staff were being asked to perform relatively mundane and un-important tasks; the level of welfare and administrative support for certain clients such as overseas students supported by the British Council was unnecessarily high; and perfectionism in such areas as communications led to extravagant use of resources. Lastly, work was being done overseas which could be done in London at considerably less cost; substantial reductions were proposed in the staffing of many overseas posts.

The report also put forward a basic principle on staffing. This was the need for greater expertise in carrying out the work of overseas representation whether in London or abroad. It suggested that there should be more specialization in many areas; that staff should have more knowledge of both the UK and the overseas side of the work (rather than knowledge of one *or* the other) so that, for example, those engaged on export promotion were familiar with both overseas markets *and* British industry; and that individuals should spend proportionately less of their careers abroad, where there was a risk of becoming out of touch with the UK. The proposed solution to these problems was to unify the Home Civil Service and the Foreign Service and to create within the combined service a Foreign Service Group, which would staff most jobs both in the UK and overseas in many of the main areas of work.

Finally, the CPRS recommended a number of institutional changes, and some changes in the geographical focus of overseas representation. The most significant proposals for institutional changes were, first, for new arrangements in the Cabinet Office to co-ordinate the UK's bilateral relations with other countries and, secondly, new arrangements for education and cultural work. Here the report put forward two options: the abolition of the British Council and of the smaller agencies in this area with their work being taken on by the Department of Education and Science and the Ministry of Overseas Development; or the retention of the Council, and the transfer to it of most of the work of the smaller agencies.

The need to switch geographical focus was illustrated by the BBC external services. Many high priority areas of the world, that is with little access to unbiased sources of news and information or to information about Britain and its culture, were receiving such a weak signal from BBC transmitters that high quality programmes were scarcely audible. The CPRS therefore suggested there should be a switch from revenue to much needed capital expenditure to replace obsolescent transmitters and equipment. Some of this could be financed by abandoning a number of the European vernacular services. The CPRS also recommended the closure of 20 diplomatic missions in countries where British interests were small and 30 consular posts (mainly in Western Europe) where improved communications rendered subordinate posts unnecessary. It argued that less work needed to be done in non-communist developed countries. On the other hand, in the Soviet bloc and many third world countries there would be a continuing need for direct government support whether in consular, or political work, educational and cultural work, external broadcasting, or export promotion.

The report was the major news story in virtually every daily paper, and the subject of a first leader in most of them. In the 'quality' press many of the report's recommendations were welcomed. Some of its assumptions, for example about the inevitability of Britain's decline, were questioned, and voices were raised in defence of the British Council and the BBC. The popular press, though also divided in its views, focused mainly on what it saw as the élite background and excessive privileges of diplomats, and generally applauded the report's critiques of these. But it was, among the popular press, the *Daily Express* which most concisely summarized what was to become the major theme of the critics of the report.

The trendies who produced this report argue that the diplomatic service needs to be cut down, largely merged with the home Civil Service, all to bring our overseas representation into line with our reduced world status.

This is a curious piece of reasoning. For as our ability to use force to protect our interests has declined, so our diplomacy becomes more important, not less (*Daily Express*, 1977).

As the weeks passed the criticisms grew louder.

The letters' column of *The Times* was full of correspondence defending the diplomatic service, the British Council, and the BBC External Services.

Reactions were sought by the press from MPs: a Conservative denounced the report as 'barmy', while another was reported as saying, 'I regard the report as naïve and full of elementary misconceptions. It suggests we should have a review of the think-tank.' The Shadow Foreign Secretary, Lord Carrington, in a BBC interview, conceded that the report was 'extremely thorough not superficial', but went on to say that its major conclusions were wrong; 'They say Britain is a non-influential deteriorating power. . . we are a reviving power.' Michael Stewart, a former Labour Foreign Secretary, said the report was 'rather disappointing but we shall get something out of it'. For example, the number of posts might be reduced, though the proposal for 55 closures might be 'overdoing it a little', and the proposals on the British Council and the BBC were 'penny pinching'. Many letters were published from the clients of the British Council or 'the satisfied customers' as the Council often called them. Expatriates living round the world wrote to deplore proposals for cutting some of the output of the BBC external services. The Managing Director of the BBC's External Services wrote himself pointing out that if the CPRS recommendations were implemented the External Services would be reduced to the level of those of Albania and the Netherlands. He omitted to mention that in the world league of external broadcasting hours Albania and the Netherlands were the next largest after the UK. Yet other criticisms of the report were published in letters from ex-diplomats and others. A few letters defended the CPRS and its report but they were unquestionably in a small minority.

The editorial columns of the press were also opened to critics of the report. A columnist in *The Times*, Lord Chalfont, suggested that the report was 'an example of what happens when you send little boys (and little girls) to do a man's job; and what is needed now is a fundamental reappraisal of the composition and functions of the Central Policy Review Staff' (Chalfont, 1977). He went on to say that

the general philosophy and approach reflected in the report is characteristic of what appears to be a widespread tendency to disparage this country, to erode its prestige and influence, and to lower its reputation in the eyes of the world.

Similarly Peter Walker, a former Conservative Minister, then a back-bench MP, in an article in the *Daily Mail* suggested that,

If the Prime Minister wanted advice on the future of the foreign services, an evening with Lord Home as a respected former Foreign Secretary, Sir Arnold Weinstock as one of Britain's leading exporters and Henry Kissinger giving a foreigner's viewpoint of our foreign service would provide him with better advice than all of the 442 pages contained in all the Think Tank's review (Walker, 1977).

In *The Times* John Mackintosh, the Labour MP for Berwick and West Lothian was willing to concede that

The Think Tank report on overseas representation is a good read because it is so provocative and it does, on occasion, hit the nail on the head. One example of this is when it says that appeals to Britain's special, long and deep experience in foreign affairs, and to the value placed by other nations on this experience, is largely self-delusion (Mackintosh, 1977).

But he chided the CPRS for concentrating too much on economic questions and export promotion, and for forgetting the purpose of foreign policy which he saw largely in terms of contributing to a flexible European response to the problems of world security.

The publication of the report marked only the beginning of its public castigation. There were several more public ordeals for the CPRS to go through before it could concentrate on processing the report through Whitehall and getting Ministers to take decisions on it. The first of these was a House of Lords debate on the subject. The debate opened with a speech in defence of the British Council by Lord Ballantrae, who until a year earlier had been its chairman. Many of the subsequent speakers also had been or still were in some way directly connected with one or more than one of the organizations being reviewed. Many of them clearly felt passionate about the need to defend these organizations. Few of them accepted the CPRS's assumptions about the decline in Britain's role in the world and the implications of this.

There were occasional favourable comments (the report was a 'useful piece of shock therapy') but these were completely outweighed by, for example, speculation about the patriotism of the CPRS team (' "Glory" is not a word in their vocabulary') or outrage at their philistinism (the report seemed not to recognize that in an embassy 'one needs to find grace, elegance and wit . . . [and] . . . places where people can have conversations on the highest level'). Out of 29 speakers, only 4 were in favour of the report (HL Deb, 1977).

The debate in the House of Lords formed one half of Parliament's contribution to consideration of the review. The other half took the form of a Select Committee report. Under the Chairmanship of the Conservative, Sir Harwood Harrison, the Commons Defence and External Affairs Sub-Committee decided to take the review as the subject of its first report during the 1977 to 1978 session of Parliament. In political terms, the composition of the committee was broadly centre and right. In terms of expertise, it was stronger on defence matters than on international economic or trade issues. One member, the Conservative Sir Anthony Kershaw, was a former FCO Minister and a member of the British Council Board.

The committee took written and oral evidence from all the main interests during November and December 1977. At the invitation of the committee, the CPRS submitted a written memorandum on its reactions to criticisms of the report. It followed this up with oral evidence, defending its recommendations and attempting to counter objections to these. More objections were, of course, expressed to the committee by other witnesses, including two former Foreign Secretaries, Lord Home and Lord George Brown.

The committee appeared more convinced by these than by the CPRS—perhaps because, as was made clear during the cross-examination of the CPRS, committee members shared the view of other critics that the CPRS team was too young for its tasks. They were unmoved by Berrill's reminder that their average age was about that of the current Foreign Secretary, David Owen, namely thirty-nine. In its report the committee rejected most of the report's conclusions and, in particular, its major premise, namely that in the modern world a country's power and influence were largely determined by its economic performance. Though the committee disagreed with the CBI's claim that 'military or economic decline can be largely offset by diplomatic skill and influence', it agreed with the Foreign Office that a decline in a country's power increased the need for diplomatic resources. The main consolation for the CPRS in the committee's largely hostile report was commendation for the research underlying the review and the comment that this would 'serve as an extremely valuable, statistical and analytical tool for determining future requirements and policies' (House of Commons, 1978).

Other less formal discussions of the report at this time included seminars or lectures at the BBC, the Royal Commonwealth Society, and the Institute of Development Studies. At most of these the increasingly familiar objections to the report were developed in different contexts. On a few occasions rather more modest defences of the team and of its conclusions were mounted.

One of the first pieces of work commissioned was a study led by the Civil Service Department of ways of increasing the amount of interchange between the Foreign Office and the Home Civil Service. The Foreign Secretary made it clear that he would not support the CPRS's preferred method of achieving greater expertise and of ensuring that the same group of staff performed certain functions at home and overseas, namely the creation of a Foreign Service Group within a unified Diplomatic and Home Civil Service. However, he accepted the need for much greater interchange between the two services, something which the CSD report claimed that it could deliver.

Departments were asked to identify uncontroversial recommendations which could be implemented without further Ministerial discussion. There were more than fifty of these. Some of them had already been implemented during the course of the review. Ministers, however, still had to work their way laboriously through the large number of more controversial recommendations.

They accepted some of these: the closure of some consular posts, cuts in the number of defence attachés, reductions in the scale of press and information work, certain changes in entry control to the UK, the need for 'mini-missions' (with only two to six UK-based staff) in certain countries, some changes in the British Council's priorities and the restructuring of educational aid and interchange to avoid duplication between different agencies, certain changes in the way aid was administered, and some reductions in the BBC's vernacular services. Perhaps the most disappointing outcome for the CPRS was the opposition of the Department of Trade to many of the recommendations concerning export promotion. Neither Edmund Dell nor his senior officials seemed to want to alter the current distribution of tasks between the Department of Trade and the Foreign Office, nor to use the chance offered by the review to increase their department's control of what was, in effect, its own overseas activities. They seemed to assume that members of the Home Civil Service could not, and would not, serve overseas—except possibly in Washington and Brussels.

Ministers not surprisingly found it difficult to review such a complex and wide-ranging set of recommendations. The Prime Minister became impatient at the detailed nature of the discussions. Other Ministers found it hard to grasp what the CPRS was recommending and why. It was easy for the Foreign Office and other departments to dissuade them from accepting those recommendations which the departments disliked. In one paper the Foreign Secretary argued against any closures of embassies or high commissions, illustrating his argument with examples of proposed post closures in specific capitals. One of those listed was the capital of a small Commonwealth country. When asked where it was, he had no idea. Nor did anyone else, at which point one of his colleagues suggested that since no one knew where it was, the case for closure had perhaps been made.

Some Ministers were well disposed to many of the review's arguments. Others, battered by lobbying from people like Lord Mountbatten (who had written to the Prime Minister to defend the British Council), seemed to feel that the political row entailed in implementing some of the more radical recommendations was not worth the candle. Potentially the most influential member of the Ministerial Group was the Foreign Secretary, not a Minister liable uncritically to accept his officials' views. However, his support for the report diminished when he found that it said nothing in favour of the 'up or out' approach to early retirement, which he thought should be introduced to rid the Foreign Office of dead wood. He also intensely disliked the CPRS's underlying assumptions about the role of Britain in the world.

The White Paper which eventually emerged in the summer of 1978 rejected many of the report's main recommendations. In particular, it rejected the central message of the report, namely that the different aspects of relationships with foreign countries require considerable expertise if they are to be handled well; and that this expertise requires an understanding of how these relationships relate to UK policies and processes as well as the overseas end of things. The best way of ensuring such expertise at home and abroad, in the CPRS's view, was to amalgamate the Diplomatic Service and the Home Civil Service and employ the same people to carry out a particular function in the UK and overseas. The government partly accepted the CPRS's premise about expertise. However, it opted for the less radical option put forward by the CPRS, of increasing interchange between the two services. As the CPRS predicted at the time, this has proved difficult to achieve on the scale recommended. The government also rejected the more radical of the two options relating to the British Council—its abolition. The alternative option was, in effect accepted—not immediately, but over time. This involved the incorporation into the Council of several smaller agencies carrying out closely related work, such as the Inter-Universities Council, greater stress on its work in developing countries at the expense of Western Europe, an increase in revenue earning activities, and a tighter definition of objectives.

Many of the report's middle-range and minor recommendations were in fact accepted at the time. Others which were not accepted or which were put on 'the back burner' pending further reviews and investigations have subsequently been implemented, usually without any reference to the CPRS's report. This is true in particular of the report's detailed recommendations on the organization of posts overseas. In many cases the object of the changes has been to save public expenditure, in others to provide a more efficient and effective service. For example, many of the consular posts the CPRS recommended for closure have been closed. There has been some reduction in the size of posts and in diplomatic service manpower. The idea of mini-missions has been accepted and implemented on quite a large scale. Some of these posts now have ambassadors at Principal level, as recommended by the CPRS. Amongst the larger posts that have been cut back, missions in Commonwealth countries such as Australia and Canada have taken substantial reductions, also recommended by the CPRS. Similarly, many of the proposals on organization in London, which focused on greater interdepartmental co-operation, have been adopted. On the staffing of overseas work, whilst there is less specialization than the CPRS thought desirable, more emphasis has been placed on training to build up expertise in particular fields. Staff now spend more time working in London and less abroad, again as the CPRS recommended.

In its examination of the various functions of embassies and high commissions the CPRS was particularly critical of information work, much of which it saw as a waste of effort. This work has since been reduced by about 60 per cent, and all but one of the detailed recommendations have been accepted and implemented. The BBC has had an increased capital programme to deal with problems of audibility and most of the vernacular services recommended by the CPRS for cuts have been cut, not always for the reasons argued by the report.

More broadly, a senior Foreign Office official told us in 1986 that the report's advocacy of the 'managerial approach' and of a more cost-effective approach to administration had been accepted. Occasionally this was thwarted by Ministers. For example, they frequently succumbed to parliamentary pressures on consular cases, which made reform in the provision of consular services difficult. He also suggested that illusions of grandeur about Britain's role in the world were disappearing. He pointed out that the CPRS report's identification of trends in relation to Britain's declining world position and substantial economic problems had proved to be entirely justified. The gradual acceptance of these realities in the decade since the report was written must have helped to secure the implementation of many of the recommendations. In other words, external events, rather than an active decision to look again at the report's proposed solutions, had imposed many of the report's recommended changes.

Whatever the intrinsic significance of the review or, indeed of its subject-matter, it raises so many issues about the role of bodies such as the CPRS, and about the processes of change in a traditional society, that it is worth dwelling on as a case-study. At least two different types of question can be asked. First are questions about the review as such. Was the CPRS right to take on the task itself? If so, should it have demanded more limited terms of reference? Whatever the value of the specific recommendations made, were they appropriate in all the circumstances? Could and should the CPRS have done more to neutralize the opposition and to rally support for its own proposals? Second are questions about the lessons that might be learned from the episode. How can would-be reformers, facing well-established and well-supported institutions, ensure that their proposals are taken on their merits and, if agreed to be sensible, implemented?

As already mentioned, a number of observers thought that the CPRS should not have agreed to carry out the review itself. The subject-matter was in some respects inappropriate, involving too much detail; the review consumed a disproportionate amount of CPRS time; the whole issue was an example of a 'poisoned chalice', since the review was found to lead to public conflict with the major institutions covered, from which the CPRS was almost certain to gain little advantage. Thus Edward Heath said on more than one occasion that this was not the kind of task he had established the CPRS to do. He felt that the

172

CPRS should concentrate on major questions of policy, including overall strategy, rather than get involved in the nuts and bolts of public administration, which much of the second stage of the review involved. The review was a misuse of the CPRS's time; in addition, the CPRS team did not have the right qualifications for the job. This view was shared by David Owen, who had not been involved in setting up the review but who, as the result of Crosland's untimely death, was Foreign Secretary during its later stages and when the report was presented to Ministers. He argued that 'it was a fatally flawed decision actually to put the CPRS on to the Foreign Office. They're not geared to that type of investigation; it went wider than their proper brief (quoted in Hennessy, 1985).

Within the CPRS, too, there were doubts as to whether the assignment should have been accepted. The review tied up around 25 per cent of the CPRS manpower for a year. Some non-members of the team felt that this too greatly reduced the general capability of the CPRS. One later said to us, 'I believe the review was a major disaster for the CPRS. Berrill should never have accepted the commission in the first place. The analysis should never have been done in public and analysts in a body such as the Think Tank cannot afford to take the long view.' Such strong views were not shared by the team. However one of its members did have reservations. 'The CPRS should not have taken on the task,' he told us. 'It was too wide and too time-consuming and, even if we had not managed to resist at the outset, we should have argued strongly for withdrawal after completion of phase one.'

An extension of this view, as implied above, was that the mistake was not so much to have undertaken the review at all, but to have undertaken it with such wide terms of reference. In the first place, these entailed too much detailed work on the day-to-day running of embassies and high commissions. Secondly, they covered an enormously wide range of institutions. To include the British Council and the BBC External Services as well as the Foreign Office, other Whitehall departments concerned with overseas matters, and the multiplicity of trade and aid quangos, the Central Office of Information, and the Property Services Agency created a huge task. This led to several problems. The CPRS had to cover so many issues that it had too little time, having collected its evidence and thought through its views, to work on the tricky task of presentation. The report itself was too long for many to grasp, with too many complex interlocking recommendations. The range of the report multiplied the number of institutions which felt themselves to be under attack. Both the BBC and the British Council had many friends and supporters in the press, the House of Lords, and amongst MPs on whom they could call to defend them.

Judgement on the terms of reference must depend on tactical considerations. It was undeniably logical to link the British Council and the BBC to the review, but logic was not the point. It is virtually certain that, had Berrill refused the last-minute proposal to extend the coverage beyond the Foreign Office and the other Whitehall departments with overseas interest, the CPRS would have had an easier task and would have run into much less outside opposition. With hindsight it would seem to have been prudent to have refused.

The wider question, whether the CPRS should have accepted the task on any terms, is harder to answer. Despite Heath's comments, the subject was in many ways ideal: interdepartmental, calling for analysis of long-established institutions and attitudes, and for rethinking of the objectives underlying these. The question of how best to co-ordinate activities in Whitehall relating to overseas issues was analogous to the question of co-ordination in relation to social or welfare issues; the CPRS dealt with this in the JASP project amid general agreement that this was a highly suitable task for the CPRS. Attempting to define, or to redefine, Britain's role in the world at large was precisely the kind of 'strategic' task that the CPRS had been created to perform in the first place. On balance, if the CPRS was wrong to accept the commission, its error was probably one of degree rather than of kind; it was right to take the job but wrong to take and to handle it on the terms proposed.

This conclusion is close to that of one of the few academic commentators who have discussed the review. Writing in 1978, William Wallace, director of research at the Royal Institute of International Affairs, noted that one of the underlying problems the CPRS faced was the lack of any clear guidance about the objectives of British foreign policy. Wallace suggested that the fundamental question was 'What do we need our structure of overseas representation *for*?' (Wallace, 1978) When the CPRS posed this question in its interim report, Ministers failed to respond. The CPRS was thus forced to fall back on its own definitions. The terms of reference of the review did not preclude discussion of these underlying issues by the CPRS but placed the emphasis on organizational matters. In considering the latter the CPRS touched on the underlying questions as part of the background, but perhaps fell between two stools in failing to address them in the depth they deserved. It might have alienated fewer of those it needed to convince if it had not considered the fundamental issue of Britain's role in the world at all. However, had it left this out it would have been eschewing tasks which it was originally set up to perform.

An oblique version of this view was that the CPRS should not have carried out the review, on the ostensibly pragmatic grounds that the manner and conclusions of the review had queered the pitch for more moderate would-be reformers within the system. More sophisticated radicals in the Foreign Office, it was argued, could have achieved far more had they only been left to get on with the task. To this familiar claim the familiar riposte may be made: given how little the alleged reformers had achieved by the time of the review, what evidence can there be that they would have achieved more in the future? In any case, even if the reformist cause was damaged by the report, there is no reason to suppose that the counter-reformation was, as a result, strengthened in more than the very short term. One senior official in the Foreign Office suggested to us that some of the reformers inside the FCO had to press their case rather harder for a brief period. He also suggested that the defensive reaction of FCO officials was heightened by their relative isolation and geographical distance from events in Whitehall. However, he did not consider these were lasting effects and dismissed the idea that reform from inside had been put back by the publication of the report.

Even if it were universally agreed that the CPRS was right to take on the review, questions remain about the way in which the process was managed. In making proposals a body such as the CPRS always has in principle to choose where to locate them on the scale 'radical/conservative'. The choice made is likely to determine how hard will be the battle to sustain the proposals and with whom. It ought also to determine the tactics used in sustaining them.

The substance of the CPRS's proposals in this case was bound to affront many influential people and interests; as William Wallace noted, many of these simply would not accept the guiding assumptions of the report, nor any of the conclusions that followed from these. The team has been criticized for naïvety in apparently failing to realize this and to take appropriate action. In fact it understood the situation very clearly. When Berrill was first confronted with the full range of the team's proposals in early 1977, he held a meeting to consider whether they should all go forward. Might it not be preferable to limit the number of fronts on which the CPRS would have to fight, and to try to ensure that at least some proposals were accepted? As one member of the team later recalled, Berrill pointed out that the team's proposals

would meet with enormous resistance, and might well lead to the report as a whole being rejected. He suggested that the alternative course of action would be to trim back in various directions, and increase the chances that our more limited proposals would be accepted. We debated this issue, and opted for the radical option on the grounds first, that it was in the tradition of the CPRS, and secondly, that we believed that initial rejection would be followed by our ideas becoming gradually more acceptable as they became more familiar, and this would lead in turn to our proposals being implemented in some form or other.

If the proposals were right, could they have been better presented? It is arguable that some of the language of the report was too blunt. A member of the team felt that it would have been better to omit the opening arguments about Britain's decline and the relationship between economic decline and political influence, as neither self-evidently true nor logically essential to much of the later argument and as 'always likely to antagonize politicians across the board'. A CPRS non-member of the team was more critical: the report

would not have been rubbished so drastically had not the introductory chapter saying that Britain had had it been written in the way it was. That was an error of judgement by Ken Berrill. Indeed one could say that he failed as Head of the Unit in not getting a grip on the insensitivities of the style and presentation of the report generally which blurred the very sensible things it was in fact saying.

Sympathetic Foreign Office officials who wanted change also blamed Berrill for failing to take a tighter editorial grip. One of them suggested that the report was 'too intellectually honest' and that Berrill and his team had paid insufficient attention to tactics and the political handling of the report when it was finished.

There are echoes here of JASP Mark I, where Rothschild's plain language upset the welfare departments. But in that case the position was retrieved by starting the exercise again from scratch. There is no doubt that the team, having deliberately decided to go for the radical options, made a tactical error in presenting these in radical language. Even the court jester, to use Hunt's appropriate analogy for the CPRS, must watch his words. But given the proposals and the language, could the CPRS have been more successful in managing the 'marketing' of the report and of ensuring that its proposals were not dismissed out of hand? In principle, it undoubtedly could have been. Two facts were basic here. Firstly, the CPRS, having partly failed to anticipate the hostility to the report, completely failed to anticipate the intensity of the objectors' campaign against it. Secondly, it did virtually nothing itself to counter that campaign.

As described above, the campaign began with the press leaks that appeared even before the circulation of the interim report. The Foreign Office, with its tight network of diplomatic correspondents, found it easy to inspire, if not actually to place, scare stories about the review team and its likely conclusions. The BBC obviously found it even easier. The report's opponents influenced parts of the media normally thought to be beyond such manipulation; a *Times* staff member told us that the proportion of letters received supporting the report was much larger than that actually published, despite remonstrations by the editorial staff. Members of the House of Lords were lobbied by and on behalf of the Foreign Office before the debate in the autumn of 1977; that debate was dominated by speakers such as governors of the British Council or former senior diplomats.

As striking as the intensity of the campaign were its form and content.

Many of the press stories contained elements both of pure fantasy and of personal malice. For example, the review team was alleged to be about to propose the abolition of the Foreign and Commonwealth Office. The folly of such proposals could be explained by the team's youth, ignorance of foreign affairs, philistinism, domination by sociologists, and left-wing beliefs. 'They seemed likely to complete Stage I . . . not only with a minimum knowledge of what goes on overseas but with no real impression of what the customer wants', reported the British Council's Assistant Director General (quoted in Donaldson, 1984).

Max Beloff, a former professor of public administration at Oxford, wrote in an article in a learned journal that it was hardly surprising that the review team's report was not taken seriously, given the team's relative juniority. Earlier reports had been

the work of a committee of men of weight and distinction, bringing to bear on their subject a wide variety of relevant experience. Sir Kenneth's team was not of this kind . . . one can see that busy public servants might well find it profitable to discuss their concerns with an eminent public servant like Lord Plowden or a highly regarded man of business like the late Sir Val Duncan and not extend the same tolerance to thrustful youngsters, with no such personal claims on their time and attention (Beloff, 1977).

To put this kind of comment in perspective, it is worth recalling that the average age of the review team, at the start of the project, was 38; and that of the team, one was a professional diplomat, one a former employee of the World Bank, one an academic economist who had worked for the Prime Minister of Ghana, and one a seconded member of the Overseas Development Administration. These were complemented by a civil servant seconded from the Ministry of Defence, an academic sociologist, and Berrill himself. It was, in short, a group with a good deal of collective experience, including experience overseas.

Insufficient effort was put into countering this kind of propaganda by circulating the facts and counter-attacking. As one official has put it, 'conducting street warfare in Whitehall effectively was crucial to the CPRS and especially to getting a fair hearing for a review involving many Whitehall vested interests'.

No one could claim that the Review of Overseas Representation was the CPRS's greatest success. Mistakes were made in the handling of the study and the presentation of the report. But the episode probably did no lasting damage. The CPRS soon recovered from the blow to its morale at the time and went on to do a number of successful studies in other areas under Berrill and then Ibbs. Its eventual abolition six years later was caused by quite different factors. Mrs Thatcher's frequent and well-publicized impatience with the Foreign Office might even have endeared some parts of the report to her. One of her senior Ministers told us that 'taking on the Foreign Office was worth while' and still hoped that 'something would come of it'. Whether more will ever come of it remains to be seen. There were a number of lessons to be learnt from this study for the CPRS. Perhaps the most important was not to take on too many parts of the British Establishment at once. The most comforting verdict for those who were involved in doing the review might be that it was a little before its time, but that new ways of seeing things and doing things always take some time to gain acceptance. Certainly an organization such as the CPRS should identify some new approaches and put them forward even if their chances of being accepted at the time are not high. The fact that many of the recommendations have been implemented subsequently endorses this. Though there can still be no final verdict, perhaps the last word should go to Victor Rothschild, who described it as 'pretty successful in the end'.

9

The Demise of the CPRS

THROUGHOUT THE LIFE of the CPRS there were times when its abolition looked possible. The first of these occasions was when Heath lost the February 1974 election. The strong personal antipathy between Heath and his successor, Harold Wilson, led the latter to regard the CPRS, as a Heath creation, with some suspicion. It is clear that he considered abolishing it—perhaps influenced also by his admiration and respect for the Civil Service. However, he decided to retain it. When Callaghan took office he showed no inclination to disturb the status quo. Again when the next change of Prime Minister took place in May 1979, there was speculation about whether Mrs Thatcher would retain it. In fact it survived her first administration. Ken Berrill's efforts at establishing a relationship with the new Prime Minister and at carving out a role for the CPRS during her early months at Number Ten were rewarded; the Prime Minister sought the CPRS's advice in a number of areas during her first year in office. Whilst some CPRS members wondered whether Berrill's successor, Ibbs, would be too mild in manner and too reticent to cut much ice with the Prime Minister, she grew to respect him and indeed to rely on him for advice on industrial policy. When Ibbs returned to ICI in April 1982, Thatcher herself selected John Sparrow to replace him.

On 16 June 1983, one week after the election and fourteen months after Sparrow's arrival in the Cabinet Office, the Prime Minister made the following announcement in a Downing Street press notice, having secured the agreement of the Cabinet that morning:

The Prime Minister has reviewed the arrangements for support to Ministers on policy analysis, and advice and in particular the role of the Central Policy Review Staff (CPRS).

The CPRS has been a valuable source of policy analysis and collective advice to Ministers in successive governments since it was established in 1971. In the meantime, however, Departments have established or expanded their own policy units for long-term planning, and the Cabinet Office Secretariat's role in preparing issues for collective Ministerial discussion has grown considerably. A policy unit has also been established in the Prime Minister's office.

In the light of these developments, and of the development of the role of special advisers as a source of general advice to Ministers, the Prime Minister has decided, after consultation with her Cabinet colleagues, that the purposes for which the CPRS was set up are now being met satisfactorily in other ways and it should therefore be disbanded at the end of July.

Virtually the same words were repeated in her answer to a parliamentary question a few days later (House of Commons, 1983).

Peter Hennessy claims in his monograph on the CPRS that, 'The first the fifteen members of the CPRS knew of their impending fate was the story in *The Times* on election day,' and that '. . . early in the week after the election . . . Sparrow made a last ditch effort to save it' (Hennessy, 1986). In fact members of the CPRS were well aware of the possibility that changes in the machinery of government at the centre might be made after the election, and that the CPRS itself could be vulnerable. In the period leading up to the election they discussed this possibility. There was a clear split between those who took the over-sanguine view that the CPRS had survived two previous elections and was now too much part of the furniture to be removed, and those who believed that all was not well with respect to Mrs Thatcher's perception of the unit and that she would feel little compunction about wielding the axe. This group urged that, if the CPRS were to have any chance of survival, Sparrow should go and put the case to her. He did so. In spite of the support of the Cabinet Secretary Sir Robert Armstrong—who has since, during a Civil Service training seminar, explicitly regretted the abolition of the CPRS—the Prime Minister was not persuaded. Members of the CPRS were told of the likely contents of the press release at their usual Monday morning meeting on 13 June, three days before it was released.

There had been little collective discussion amongst Ministers. Mrs Thatcher asked her colleagues briskly whether the CPRS was of any help to them—adding that it was of none to her. Nobody spoke out in its defence. *The Times* had run a story anticipating its abolition a week before it took place. Within Whitehall senior officials close to the centre of the government machine were aware that Mrs Thatcher had become impatient with the CPRS and had little confidence in its head, in spite of the fact that she personally had appointed him. She had in fact decided before the election that the CPRS was a liability and should be abolished. Her electoral victory sealed its fate. Her massive majority presumably helped to confirm her conviction about the rightness of her policies, and made it easy for her to dispose with confidence of an organization whose role, in part, was to advise her about the implications of those policies and even of alternatives to them.

The Demise of the CPRS

Most of the newspaper comment about her decision to close down the Think Tank was critical. *The Times* in its leader columns disapproved strongly. It argued that Ibbs and Sparrow had been chosen by the Prime Minister and if they failed her she had either picked badly or given them unsuitable tasks; 'If an intelligent woman cannot profitably use fifteen of the best and brightest that Whitehall, the City, industry, the universities and the professions can provide, there is a gap in her make-up . . .'. It commended her decision to strengthen the Policy Unit but claimed that this was quite compatible with retaining the CPRS, which served the Cabinet as a whole (*The Times*, 1983).

The *Guardian* was equally critical:

The rationale for twenty or so licensed free thinkers, drawn in roughly equal proportion from within and outside Whitehall, was that they could span departmental divisions, pick up strategic issues ignored in the daily humdrum, and act as an independent counter-weight to the conventional wisdoms of the ministries . . .

It went on to argue that abolition of the CPRS only made sense if there were to be a decline in Cabinet government and collective Cabinet decision-making:

The prime raison d'être of the Think Tank was to provide non-departmental advice to any member of the Cabinet who so wished, but perhaps that non-departmental advice is instead to be extended solely to the Prime Minister through an expanded Downing Street unit (*Guardian*, 1983).

In Whitehall the abolition of the CPRS was greeted with widespread regret. Many senior officials were critical of the decision, in spite of the irritation the CPRS had caused them in the past. Peter Hennessy of *The Times* claimed that Permanent Secretaries were unanimous in their condemnation. Richard Norton-Taylor wrote in the *Guardian*, '. . . its demise yesterday was widely criticised on the grounds that the Think Tank was designed to serve the whole Cabinet not just the Prime Minister.' He quotes one close observer as saying, '. . . the stronger the Prime Minister the more you need a strong and independent Think Tank to counter the influence of her camp followers' (Norton-Taylor, 1983). That remark perhaps reflected Whitehall's own self-interest as much as its support for the CPRS. Even the Think Tank was more acceptable than some of the Prime Minister's kitchen Cabinet.

The abolition of the CPRS was in fact the final implementation of a plan which had long been in Mrs Thatcher's mind. She had never been a strong supporter of the CPRS. She in fact took the trouble to consult Rothschild about abolition. Any doubts she may have had were reinforced by him; he did not make a strong case for retaining it. Only the intervention of her own adviser and first head of her Policy Unit, Sir John Hoskyns, saved the CPRS when she first became Prime Minister in 1979. Hoskyns, as later became clear, was a fierce critic of the senior Civil Service and believed that alternative sources of advice from within the machine with less reliance on departments was desirable.

How far can the reasons given in the statement she issued be accepted as valid? How far were they concocted to provide public justification for, or a rationalization of, a decision taken on other grounds? Three specific reasons were put forward: first, departments had established and expanded their own policy units for long-term planning; second, the Cabinet Secretariat's role in preparing issues for collective Ministerial discussion had grown considerably; third, a policy unit had been established in the Prime Minister's Office. Finally and more generally, the CPRS had played an important part in the past, but it no longer had a role because its work was now being done by others.

However, none of the three other institutions cited could adequately replace the CPRS. The reasons were different in each case. Useful though departmental policy units can be, and indeed the CPRS advocated strengthening them at various times during its twelve-year history, such units are, at best, an integral part of their own departments. They service their own Minister's interests. They rarely challenge the assumptions underlying departmental policies. In other words, they are unlikely to be concerned with the interests of the government as a whole and with its overall strategies. One of the most important *raisons d'être* of the CPRS, which we hope that we have demonstrated throughout this book, was its capacity to take a non-departmental view of government activities. In that sense, by definition, departmental policy units could hardly replace it. In any case, even when such units exist they all too often degenerate into mere speech-writing and fire-fighting adjuncts of Ministers' private offices. In some departments, at some or all times, they do not exist at all.

The Cabinet Secretariat is an equally inadequate substitute for the CPRS. As its name implies, its job is to run the Cabinet and Cabinet committees. It is not staffed or organized to do medium- or longer-term thinking, still less expected to ask searching questions about the merits of the decisions which it so smoothly promulgates. Throughout its life the CPRS worked closely with the Cabinet Secretariat; the two organizations supported each other by the sharing of information and occasionally through the exchange of ideas, which might be incorporated in the briefs for Chairmen of Cabinet committees. But their roles were fundamentally different and they complemented each other rather than competed with each other. The earliest arguments for creating a central capability, for example, the report of Lady Sharp's group or the memorandum by Lord Plowden and Lord Roberthall, had referred specifically to the inadequacies of the Cabinet Secretariat in this respect. Despite the efforts of Sir John Hunt, there had been little change by 1983.

Nor could, or did, a Prime Minister's Policy Unit fill the gap left by the CPRS. The job done by the Donoughue unit for Labour under Wilson and Callaghan, and by the Hoskyns/Mount/Redwood unit for Mrs Thatcher, was completely different from that of the CPRS. In the first place, to quote James Callaghan (referring to the unit in his time), '. . . the Policy Unit tended to be more ideological, the CPRS more pragmatic and expert. Both were necessary; a P.M. tends to get very isolated.' The real danger of 'group thinking' around powerful leaders makes it essential that their circle includes some licensed dissidents who do not necessarily share every conviction. Secondly, the special advisers in the Number Ten Policy Unit worked for the Prime Minister alone; the CPRS, though it had always done special jobs for the Prime Minister of the day, was there to serve the Cabinet as a whole. Finally, the Policy Unit did not normally engage in the large-scale, longer-term studies which led to both published and unpublished CPRS reports. Again, the two organizations were complementary rather than direct substitutes for each other.

None of the reasons put forward can therefore be accepted at their face value. Some of the newspaper comment in the immediate aftermath of the CPRS's abolition suggested that it had been abolished primarily because it was a source of leaks. One of the exponents of this view was Jock Bruce-Gardyne who had been a junior Minister at the Treasury during Thatcher's first term of office. In a rather silly article headed, 'What use a Tank that leaks', he argued that '. . . the real reason they were given their tickets was simply that they had apparently become as water tight as a collander. *Time Out* magazine seemed to be plugged into their office Xerox' (Bruce-Gardyne, 1983). As described in Chapter 5, there had, it is true, been a major leak of a CPRS report some six months before which had caused the government considerable embarrassment and forced it to do some rapid backtracking, including denials that it was planning to dismantle large parts of the welfare state. It would not have been in the CPRS's interests to leak such a document though it might have been in the interests of some Ministers and some departmental civil servants to do so. Members of the CPRS who had access to a great deal of classified information were always particularly sensitive about leaking, studiously avoiding it as a tactic since they were highly vulnerable to accusations of leaking. In this case, John Sparrow wrote to the *Times* refuting the suggestion made in Bruce-Gardyne's article. His letter, however, appeared to have only a limited effect on further newspaper comments, which continued to suggest that the CPRS itself had been the source of many leaks. Far more important, however, it had no effect on the Prime Minister herself; when asked why she had abolished the CPRS, she gave as her first reason, 'All those leaks!' (conversation with author).

But if the alleged leakiness of the CPRS was the immediate cause of its abolition, the origins were considerably earlier. Even as a departmental Minister Mrs Thatcher had never been greatly impressed by the CPRS as an institution. When she came to power as Prime Minister in 1979, with, as she saw it, a mandate to abandon consensus politics and to reorientate the nation as fast as possible, she had even less time for the kind of careful, often cautious, analysis that the CPRS was by then offering. 'We had more time for research in those days', she said looking back to the early 1970s (conversation with author).

Hugo Young, never a great supporter of Mrs Thatcher, suggested that she got rid of it because there was no longer a place for a body which challenged the prevailing orthodoxy. The CPRS, he said, provided an alternative view to the conventional wisdom of Whitehall. But:

The very need for a separate fount of unorthodoxy is apparently reckoned to have expired . . . This is ominous at several levels. Can one seriously suppose that innovative thinking, of the quality shown by the CPRS at its best, will emerge from self-interested departments with corners to defend?

He concluded that a new Thatcherite orthodoxy had been established and that '. . . instead of opening minds, a new set of unchallengeable verities has begun to close them' (Young, 1983).

Other commentators, inside and outside the CPRS, agreed with Young. Conviction politicians such as Mrs Thatcher find it more difficult to make use of an organization such as the CPRS, than those who are both less ideological and more open-minded. For those confident that they know how to tackle the major problems of the day, policy analysts who are trying to seek answers to them are liable to seem redundant.

What such politicians want from policy analysts is advice on how to implement the solutions. But implementation was not a central part of the CPRS's role. Mrs Thatcher is in fact a particularly difficult client for an organization such as the CPRS. She has strong ideas on where she wants to go, and wants advice about how to get there; she does not relish being distracted by suggestions of other options or by apparently faint-hearted assessments of the cost.

Ibbs's strategy for the CPRS took account of these attitudes on the part of its principal client. Ibbs himself, as we have pointed out earlier, did succeed in establishing an excellent working relationship with the Prime Minister. Concentrating CPRS efforts on only a limited range of subjects (mainly in the industrial field—see Chapter 7), he was careful never to produce a CPRS report in which he was not completely confident of his own ability to speak. A senior Minister observed that Ibbs was also careful not to provoke confrontation with the Prime Minister; 'I think Margaret Thatcher told the CPRS what to do papers on, whereas Victor Rothschild decided'.

The result was that Ibbs's standing with the Prime Minister rose hig
the CPRS, as such, shared in her goodwill to a much more limited extent.
doesn't think in terms of organizations, but of people, as people', comment
one senior official. 'She didn't seem to understand what the CPRS, as such,
could do, although she from time to time quite genuinely tried to think of areas
where it could be useful.' Nor did she seem to appreciate how far the value of
Ibbs's advice on a wide range of industrial policy issues depended on the
support and analysis he was getting from the CPRS. Her lack of awareness of
the CPRS as an organization was to have disastrous consequences for it when,
in March 1982, Ibbs was recalled to ICI and was replaced, at Mrs Thatcher's
instigation, by John Sparrow. Sparrow was a director of the merchant bank
Morgan Grenfell; he had earlier established a relationship with the Prime
Minister when nominated by the bank, which she had asked to provide her
with a personal adviser on financial matters.

The skills required for personal financial advice were quite different from
those required to run the CPRS. Sparrow, not unreasonably, seems not to have
seen the relationship between the Prime Minister and himself, in his capacity
as head of the CPRS, as a purely personal one; he hoped to act as the conduit for
advice coming forward from the CPRS as a group of advisers. Unlike Ibbs, he
recognized the need to make Mrs Thatcher acquainted with the staff of the
CPRS, and attempted to rectify earlier failures to do this.

One manifestation of this was a dinner arranged with the Prime Minister. In
the Summer of 1982 a member of the Number Ten Policy Unit gave a leaving
party attended by Mrs Thatcher to which the CPRS was also invited. The fact
that few CPRS staff had ever met the Prime Minister was a matter for comment
on this occasion. This created an opportunity for John Sparrow to suggest that
this should be rectified. The outcome was a dinner in Number Ten to which
some half a dozen CPRS members were invited as well as several Cabinet
Ministers. The agenda was the CPRS's future work programme. According to
one participant, it was a prickly affair without much meeting of minds; in
addition, any value it may have had was soon dissipated by the leaking of the
CPRS's paper on public expenditure, described in Chapter 5.

Inexperienced in politics and in government, Sparrow lacked some of the
skills to manage the difficult processes either of generating or of offering
advice. Under him, the products of CPRS thinking were 'curiously in-
sensitive', commented a senior civil servant in a central department. 'The
CPRS claimed to offer more than the stimulating ideas of bright people, it
purported to produce in-depth studies, but the authors weren't real experts.
Their conclusions were often jejune.' Mrs Thatcher herself described them as
'. . . guffy stuff, like Ph.D. theses. We could do that kind of thing ourselves'
(conversation with author).

If the 'guffy' quality of CPRS reports reflected Sparrow's inability to manage his staff or to edit their work, this flaw was compounded by the difficulties which he faced when trying to present their conclusions to Ministers. He had, almost deliberately, abandoned Ibbs's approach of focusing on only a limited range of topics with which he felt at ease. On the other hand, he lacked the charisma, nerve, and 'deviousness' which had enabled Rothschild to give convincing presentations even on issues relatively unfamiliar to him. On too many occasions Sparrow, and the CPRS, for which he spoke, found themselves out of their depth. Increasingly, the Prime Minister disregarded his interventions at Ministerial meetings. 'She almost stopped him speaking before he'd started', recalled one of her colleagues. To be fair to Sparrow, any head of the CPRS would probably have experienced some difficulties in getting through at this time, since in the run-up to a general election party political needs often tend to dominate over governmental needs.

Nevertheless, clues of this kind from the Prime Minister were extremely obvious, and were instantly noted by other members of the Cabinet. 'As a Minister you don't read the papers. You're so overwhelmed that if, reading the [Cabinet] papers at 3.00 a.m. you think, this [a CPRS document] isn't going to go, you don't read it.' Some felt that in any case the CPRS was contributing nothing of value to collective discussions. In failing to challenge Mrs Thatcher, the Prime Minister, it was simply '. . . augmenting the prejudices of the Prime Minister', said a Minister at the 'wet' end of the political spectrum, 'and becoming a second mouthpiece for the Treasury'. Moreover, the CPRS was tending more even than in the past to produce collective briefs which asked pertinent questions but did not make clear recommendations. Busy Cabinet Ministers look to such briefs for recommendations for action, rather than an analysis of the problem. The frequent failure of the CPRS to make firm recommendations may be a further explanation of Mrs Thatcher's reference to 'guff' (although an ex-member of the CPRS noted that Mrs Thatcher's view of a paper was often determined by her approval or disapproval of particular points rather than being based on a judgement of the paper as a whole).

Finally, the lower profile adopted by Rothschild's successor had its own costs. The CPRS of the early 1980s was not the CPRS of a decade before. 'It seemed to have drawn in on itself', said a senior member of both Conservative governments: 'Victor Rothschild's chart and blackboard had gone'. The CPRS of Berrill and Ibbs, added one of his colleagues, lacked Rothschild's 'dynamic and irreverence'.

With the dynamic and irreverence there went, at least during the last year or so of the CPRS's life, something else. Some of its members felt that the *esprit de corps* or team spirit that had been so marked during the first ten years had been dissipated. There were a number of bitter internal wrangles about particular projects, such as the study on higher education. Furthermore, well before Sparrow arrived, the group who worked on industrial policy and the nationalized industries had become somewhat separated from the rest, who acted as a dissatisfied rump trying to devise acceptable projects in other areas. As one ex-member of the CPRS put it, they 'progressively stopped being a happy band of travellers working as a multi-disciplinary corporate group, becoming instead a rather rigidly organized and defined small group'.

There were also, it was suggested, subtle changes in the staffing of the CPRS. More specialists were recruited who were technically highly competent but who, some thought, were rather 'grey'. There was a loss of flair; and, some have suggested, a loss of political understanding. Perhaps this was inevitable under an ideological government which looked to the CPRS for advice not on the merits of Ministers' proposals but on their implementation. It was probably also a mistake not to have recruited a monetarist, given the prevalent economic ideology. Another ex-member of the CPRS suggested that there was less lateral thinking going on. He added that this might have been connected with the decline in the number of women in the CPRS. However, it probably had much more to do with the type of men that replaced the women than just with the fact that they were men. There were fewer mavericks, and the mavericks who were left felt constrained about speaking as such because they were isolated. This view was not shared by everyone associated with the CPRS at the time. One ex-member claimed 'that the team spirit remained high . . . lateral thinking remained very much our brief and there was still outspoken comment and discussion. The CPRS remained a stimulating environment in which to work.' But most of the comments made to us point to an organization that had begun to lose some sense of purpose and direction.

Some of these changes had already started to take place during Robin Ibbs's period as head of the CPRS. It is easy to blame Sparrow for its demise, but probably unfair. The seeds of the destruction may have been sown from the day Margaret Thatcher arrived in Number Ten; Ibbs, despite all the care he had taken to foster a successful relationship with the Prime Minister, had been able only to delay the inevitable end. Certainly, some of the changes described above had already started to take place in his time. He took a number of decisions, for example that reports should not be published and that a group separate from the rest of the CPRS should work on the nationalized industries, which subtly changed the way in which the CPRS operated. He believed, however, that such changes were necessary to secure the CPRS's survival in a changed climate. This view was endorsed by many of his colleagues in the CPRS. As one of them put it, the CPRS had to be chameleon-like with the changes of government and of Prime Minister. It could not keep going as if nothing had happened. However, whilst the Ibbs chameleon was able to survive in the short term by blending with the foliage that surrounded it, this very tactic may have weakened its longer-term capacity to survive. Its eventual disappearance may have been all the easier because of its increasing invisibility.

There are several respects in which this might be true. First, the growing concentration by the CPRS on a single client, and on one or two senior Ministers close to her, was a high-risk strategy which may have in the end made it more of a victim, heavily dependent on her whims (to put it pejoratively) or on her personal perception of its value (to put it more positively). Its relatively low profile amongst the Cabinet as a whole meant that there was not a wider group of satisfied clients, prepared to defend it and to fight against the threat of extinction. Yet in the short term Ibbs's strategy was perfectly comprehensible and defensible. In a government so dominated by the Prime Minister, there was much to be said for getting on to her wavelength and trying to provide advice in areas of concern to her. More generally, there were, in any case, good reasons for increasing the amount of CPRS work directed towards the Prime Minister rather than the Cabinet as a whole. The small size of the Prime Minister's Office and the increasingly complex nature of the briefing required on subjects ranging from summit meetings to major industrial disputes, such as the miners' strike, means that Prime Ministers have a growing need for more and better advice from outside the Number Ten private office. It is not surprising that the CPRS should have tried to help this need. Its problem was that the Policy Unit did this too and could do it more intimately and discreetly.

The second and related short-term expedient adopted by the CPRS under Thatcher was to concentrate a high proportion of its time and effort on industrial policy and, during the Ibbs era, on the nationalized industries in particular. This was always a central part of the CPRS's work, but it came so to dominate CPRS activities as to prevent it from realizing its original objective of covering a wide range of government policies. The fewer the Ministers who were getting useful advice for the CPRS on issues of concern to them, the fewer there were at the end to defend it. A Tory Minister who regretted the closure of the CPRS felt that it should have devoted more time to certain fundamental problems such as the future of work, or to certain areas of social policy which he considered were 'in a mess', such as the future of the prison service. On the other hand, another Conservative Minister who also deplored the abolition of the CPRS told us that he did not consider that the CPRS concentrated too much on industrial questions. He believed that economic and industrial policy issues were central to the government's concerns and therefore should be central to the CPRS's work. And he cited alcohol as a topic too peripheral to have occupied CPRS's time. But even he admitted, with some regret, that he had not had much contact with the CPRS during its latter period, perhaps because he was not reponsible for industrial or economic policies.

The third change was the fact that CPRS reports were no longer being published. Again the reason was ostensibly a good one at the time; the Prime Minister preferred that they were not published. However, it followed that no one outside Whitehall knew what the CPRS was doing. This encouraged commentators to write it off as having been incorporated into the machine. This view may have contributed to a climate in which the CPRS was perceived as expendable.

Whether the CPRS is reinvented or not will in the end depend on how far any government which replaces the present one takes a collective approach to decision-making. There is a potential for a body whose aim is primarily to give collective advice only where a collectivity exists to which the advice can be directed. Part of the problem for the CPRS under Thatcher was that she led from the front, putting forward the decisions herself rather than allowing the Cabinet to discuss and explore the options before coming to a collective decision, except on those occasions where a sufficiently powerful group of Ministers got together to persuade her that she was wrong. In the circumstances a strengthened Number Ten Policy Unit, which Mrs Thatcher created when she abolished the CPRS, was probably more appropriate. The Policy Unit had certain distinct advantages over the CPRS. First, its members were able to be much closer to the Prime Minister herself than all the members of the CPRS, other than its head. Secondly, it could operate privately. Because the CPRS gave advice to all Ministers its papers were seen by them all and by their departments. To avoid being criticized for factual errors the CPRS often cleared its papers in draft with departments. Departments consequently had advance warning of proposals to which they might object and, if they did, had ample time to work at having these killed. Alternatively, the CPRS could take the risk of not consulting departments. This exposed it to the possibility of ridicule if its facts were wrong or its judgements, perhaps, simplistic. The Policy Unit did not have this dilemma because departments rarely saw the advice it gave.

Nor was it easy for the CPRS to make a contribution to discussions on strategy under Thatcher. She relied on her own instincts and believed that she could develop and steer the government's strategy herself. This does not mean that she did not want ideas put to her. Perhaps more than her predecessors, she valued a separate and independent view from the Whitehall machine. What she also wanted was not to be reminded of her objectives but to be given facts and arguments about particular problems which the departmental civil servants had failed to provide, and which she could use to counter the departmental viewpoint. Her Policy Unit apparently provided her with this. When the CPRS tried, she was apparently often disappointed in the results, partly because the CPRS was not always on the same political wavelength as herself. Departmental objections to CPRS proposals or to the proposals on which the CPRS had been asked to advise sometimes led to leaks. Where the CPRS seemingly also lacked political sensitivity, the risk of departmental leaking became greater and the insensitivity made the leaks especially newsworthy. In these circumstances her decision to abolish it, though regrettable, was not surprising. Sir Patrick Nairne in a letter to *The Times* (27 June 1983) sums it up well. Without the backing of the Prime Minister, he agreed, a CPRS can achieve little; with it, it can achieve a great deal. But '. . . as things were, it seems best that the axe should have been struck. But government will be poorer for the loss of a small and vigorous "loan collection" from inside and outside Whitehall licensed to break new ground and challenge the accepted view.'

10

Conclusions

WHEN WE EMBARKED on this book the CPRS was still in existence. At that point the main task for this chapter would have been to assess the contribution of the CPRS to policy-making and, perhaps, to speculate about its future. However, before we had made much progress, and as related in the last chapter, the CPRS was abolished in 1983. The need for assessment remains; but the secondary question to which assessment can contribute is whether a future government, of any party, should recreate a central policy review staff of some kind and, if so, what kind.

The problems faced by 'rulers', as outlined in Chapter 2, have certainly not diminished in the fifteen years since the CPRS was created. Indeed, it could be argued that it was during the 1970s that both the severity of the problems, and the obvious incapacity of most rulers for dealing with them, first came to be fully understood. The pace of political change, the poor performance of the world economy, combining high unemployment and high inflation, and the concomitant loss of faith in Keynesian remedies, the growing role of violence as a political tool, the internationalization of local political crises, the merciless scrutiny of the mass media, especially television, and, partly derived from this, the constant expectation of personal interventions by individual rulers, have by the 1980s made the job of Prime Minister, or President, one of the few in which failure, in some sense, is ultimately more probable than success. At least in principle, the case remains strong for ensuring that somewhere in government is the capability to perform the tasks originally given to the CPRS.

Professor Dror suggests several ways in which policy analysts, grouped into 'islands of excellence' close to the rulers whom they advise, can help their clients (Dror, 1984). They can offset what he calls 'fallacies' in the decision-making process, by challenging both established orthodoxies and new ones as they develop, especially in the process of collective self-delusion which has been dubbed 'group think'. They can provide comprehensive and long-term perspectives. They can diagnose situations and problems and, we would add, solutions to solve those problems. They can contribute innovative and unconventional contributions to decision-making and can also help ensure that decisions are implemented. At a rather different level, they can provide help in particular situations, such as bargaining and negotiations. They may have a distinctive part to play in the budgetary process. However, all these ways of contributing must be based on the recognition that ultimately certain decisions are political.

The CPRS acted in all these ways at different times although the weight given to any of them varied. The Rothschild era saw much more emphasis on the mode of challenge and on the long-term, comprehensive perspective. Berrill, the supreme committee-man, made an important contribution to bargaining and negotiation. He also secured the entrée to discussions of public expenditure which, despite the successful contributions made by Dick Ross, had largely been denied to Rothschild. This right was let slip again by Ibbs and Sparrow. Ibbs's distinctive contribution lay in reinforcing the Prime Minister's power to implement specific policies which she thought important, notably towards the nationalized industries. Throughout most of its life the CPRS contributions to decision-making were, by the conservative standards of Whitehall, innovative and unconventional. If the cumulative impact of all this was not, in the end, a marked improvement in the performance of British government, did the reasons for this lie in the techniques, the tactics, the composition, the style of the CPRS itself? Or was it due to some inherent characteristics of British central government, proof against the CPRS as against so many other critics and would-be reformers, before and since?

Assessing the impact of the CPRS on outcomes is inevitably difficult. As Peter Hennessy points out in his booklet on the CPRS, its contribution 'was only one of many ingredients in a haphazard mix of prejudices, pragmatism, and analysis which is flattered by the name of policy-making' (Hennessy, Morrison, and Townsend, 1985). And, as he also points out, whatever the final verdict, it was hardly a great draw on the nation's resources and could even be said to be cheap at the price. In answering the question on whether the CPRS delivered, he wrote:

On a value for money level, the answer is an unequivocal 'yes'. At just under £1 million a year at 1983 prices, its running costs were tiny. Its output certainly justified an expenditure on that scale. On the grand strategy level, in answer to the question did the CPRS in fulfilling its remit of diverting ministerial attention to the long-term, help halt and then reverse Britain's relative economic decline? The answer is an unequivocal 'no'. In between the poles established by the two questions, the assessment of impact becomes highly problematical (Hennessy, Morrison, and Townsend, 1985).

Even to suggest that an organization such as the CPRS could reverse the decline of Britain would clearly be naïve. A small group of people with no more than an advisory role, even though it had the privilege of potential inside influence, could hardly make more than the most minimal of contributions to such reversals. The more interesting question is whether it made a contribution of any value in the form of practical proposals which might help to halt the decline. Given the complexity and depth of the problem grand strategies were unlikely to get deeply enough into the issues at stake. Instead an enormous range of changes are probably needed in many spheres ranging through education and training, industrial relations, investment policies, the marketing of exports, the successful development of new ideas derived from scientific and technological research, pay and prices policies and so on. Many of the problems in these areas need to be faced in a pragmatic and piecemeal way. Yet at the same time there is a need to recognize and understand the connections between them.

The CPRS did make recommendations in all the areas we have just listed and it was in a uniquely strong position to take into account the interconnections. One of its earliest collective briefs warned Mr Heath's Cabinet of the dangers of supporting the 'lame duck' Upper Clyde Shipbuilders and, in so doing, abandoning the government's selective industrial assistance policy almost before the policy had begun. The report on ICL focused on the inherent weaknesses of a policy of support for key firms which took no account of the managerial competence of such firms. The motor car study, above all, spelled out the facts about productivity in British industry in a way that had never been done before; the government lacked the courage to follow the prescriptions for policy but they and the analysis remained valid. Although largely unheeded, the CPRS warned of the likelihood of a large increase in oil prices in 1973 and the consequences for other policies. In another sphere, the analysis and conclusions in the race relations report have grown tragically more relevant every year since they were first shown to, and ignored by, a Conservative then Labour government; while despite Mrs Thatcher's horrified public reaction to the 1982 report on future options for welfare spending, nothing has ever been said to suggest that its analysis was faulty. Most significant of all, in political terms, was the desperate debate during the miners' strike of 1973–4; the CPRS thoughts on this, had they been listened to, might have avoided the disastrous path down which Mr Heath led the Conservative government.

The CPRS on a number of occasions also pointed out the extent and nature of the economic decline that had already taken place and the need to make certain adjustments in the light of that and to avoid further decline. These occasions included Rothschild's Wantage speech in late 1973 and the opening chapters of the Review of Overseas Representation in 1977. The hostile reactions to both of these indicate the resistance on the part of government and other parts of the Establishment to accept the central facts of the matter.

It was, of course, necessary to do more than purvey gloom and despondency by analysing the decline. Ways had to be found to turn things round. None of the CPRS's solutions were especially radical or original whether in, say, incomes policy, industrial policy, training programmes, or export promotion. But all of them were chipping away at existing approaches which in one way or another were failing the nation. Many CPRS recommendations could have been or were made by others. This was indeed one of the main comments made by critics of the CPRS. The obvious riposte to that is that 'there is nothing new in the Bible'. Totally new ideas in the world of government policy are rare unless the thinking is of a very long-term variety. Many of the problems the CPRS studied were extremely intractable. Northern Ireland is a good example. The CPRS made three separate attempts to throw light on how to resolve the semi-permanent political crisis in which that province struggles on. The first was under Rothschild during the Heath government, the second under Berrill during the Wilson government, and the third under Ibbs during the Thatcher government. Three different Prime Ministers, three different Directors of the CPRS, and three different sets of CPRS staff made little difference to the outcome. The CPRS could not come up with a new and radical solution, though limited advice such as 'refrain from further initiatives for the time being' may have its uses even if it appears something of a damp squib. Peter Hennessy quoted a conversation with Sir Frank Cooper, who was Permanent Secretary at the Northern Ireland Office from 1973 to 1976. Cooper's claims are hard to dispute.

Northern Ireland is a quagmire for anyone however long they may or may not have been involved. And I think it was probably very unlikely that some relative newcomer could come and throw some brand new light on the whole situation . . . Certainly, there was no opposition in the Northern Ireland Office to the Think Tank having a look.

We didn't have any great hopes that it would bring some blinding flash of new insight . . . simply because the people who were working in the Office were totally immersed in it. They'd found it difficult enough to get to know something about it. And although Robert Wade-Gery[1] is a man of outstanding ability, I think it's unlikely that he or anyone else involved could have produced something which gave an absolutely revolutionary view of the situation which was going to work (Hennessy, Morrison, and Townsend, 1985).

These were fair comments. But the fact that the CPRS was reiterating ideas, or proposing solutions, already put forward by others did not necessarily mean that they were not valid. It may have meant instead that further advocacy was not needed. Alternatively, if the timing was right and the presentation effective

---

[1] The author of the first CPRS report on this subject.

the CPRS, like any good management consultant, could make more headway than line managers in promoting new ideas to top management, that is amongst Ministers and those that surround them. More generally, it is clear from some of the comments made to us and to others by former Ministers and Prime Ministers, that they felt that the CPRS had been useful to them in influencing the course and the outcome of debates in Cabinet and elsewhere. James Callaghan was grateful for Kenneth Berrill's role on aerospace matters, a role performed largely by virtue of his chairmanship of the relevant interdepartmental committee rather than as the leader of a team of analysts.

In any case, dismissing the proposals of policy analysts as unoriginal is simply one of two negative responses immediately available to line managers; the other, of course, is to condemn them with even greater force as being unacceptably radical and impracticable. As familiar, and as effective, was the combination of the two: not only is a proposal completely old hat, but it has long since been shown to be worthless because of its radical implications in terms of cost, political support, legislation, and so on. The choice between these on the part of departments was simply a question of tactics.

The views expressed by the CPRS were sometimes unacceptable elsewhere in Whitehall. So too were the subjects on which it expressed views. A problem inherent in large organizations is the difficulty faced by those at the top in setting their own agenda. The issues which they find themselves discussing are typically forced on them by external events, by the evolving needs of the organization itself, and by their subordinates. Thus a Cabinet, however much it may want to stand back and consider its long-term foreign policy, may well find the agenda taken up with a power workers' strike, with new proposals for Civil Service pay, and with a draft Bill tidying up long-standing anomalies in the social security system. The power of the British Cabinet Secretary derives in large part from his role as formal agenda-setter for the Cabinet and the Prime Minister.

In this context the job of the policy analyst as adviser is to help rulers at least to influence the agenda, to elicit what is on their minds and to structure the issues for discussion and, more problematically, to infer what ought to be on their minds and to persuade them that they should discuss it. This was what was intended in the CPRS's work on strategy. In doing this, of course, the policy analyst needs great discretion in setting his own agenda. Rulers' other advisers have their own agendas and are likely to resist additional items intruding from outside. It follows that they will also try to influence the policy analyst's own agenda or work programme. The analyst thus faces two difficult tactical choices: first, should he try to enlist the political support of the Ministerial clients for work on issues about which he knows that the official machine is likely to be uncooperative and thus possibly stir up opposition at the outset; or should he covertly start work in the hope that by the time the bureaucrats discover, he will have gone too far to be stopped? Second, how much weight should he give to proposals from his clients and the bureaucracy for work on issues of interest to them? Should he accept these commissions simply because they do interest his clients, regardless of his own views of their significance or his own capacity for tackling them? Conversely, how much work should he do on issues which he believes to be important but which plainly do not interest his clients?

In general, the CPRS thought it wise to collaborate with the bureaucracy, not least because the latter has a near monopoly of so many of the available facts but also because this was in most cases a more cost-effective approach. In the early days of the Heath government, and in a limited way for a period under Mrs Thatcher, the process was formalized: a Cabinet committee of Ministers had the task of approving the CPRS work programme. This was a relatively high- risk approach, under which topics might be formally vetoed but, if not, acquired an equally formal seal of collective Ministerial approval which made it hard for departments to refuse to collaborate. It also meant that at least some Ministers were made aware of what the CPRS was doing and might have some pride of ownership in its programme. Although few regretted the passing of the Heath 'Committee on the Central Capability' some always felt that, if it had survived, the CPRS and Ministers might have worked more closely and more effectively together than they did.

Any Minister and his officials were liable at any time to try to keep the CPRS out of his territory. In this respect there was little to choose between different departments at different periods. Some Ministers, for example Tony Benn, came to see the CPRS as an instrument inherently hostile to them and their policies, and resented its activities accordingly. Others more realistically recognized that the CPRS was as likely to support as to resist their line, whether against the Treasury, other departments, or the Prime Minister, and saw it as broadly neutral. The result was that the CPRS was, in general, fairly free to roam and to investigate where it wished in the Whitehall jungle. There were exceptions to this. The CPRS found great difficulty in penetrating into one or two particular thickets and to counter the argument that this was unsuitable territory for them. For a long time this was true of economic policy, especially taxation. It remained true of defence and foreign policy. Sir Frank Cooper, formerly Permanent Secretary at the Ministry of Defence, told Peter Hennessy that these

are not areas where there is a great deal of widespread expertise in this country. In defence in particular there are very few other experts and [the Ministry of] Defence has a near monopoly. In terms of foreign affairs? Well, people certainly write history and write pieces about foreign affairs. But again there is a limited knowledge of the real relations that one country has with another (quoted in Hennessy, Morrison, and Townsend, 1985).

As Sir Frank went on from the Northern Ireland Office to be Permanent Secretary at the Ministry of Defence his 'keep off' attitude is perhaps not surprising. A counter-argument is that the very fact that the Ministry of Defence had a monopoly was reason enough for encouraging others to examine the policies it promulgated. Monopolies can turn into strangleholds and lead to the ossification of ideas. Nor was there any necessary reason why the CPRS should not look at foreign affairs. And the CPRS did discuss foreign policy questions from time to time. In the mid-seventies it considered putting in a paper on ways of extricating the UK from the Falklands. In the end the CPRS did not pursue it. It is possible that even had the CPRS done so, the subsequent course of history would not have been altered. There will always be issues on which passions run so high that the still, small voice of the policy analyst at best goes unheard and at worst invites ridicule or contempt.

It can be argued that the most important dimension of relations with other countries is economic. The CPRS was no less well placed to study this dimension than many other areas of policy on which it advised. Apart from the Review of Overseas Representation, which was not concerned with foreign and international economic policy as such, the CPRS in fact ventured relatively rarely into either defence or foreign affairs. There were occasional exceptions, such as policies on the continental shelf, the work that the Chief Scientist did on scientific relationships with other countries, and from time to time aspects of defence expenditure, the 'North–South dialogue', aid and trade and international commodity policy. It was certainly Rothschild's view that the CPRS should be able to cover the entire range of government policy without some parts being excluded as 'no-go areas'. He maintained that even security questions of a highly classified variety should not be excluded and that it was not essential that the head of the CPRS should be fully party to the details of work done by his staff on questions of this kind. One member of the CPRS who was himself involved in two such studies did not agree with this assessment. His grounds were that highly classified work involving only two or three members of the CPRS cut them off from their colleagues and weakened the organization's collegial spirit. Rothschild also did not accept the Cooper argument that defence and foreign affairs were unsuitable topics for the Think Tank. Certainly the claim that these areas required more expertise than many others in which the CPRS was active seems a little difficult to sustain. Many parts of the operation of the social security system, for example, are complex and difficult to master.

In general, machinery of government questions were effectively barred to the CPRS, except for those covered in the study of overseas representation. In principle, the CPRS, with its bird's-eye view of Whitehall from the centre, was ideally placed to comment on defects in the processes and structures for government decision-making. It did implicitly comment on the archaic procedures of the Cabinet[2] both in introducing 'strategy' meetings and in the new styles of presentation, which it used. It also did some work on the question of whether there should be more 'open' government. In practice, however, the CPRS in trying to concern itself with 'process' questions, with the exception of 'open' government, was in Whitehall's eyes guilty of heresy, in one or other of two senses. Any attempt to exploit its central perspective was heretical in that the only people at the centre normally licensed to discuss these matters are the Prime Minister and the principal official adviser, the Cabinet Secretary. Decisions and discussion of process and structure are reserved to them for the very practical reason that changes in these are powerful political tools, to be used pragmatically as the Prime Minister wishes in manipulating his colleagues. An obstreperous colleague can be neutralized by excluding him from a special Cabinet committee set up to consider an issue on which his views are 'unsound'. A faction in the government can be placated by creating a new department to be headed by one of its members. Moreover, the skills of the higher Civil Service, especially at the very top, are essentially political rather than managerial or analytical; senior officials in general neither understand nor are greatly interested by the principles of organization and process. There has never been an adequate competence at the centre, whether in the Treasury, the Civil Service Department, or subsequently the Management and Personnel Office, for advising on these issues.

CPRS attempts to influence the working of constituent parts of Whitehall were equally heretical. One reason for the absence of central expertise about these matters is the strongly entrenched tradition that the working of Whitehall departments is the almost exclusive preserve of those departments and their heads. Occasional suggestions from the CPRS that a particular policy might be more effective if certain changes were made in departmental organization tended to be greeted with the comment 'That is a matter for the Permanent Secretary to decide.' A CPRS project to review departments' capabilities for planning and analysis was stillborn in the face of unanimous opposition from departmental heads. In general though, the CPRS had remarkable freedom and success in planning its own work programme. This gives greater force to the question of whether the programme was correct.

---

[2] Of which Sir John Hoskyns later commented: 'Cabinets and Cabinet Committees involve too many people. The meetings are too formal. There isn't enough time. People are not allowed to take their coats off. Visual aids are regarded as in bad taste. Such meetings consist of the rehearsal and negotiation of departmental positions and seldom produce new insights or new ideas' (Hoskyns, 1986).

Conclusions

Were there topics that the CPRS should have tackled but did not and others that it did tackle but should not have done?

One of Mr Callaghan's closest advisers commended the CPRS's work at this period on various industrial issues; the CPRS was 'more realistic and better informed' than the Department of Industry. On social policy and economic policy the CPRS's main contribution was to see the interrelationship between different parts of the jigsaw and to start its analysis with the needs of the citizen for social services. 'Though the CPRS was erratic, it did manage to analyse policy into basic options whereas Treasury papers were orientated towards the Treasury's own interests.'

Inevitably many people had their own favourite topics on which they would have welcomed a CPRS contribution: 'prisons policy,' said a senior member of Mrs Thatcher's Cabinet, 'Nobody knows what kind of prisons to build. Or work, over the next fifteen years, what to do with our people.' The same speaker went on to speculate about the kinds of issue on which the Prime Minister might have welcomed a CPRS paper. 'She'd love to get at the Foreign Office on some major issue. The Foreign Secretary's in the UK so rarely that it's very hard to catch him.' There was widespread agreement on at least some projects that the CPRS should not have done. Top of many people's list was the Review of Overseas Representatives. Edward Heath and Sir Douglas Wass have both publicly criticized the CPRS's decision to work on this at all, regardless of its conclusions. It 'could well have been done by the Civil Service Department', said Wass in his second Reith Lecture (Wass, 1984). 'Neither trans-departmental or government-wide', said Heath. 'Its recommendations were ridiculous. The way in which it was handled made it harder for people who wanted sensible reforms to handle them' (interview with authors). As Chapter 8 showed, some members of the CPRS were also critical, less on the grounds of the subject-matter than because the study used up such a large proportion of scarce manpower. Others felt as strongly that comments of the kind made by Heath uncritically reflected the 'rubbishing' campaign led by the Foreign Office and took no account of the facts: they argued that the review was certainly 'government-wide' and probably the most thoroughly 'trans-departmental' of any study done by the CPRS.

In the later years of the CPRS some of its members, and others, felt that too many resources had gone into the work, managed by Robin Ibbs, on nationalized industries. 'Very distracting', said one. 'The CPRS progressively stopped being a single multi-disciplinary team and became a collection of teams communicating and linked with each other mainly through top management.' A senior Cabinet Minister disagreed: 'This was a problem on which Ministers needed advice.'

Sir Douglas Wass felt that the CPRS should not have tackled the British car industry: 'something that could have been done by the Department of Industry' (Wass, 1984). The argument here seems to be that the CPRS should have stuck to interdepartmental issues rather than those that fell within the purview of a single department. Many senior civil servants expressed similar views about CPRS studies on subjects for which their departments were responsible. This was hardly surprising. The implicit argument often ran, 'My department knows a lot about X. The CPRS, at least at the outset, knew little about X. Therefore, my department should have done the study of X.' The basic flaw in this line of reasoning was that the department in question all too often had seen no case for making such a study and had had no intention of doing so.

Moreover, departmental knowledge of a subject was no guarantee of an effective study. Wass's objections above show quite unjustified confidence in the capacity of departments to take on the vested interests likely to resist both the principle and the conclusions of an inquiry—car manufacturers and unions—or the many entrenched institutions which comprise Britain's system of overseas representation. It is also worth noting that the Civil Service Department, during the period of the review of overseas representation, had proved incapable of delivering even quite limited cuts in Civil Service manpower. In a note entitled 'Epistle to a Prime Minister' Rothschild commented on Wass:

The fallacy of making generalisations from particular instances needs no emphasis and, as a matter of fact, the examples were unfortunately chosen. It is true that the Think Tank study of the Foreign Service was clumsily handled; but it is also true that many of the recommendations made in the study have been implemented. Sir Douglas Wass's other example, the Think Tank study of the car industry, was equally fallacious. The Think Tank would not have undertaken such an inquiry except at the request of the Prime Minister and/or the Cabinet. The fact that it was asked to do this merely shows that the relevant department was unable or unwilling to do so; and this can happen in spite of Sir Douglas's departmental dreamworld (Rothschild, in Hennessy, Morrison, and Townsend, 1985).

A cross-cutting question is whether the CPRS struck the right balance in terms of types of activities: did it neglect the long-term in favour of the immediate, or vice versa? Some commentators answered both questions at once. A former Labour Minister, looking back at experiences between 1974 and 1979, said that the CPRS should have given more weight to medium- to long-term issues, such as regional policy or skill shortages. It had failed to prevent the 'nonsense' and waste of resources involved in siting, with massive government help, an aluminium smelter at Invergordon, which it later advised should be closed. (The CPRS did in fact work on regional policy before 1974, but since the results were unpublished Labour Ministers had no way of knowing this.) The same Minister commented that reactive collective briefs were useful but that they inevitably distracted the CPRS from the larger, longer-term issues. On the other hand, Mr Callaghan, looking back on his time as Prime Minister, expressed the opposite view: 'I often found when I received the one sheet of paper, which was mostly what the Think Tank wanted to put down, the following questions and I would ask questions, then you began to see whether the minister was stumbling or whether he had the answers. The Think Tank was an invaluable way of reaching the right conclusions' (House of Commons, 1986).

This was in fact one of the central issues for the CPRS throughout its life. Its functions undeniably included looking ahead whenever possible, trying to anticipate future problems and to identify the implications of these for government policies. Not only many outsiders but some of its members came to think of it as a 'think tank' in the true sense, ranging free and widely in its activities, looking as far ahead as intellect allowed, proposing major shifts in policy which would be practicable only in the very long term. 'We did get caught up in the shorter-term aspects of policy and failed to take a broad and long view', said a member of staff looking back at the end of the 1970s. 'The CPRS must consciously resist the tendency to do too much on the short term.' This thought was echoed by many of the commentators who at different times dismissed the CPRS as having been 'captured by the mandarins'. If the CPRS found itself concerned with the same limited time-scale as preoccupied Ministers and civil servants, it had much less that was distinctive to offer; the mandarins, it was suggested, were far happier with the CPRS acting as an additional fire-fighter than trying to raise fundamental questions the answers to which were likely to leave Ministers dissatisfied.

But the practical case against overemphasis on the longer term was a strong one and simply stated. One statement may stand for many, by one of Mrs Thatcher's Ministers, broadly sympathetic to the CPRS and its objectives:

She abolished it because it wasn't doing any good. And she worried that it wasn't producing papers that had much relevance to issues of the moment. Its papers were deliberately pointed in the interests of the longer term. This isn't of much interest to the Cabinet.

For most of its existence the CPRS had avoided this danger. Rothschild later wrote that the propagation of the view that the CPRS should focus on the longer term had been of great potential value to the opponents of the CPRS,

its programme should be a mix of short, medium and long-term work. The short-term work, has, apart from other considerations, an important role in maintaining morale, enthusiasm and interest of the members of the CPRS. They do not want, as some Permanent Secretaries have proposed, to be wholly engaged in long-term work (as remote from Whitehall as possible) studying such questions as Energy in the year 2000; or intractable problems such as Regional Policy. They don't want to be a dustbin in which hopeless issues are deposited. They want to be part of the hurly-burly of Whitehall, to participate in the solution of immediate problems and, in fact, to be wanted now (Rothschild in Hennessy, Morrison, and Townsend, 1985).

Kenneth Berrill was strongly of the view that Ministers were the CPRS's main clients and that they needed advice about their preoccupations, which were often short-term ones. He was right. The CPRS would have been abolished much earlier had it got itself bogged down in futurology.

A ten-year-ahead perspective in terms of analysing the consequences of alternative states of the world was probably about as far forward it was realistic for the CPRS to look. Beyond that the uncertainties became too great in most areas for Ministers to be able to take much serious interest. This is not to say the governments do not need advice about the long-term future, but this is probably better given by outside research organizations, or think tanks in the true sense. Where looking forward involves taking account of how a particular policy will perform in the future on the basis of a broad extrapolation of the present it is sometimes possible to look further ahead. A good example of this is changes in pension schemes (see Chapter 6).

Overlapping the long-term versus short-term issue was the question of whether the CPRS was right to focus on discrete departmental programmes and decisions in the first place. Those who recalled the language of the 1970 White Paper pointed out that the new staff had been created to help governments not to lose 'sight of the need to consider the totality of their current policies in relation to their longer term objectives', and to help Ministers 'to establish the relative priorities to be given to the different sectors of their programme as a whole'. This was a task, some argued, which almost by definition should have kept the CPRS from involvement in the details of diplomats' entertainment allowances or motor car production lines. Douglas Wass suggested that the CPRS had tried to do not only the wrong things, but too much:

The role that it was given was too ambitious. I do not believe a small central staff by itself can be expected to identify new areas of workable policy which have somehow escaped the attention of the expert department. Nor can it really evaluate the implications of alternative courses: that too is best left to the specialists.

What the Think Tank should have concentrated on was what I have called 'the balance of policy', in other words the way the government's programmes fitted into its strategic objectives and the way it orders its priorities. It should also have taken more seriously the job of criticising departmental proposals where it had evidence that they had unperceived implications for other parts of the programme (Wass, 1984).

There are two flaws in Wass's argument. The first is that it is hard to imagine how the CPRS could have confined its work to overall strategy and the setting of priorities without either becoming far too political a unit to be acceptable to Ministers, or getting lost in the stratosphere never to return to earth. Second, considering questions of strategy and priorities is certainly helped by some understanding of the component parts, even if that understanding is inevitably more superficial than that of the responsible departments. Criticisms of departmental proposals because of their implications for other parts of the government's programme were far more likely to be soundly based if the CPRS had done some work on those parts.

Another difficult judgement the CPRS had to make related to the balance of effort it put into its larger detailed reports and collective briefs. The two types of activity were certainly not mutually exclusive. Indeed to some extent one could derive from the other. Thus many short collective briefs put in to Cabinet committees were based on work done for some of the big reports. Peter Hennessy suggests that

It is for its big, one-off reports that it is most difficult to claim an impact for the Tank. But a case can be made even for the most unpromising examples. Take the Review of Overseas Representation. Universally rubbished when unveiled, by the mid-1980s a great many of the economies it recommended had been achieved by Conservative ministers keen to create a more streamlined machine both within Whitehall and its extensions overseas . . . The inquiry into the volume car industry became the source document in Whitehall for several years after and is credited by some outside the Tank with helping create a new climate of reality in the motor industry. A similar delayed-reaction can be claimed more clearly for the 1983 review for long-term spending. The Treasury Green Paper on taxation and spending into the 1980s published a year later was a belated and much watered-down attempt to cover the same ground (Hennessy, Morrison, and Townsend, 1985).

It must be said that whilst a collective brief could have a more immediate impact, this was usually ephemeral. The advantage of the larger studies was that even if they had little immediate impact, they were much more likely to be returned to later than collective briefs, which were geared to a particular meeting of a Cabinet committee and would be unlikely to be looked at again until the Public Record Office opens the files in thirty years' time. In any case, many collective briefs were supported by evidence which the CPRS had gathered in undertaking its larger studies. CPRS papers were frequently, we believe, better argued and based on a more secure foundation of knowledge and understanding when the CPRS itself spent substantial amounts of time working in the subject area or one related to it. Thus collective briefs on energy policy, the nationalized industries, or information technology, to name just a few areas, benefited from the fact that the CPRS had established its own expertise and was not simply reacting to papers put forward by other departments. For these reasons we do not agree that collective briefing was intrinsically more valuable than the 'red book' studies. The two were in fact complementary, each feeding into the other. John Ashworth sums up the case for the major studies well:

Their production helped build up, amongst the members of the CPRS, a specialist competence in certain policy areas. This was necessary both for other activities and for the maintenance of a high degree of professionalism in certain kinds of policy analysis (Ashworth, 1985).

Three closely linked issues concerned the relationships between the composition of the CPRS, the nature of the views that it developed, and the way in which those views were presented to Ministers. This relationship was in principle a circular one. The types of views expressed in a CPRS paper were a function both of those who expressed them and of the expectations, or supposed expectations, of their Ministerial clients. How far was the CPRS neutral in relation either to specific policies or to party ideology and how far should neutrality or partisanship be reflected in its submissions to Ministers? Even more specifically, should those submissions end with firm proposals for one course of action rather than another? The dilemma is a familiar one. 'Some analysts', Meltsner has observed, 'feel that they are not advisors. In their view, all they do is provide information to policy makers. The word "advice" sounds too much as though they were making, or at least suggesting decisions' (Meltsner, 1986).

This view was always strongly represented within the CPRS. So was its opposite. Rothschild was quite clear:

One of the rules I made at the start . . . was that we should not make reports of presentations unless they ended with precise recommendations for action. I did not think we were in business just to produce information (interview with authors).

In his day this rule was usually followed. Reports and recommendations were made, in language often too blunt for more circumspect regular officials. But this pattern was not always followed, especially under Rothschild's successors. Collective briefs often used to end not with a positive recommendation but with a short list of issues which Ministers were advised to consider before making up their own minds. This approach was advocated, and brought to a fine art, by Dick Ross. It had the virtue of leaving Ministers to draw their own conclusions and to decide where there were clear issues of political choice. It drew their attention to the consequences of different actions. As James Callaghan said:

In terms of sharply pointing out the weaknesses in Ministers' papers and saying to the Prime Minister: 'suggest you ask the following questions one, two, three, four . . .', that was its great value to me . . . If I can expose weaknesses . . . so other colleagues can make up their minds between Ministers' points of view and the arguments to follow up when they are asked rather pointed questions, that is the way to get the right decisions (Evidence to the Treasury and Civil Service Committee, 1986).

But this approach had the disadvantage of failing to give Ministers a firm lead towards particular solutions, when that was what they often desperately sought. Some CPRS papers had so little to say that their only justification seemed to be the feeling that 'there ought to be a CPRS paper'. A Ministerial adviser told us that they would have been better 'if they had been less wishy-washy; Ministers often said to me that they couldn't see the point of them. The most effective were those with some real substance, or which took a strong line, or which helped to clarify really complex issues, for example in discussions of economic policy.' The same feeling is well illustrated by a passage in Barbara Castle's diaries. She describes a meeting at Chequers on government strategy on a Sunday in November 1974. The afternoon session was opened by Dick Ross. Mrs Castle outlined his remarks and commented:

'There was' he said 'no surefire recipe for economic growth.' He can say that again! There was a role for general incentives and also one for selective assistance. We needed to find a balance between them and help the regions to help themselves.

As I listened to him I thought how good these expert advisers always are at analysing a problem on an 'either, or' basis, when what ministers are yearning for is a clear indication of what policies will do the trick if only we politicians will have the courage to pursue them. In fact, the experts can't even agree on that. The more I listen to them the more I respect my own amateur profession of politics (Castle, 1980).

Listing several questions put later by Ken Berrill, she noted 'Wouldn't we like to know!' She wanted the answers rather than the questions. It is, however, worth pointing out that she was one of the most experienced Ministers in Wilson's last government. At the DHSS she had a clear sense of her own priorities in a department with more clearly defined boundaries than some others. She also had one of the strongest teams of political advisers any Minister has had since this particular animal was invented. As such she was certainly less likely to need CPRS advice, to which she had 'a high level of indifference' said one of her closest advisers, than many of her colleagues. But she was not alone in her views. One of Mrs Thatcher's closest advisers told us that, as far as Mrs Thatcher was concerned, Rothschild had been right; CPRS briefs that ended with questions rather than with proposals were not very helpful.

We are inclined to agree. With hindsight, it can be argued that boldness more often might have paid. On the other hand, as the more cautious members of the CPRS might have argued, had the CPRS constantly raised its head above the parapet it would have risked being shot earlier than eventually happened.

The decision in any particular case whether or not to give a strong lead to Ministers depended partly on whether the CPRS, or members of it, themselves had strong views on the issue. In some cases they did; there were inevitably issues on which the CPRS, like Churchill's Statistical Section before them, developed its own collective 'prejudices', to use MacDougall's term. The operational question was whether such prejudices should inform a general CPRS line which individual members of the Tank could put forward when participating in Whitehall meetings of various kinds. One of the conventions of Whitehall is to invite individual civil servants at interdepartmental meetings to speak on behalf of their departments. 'What', the Chairman might ask 'does the Ministry of Agriculture think about that?' Similar questions were addressed to members of the CPRS at such meetings. 'What is the CPRS view?' they were asked. The CPRS was more likely to have such a view on issues on which it had done work of its own. But it was often rather difficult to give a CPRS view in the sense of one reflecting the collective thinking of the organization. Because the CPRS had to cover so much ground it could not develop a collective view on every issue. Moreover, a departmental view is often moulded by the objectives of Ministers in the department concerned. The CPRS, whilst formally accountable to the Prime Minister, certainly did not go to committees speaking on behalf of the PM. Therefore its representatives were not constrained by Ministerial views, as would often be the case for civil servants from the departments. One consequence of this was that individual members of the CPRS—especially if they were the only person working on, or expert in, a subject—could find themselves speaking on behalf of the CPRS without having a clear and agreed line from their colleagues. They were thus to some extent speaking for themselves. Since turnover in the CPRS was quite rapid this could lead to changes in the line taken when the CPRS spokesman in a departmental group was replaced by another with different views.

The 'CPRS line' expressed thus occasionally reflected individuals' personal bias. This was probably inevitable. As John Ashworth has argued, it is

foolish to pretend that there can be such a thing as truly 'objective' advice—much better to admit and expose at the outset the inevitable personal prejudices to those to whom the advice is proffered and allow them to make such allowances as they feel necessary. This, by the way, is one of the skills which seem to be acquired by all good politicians, certainly all I've met have been very good detectors of, and allowers for, personal bias. Sometimes, I must confess, seemingly overly cynical about this but that too I imagine is an occupational hazard.

Of course, there are those who will claim that on technical, professional matters it is possible to give 'objective' advice and they would claim that many issues of scientific (if not technological) interest fall into this category. If they do, all I can say is that I never saw any of them (Ashworth, 1985).

Conclusions

The nature and quality of the advice, or information, tendered by the CPRS inevitably depended on its make-up. The three main issues in this context were its overall size, the skills and experience of its members, and their political or temperamental bias.

The size of the CPRS never rose above twenty professionals and a small number of support staff. Though this was incontestably the right size to sit round the Director's conference table, it was almost certainly too small for most other purposes, unless considerably greater use had been made of outside consultants to support the in-house work than actually occurred. Professor Dror suggests that 'The minimum size of a useful policy analysis unit for advising Rulers is probably somewhere around ten to fifteen persons, with twenty-five to thirty being a preferable number' (Dror, 1984). The CPRS could not be active in more than three or four policy areas at once and a large study such as the Review of Overseas Representation could use up as much as a quarter to a third of the staff for some of its duration. The range of different skills and disciplines available or different policy sectors or outside interests represented was restricted to such an extent that some major policy developments had simply to be ignored on the grounds that the CPRS had neither the in-house staff nor even the outside contacts to deal with them adequately in the time available. Alternatively, members of the CPRS with skills or expertise in one policy area would find themselves trying to comment intelligently on others about which they knew little. Many individual members were required to monitor a wide range of policy areas. This meant the risk of dilettantism was often present. Criticism of the CPRS as ignorant, amateurish, or superficial was liable to be heard. The best way to counter this danger was to rely on the help of experts from outside.

If the CPRS were to be reinstated, a staff of around twenty-five would probably ensure a more professional organization, able to proffer better informed advice on a wide range of subjects. As we explained in Chapter 3, the background of the staff was varied and, given its size, the composition was probably satisfactory. There was a balance of civil servants from spending and non-spending departments, from those with substantial overseas interests and those operating largely within the UK. Amongst outside appointments there was also a reasonable balance between the private and public sectors. Most of those from the public sector were academics. There was a reasonable mix of scientists and social scientists with more economists than others. This mix of training and experience rarely produced serious frictions or misunderstandings in working relationships. The varied staff worked well in a complementary fashion. There could have been more appointments from nationalized industries and local government. Appointments might also have been made from time to time from the voluntary sector and the trades unions.

It is a familiar criticism of the upper echelons of the Civil Service as a whole that its members suffer from the delusion that expert knowledge is insignificant; they believe that all that is really required is a good analytical brain, drafting ability, and some political 'nous'.[3]

In some ways the CPRS was the ultimate manifestation of the notion of the gifted amateur. It was based on the idea of bringing together a group of able people from a variety of backgrounds, each with some expertise in their own areas but required to work not only in these areas but also in others of which they knew little or nothing. One of the hopes behind this was that fresh thinking could be applied and that bringing together people who had no commitments to the conventional wisdoms or to current systems would allow and indeed encourage the proposal of more radical solutions. Undoubtedly there is some truth in this.

However, there are powerful counter-arguments. Those who have little knowledge of the constraints on the implementation of policy may produce solutions which are naïve because they are not implementable, although in theory they may be the most rational way of proceeding. For example, some experience of the way power is distributed between professionals, bureaucrats, and clients in the social services is important in considering changes in social policy. Some experience of the relationships between management and the trades unions may be important in some areas of industrial policy. Certainly civil servants in departments sometimes thought the CPRS was naïve and too distant from the real world of actually implementing policy. Undeniably, the CPRS needed to make a substantial investment of time in learning about some problems before it could comment authoritatively on them. This in turn limited the number of subjects in which the CPRS could be engaged at any one time, as well as limiting its overall output. Because of the frequent turnover of staff, pooled knowledge that had been acquired constantly needed replenishing.

Another issue relating to the composition of the CPRS is whether it should have been more overtly party political. Should there have been a core of known Labour supporters during the Wilson and Callaghan governments and of Conservatives under Thatcher? Rothschild and indeed Berrill and Ibbs were strongly opposed to any politicization of the CPRS in this way. Rothschild has subsequently argued:

Excluding extreme ideological positions the political views of members of the CPRS are

[3] This is of course only a subset of Martin Wiener's criticism of the baleful influence on the British professional classes of the public schools in the later 19th century. 'Their disparagement of specialised and practical studies reinforced the traditional content of the professional ideal, the limitation of the leisured landed gentleman, at the expense of the modern role of the professional as expert' (Wiener, 1982).

less important than many politicians imagine. Those of the first CPRS were largely unknown, if only because its members were too busy and committed to their work to express them. It was known, however, that one member was a Conservative, whereas another was Labour. Others had seen too much of Whitehall and Westminster to be anything but neutral and neutered. Their personal idiosyncracies were irrelevant to the work in hand; and in any case the CPRS realised that it was the job of the politicians to inject the politics into their recommendations. So Neil [Kinnock], if it is you, you don't need and should not have, half a dozen Tessa [Blackstone] clones in your Tank (Rothschild, in Hennessy, Morrison, and Townsend, 1985).

The problem is that what 'politicians imagine' cannot be ignored. It is vitally important that Ministers should feel confident of the loyalty of the members of an organization such as the CPRS. Any suspicion that the CPRS was out of sympathy with the political aims of the government could dent that confidence. We suspect that there were times both during the Labour governments and during the Thatcher administration when Ministers suspected the CPRS of being out of tune with its political objectives. Sometimes they were right. One of these occasions was when the CPRS produced a paper for the Callaghan Cabinet on economic strategy. This paper had a great deal to say about the problems of inflation but virtually nothing to say about the problems of unemployment. It did not go down well.

It would not, in our view, be right to have turned the CPRS into a unit giving advice of a party political kind which always suited the party prejudices of Ministers. Being politically sensitive did not require that. Trust in an analyst should primarily be based on the quality of the analysis rather than political sympathy.

However, there was a case for some members of a body working so closely with Ministers to be at least broadly in sympathy with the party in power, and known to be, if only to help sustain the trust and ensure the political sensitivity of the analyses.

Until recently it has been widely accepted that civil servants are apolitical and that they can advise Ministers objectively whatever their personal views. As a principle of good government, this has come increasingly under attack in relation to the Civil Service in general. It looks even more threadbare when applied to a group such as the CPRS, working—or intended to work—closely with Ministers and very closely involved in the process of relating the government's political 'commitments to administrative necessities'. It might have been preferable, as some CPRS members have argued, to have acknowledged both that the theory was probably inapplicable in principle, and that it had been most imperfectly applied in practice, and to have accepted that the style and the politics of a truly effective CPRS might and probably should change with the government. This would have helped to avoid the problem, mentioned by one of Harold Wilson's senior advisers, that the incoming Labour government of 1974 was suspicious of the CPRS as a Tory Trojan horse; reluctant to ignore the long-established convention that civil servants should not be moved around for political reasons, their initial thought was not to replace individuals with others in whom they had more confidence, but to abolish the CPRS altogether. That in the end was what Mrs Thatcher did. To avoid a future CPRS suffering the same fate we believe it would be advisable to accept the need for some changes in personnel when the government changes.

This applies above all to the head of the CPRS. He, or she, had to work closely with Ministers, in particular the Prime Minister. Whilst shared political views are not essential in this relationship, they hardly seem likely to undermine it and may well serve to strengthen it.

At the very least, the head of the CPRS and, if possible, one or two of his key colleagues, must have some 'feel' for politics. There are two dimensions to this. First, he must understand the perceptions and likely reactions of politicians, on the Government and on the Opposition side, to the world in general and to particular events and advice offered (including by the CPRS). Not all heads of the CPRS had this quality; even Rothschild, said one of Edward Heath's advisers, 'had Heath's confidence but never seemed to understand politics'. Second, in understanding politicians the head of the CPRS and the unit as a whole must see himself as basically on their side. His role is to help Ministers effectively to manage the permanent bureaucracy, as far as possible in the framework of a constructive working relationship. He must try to avoid the scepticism about the capacity, resolution, and motivation of politicians so widely found throughout the permanent Civil Service.

By any standards other than those of Whitehall, most members of the CPRS were not radical in their views. They tended to be clustered round the political centre. Neither the radical left nor the radical right secured much, if any, representation in the CPRS during its twelve-year history. This was consistent with the CPRS policy, from the outset, of aiming for collaboration with Whitehall rather than conflict. Only thus, it was felt, could the CPRS acquire the information it needed and could try out its ideas on Ministers' official advisers before putting those ideas to Ministers. The risk in this approach was, of course, that of becoming over-consensual, too anxious to reach accommodation with the rest of Whitehall and, in effect, of being 'taken over' by them. There were a number of media stories to this effect in the later 1970s. Tony Benn, whose views on this issue became more extreme over the years, saw the CPRS as an instrument of the Civil Service, a kind of back-up device for blocking Ministerial proposals which they had failed to stop at an earlier stage (Benn, 1980). His views were later dismissed as inaccurate by Edward Heath and, we believe, quite rightly so (House of Commons, 1986). As for the media, the contrasts which they made between early independence and later subservience were equally overdrawn. If in the early days of the CPRS the media grossly exaggerated Rothschild's ability single-handed to change the course of government, they equally exaggerated the emasculation of his successors, Berrill and Ibbs.

To some extent the belief that the CPRS had been taken over by Whitehall conflicts with the idea that it got into fields where it did not belong and trampled insensitively on what should have been the prerogative of individual departments. If it had been incorporated into the Whitehall machine it could hardly have undertaken the many studies which some departments considered they should have done. Our view is that the CPRS never was incorporated in quite the way that has been claimed. Whilst in its last two years its output was not published and in that sense remained, like most of the work done by Whitehall, for internal consumption only, it continued to take a robust and independent line in many of its recommendations. And it is on the basis of its output that it must be judged, not by the degree of its collaboration with the Whitehall machine or by the friendliness of its relations with key officials. These relationships never stopped the CPRS from seeking the views of those outside Whitehall too, nor from proposing solutions which were not necessarily favoured by the insiders.

There were undoubtedly times when the CPRS could have been more radical. However, we doubt whether a too cosy relationship with Whitehall was the source of this. A more likely cause was the composition of the CPRS itself. This perhaps led to a rather middle-of-the-road consensus-minded approach at times. However, there is a danger perhaps in perceiving being radical in conventional left and right terms.

Although formal political affiliation played no part in appointments to the CPRS, some attempt was made by the directors to choose people with the right blend of characteristics for posts very different from most in Whitehall. Dick Ross once summarized the main qualities required as being analytical ability, imagination, conceptual ability, versatility, open-mindedness, presentational skills, initiative, and temperament. The last is so important that it is worth quoting Ross's prescription in full:

a temperament which will put up with a fluctuating work-load and a very fluctuating success-rate; not being liable to succumb to depression in the face of constant rejection of one's advice; nor developing that cynicism about the unperfectability of the world which characterises so many perfectly intelligent Departmental officials (unpublished minute, 1976).

This was written some years before Sir John Hoskyns had announced that the first thing to realize about British civil servants was their belief that the country could not be saved (Hoskyns, 1983). Ross's stress on the right temperament was important because so many otherwise apparently suitable people, including some of those who actually worked at the CPRS, turned out to lack it. Some civil servants, in particular, evidently suffered from a kind of 'culture shock' at finding themselves in an environment where so little was structured, constrained by legislation, implemented through a formal hierarchy, or intended to maintain the status quo. Some clearly also felt frustrated at being always in the position of adviser, never of implementer. Some were not self-starters who could initiate work without instructions from above; or they failed to respond to the collegial spirit of the CPRS; or they lacked the versatility and the confidence needed to work effectively in an organization like the CPRS.

Other civil servants, however, responded with zest to the change in environment. They were in general liable to be just as radical in their proposals as any outsider from commerce, industry, or the academic world. It was conveniently overlooked by most critics of the Review of Overseas Representation that the CPRS team which produced such 'ridiculous' proposals included senior officials from the Foreign Office and the Ministry of Defence, and, for part of the review's duration, the Overseas Development Ministry. Nor did many of the civil servants on secondment to the CPRS shirk from criticizing their own departments. Indeed in some cases it provided them with a heaven-sent opportunity to voice criticism or reservations about departmental policies.

There were some misfits in the CPRS, but they were few in number. It was probably inevitable that some mistakes in recruitment were made. In some cases the blame lay as much with the organizations from which they were sent, who should have known better, as with the head of the CPRS who engaged them, with only the recommendations of others and a short interview with the candidate on which to base his judgement. One or two of the misfits escaped by leaving before the normal two-year stay was completed. Others coped.

Some people have suggested that in the last few years of the CPRS's existence the people recruited were less appropriate than earlier. In particular they lacked the creativity and sparkle of the seventies CPRS. There is, we believe, not much evidence to support this view. It was the context that was different, not the individuals that constituted the membership. The staff in 1983 were not dissimilar to the staff in 1973 or 1978 in terms of their experience, ability, and talent. But it was more difficult for their talent to flower in the cold climate of post-Falkland War Thatcher government.

Clearly the composition of the CPRS and the quality of individuals recruited was of great importance. Its departmental location was also important. The options for locating a unit such as the CPRS seem to us to be few. It could have been in Number Ten. It could have been, without any departmental base, in its own building, preferably somewhere not too far from the geographical centre of government (Downing Street). It could have been—and was—in the Cabinet Office. Given that its role was to advise Ministers collectively, Number Ten would not have been the right location. Cabinet Ministers would have been suspicious that it was purely an instrument of the Prime Minister and this might have led to some unwillingness to commission work from it. The second option of complete independence from any department has some superficial attractions in that the risk of being swallowed up by Whitehall would be smaller. But the risk of being isolated from the machine and denied access to Ministerial correspondence and interdepartmental and departmental papers would be greater. Location in the Cabinet Office provided the CPRS with vital information about the workings of Cabinet committees, close proximity to Number Ten, and regular access to the Cabinet Secretary. It was the right decision to locate it in the Cabinet Office in 1970 and that would be the right place to put it if it were re-established.

Was the CPRS a success? A satisfactory answer to this question requires subjective interpretation and judgement. To be answered satisfactorily the question must be broken down and related to several distinct issues. The first is 'strategy' and the attempts by the CPRS to give Ministers a non-departmental overview of the direction in which the government was going in the medium to longer term, and to ensure that this was consistent with the government's objectives. The second concerns the 'fire-fighting' role of the CPRS in picking up particularly tricky policy issues, solutions to which often cut across two or more departments. The third concerns the lasting value, if any, to be derived from efforts to introduce more rigorous policy analysis and to subject existing programmes to more methodical measurements of results and cost-effectiveness.

The 1970 White Paper made much of the role of the CPRS in helping Ministers to consider longer-term strategy. But for much of the CPRS's existence this was a fairly marginal activity. This does not mean that nothing worthwhile emerged from work done on strategy. But this work was not sustained in a consistent way over the years. There were no repetitions of the meeting in July 1971 when the whole of the CPRS discussed government strategy with Edward Heath in the garden of Number Ten with only Burke Trend and Douglas Hurd in attendance. The authors of the White Paper would be justified in pointing out that only in the early years did the CPRS perform its role in relation to strategy as intended. There are, we suggest, two main reasons for this. The first reason is what might be called the irritation factor. Douglas Hurd, who was not only present in the Number Ten garden but also at the Chequers strategy meetings with the entire Cabinet in the early seventies, later commented on a television programme on Cabinet government: 'These were deeply uncomfortable occasions . . . I sat on the window-seat gaping at the sight of these very exalted senior people being lectured really. Now that faded, I mean the CPRS which was done away with a year or so ago was not any longer like that at all. It had become a much more subfusc or grey-suited body.' Hurd was certainly not suggesting that such discomfort was out of place. He went on to say, 'I think there is a case for the grit which makes the oyster . . . for something quite small but good and buccaneering at the centre of the machine. It obviously cannot run roughshod over Permanent Secretaries in the whole ladder of authority. So it's got to be kept in some sort of restraint but I think a little bit of stimulation at the cost of the machine is a good thing' (Hurd, 1986). The question as far as strategy was concerned was how much grit, stimulation, or lecturing the Cabinet or the Prime Minister could take. Edward Heath was probably unusual in being willing to accept, and to persuade his Cabinet colleagues to accept, critical comments on his objectives and on the policies he was pursuing to achieve them. But such 'uncomfortable occasions' are bound to irritate some Ministers. They would resent the idea of non-elected people without the daily pressure of political office giving their view of how to approach strategy. Once Heath had gone, it was more difficult for the CPRS to push strategy presentations or papers, partly because of the irritation factor.

The second reasons for the demise of strategy work might be called the 'distraction factor'. There were plenty of other things for the CPRS to do, some of which were explicitly requested by Ministers. In particular it was distracted by the large one-off studies that led to 'red books' and which we have described in earlier chapters. Difficult as the issues were, it was usually easier to immerse CPRS teams in this kind of work than to become involved in the broader issues of across-the-board strategy. These studies were easier to handle intellectually, if only because they were much narrower in coverage, and they were usually less risky politically. Individual Ministers might disagree with the recommendations but they were unlikely to offend the Cabinet as a whole. Strategy papers, on the other hand, did risk causing offence by challenging a government's performance in relation to its own objectives. However, some commentators regretted the escape into the one-off studies. David Howell later said that after the Conservatives returned in 1979

the CPRS had become a sort of troubleshooting body . . . it had been asked to do strange one-off affairs and its reports had been leaked and bandied about in Parliament and any role it was originally supposed to have, as a systematic, regular bringing together of reports of programme analysis throughout Whitehall to present an overall strategic picture to the Prime Minister in the Cabinet, had long since disappeared. It had become a sort of one-off adventure (quoted in Hennessy, 1986).

Conclusions

We have already referred to Douglas Wass's view that the CPRS was asked to do too much when it should have concentrated on strategic objectives and the ordering of priorities.

Work on strategy could be done successfully only with the active support of the Prime Minister. Perhaps the heads of the CPRS should have sought this more frequently in the post-Heath days. However, we doubt whether Wilson, Callaghan, or Thatcher would have welcomed frequent strategy discussions informed by CPRS analysis. Under the two Labour Prime Ministers there were two or three occasions when the CPRS produced strategy papers; there were none under Mrs Thatcher. We have argued throughout this book that the CPRS had to be adaptable as governments and Prime Ministers changed. It is easy to lament the lack of time devoted to strategy for much of the CPRS's history. Is it, however, realistic to argue that the CPRS could have carried on this work regardless of Prime Ministerial indifference? Mrs Thatcher in particular, with her special brand of conviction politics, seems to have felt little need for analysis about strategic objectives. Indifference could soon have turned into hostility; it was probably wise to let this function atrophy. If our view is accepted that the 'strategy' function is important and should be performed, a future reconstructed CPRS ought to ensure that this function is formally written into its job specification. This might perhaps commit the CPRS to report once or twice a year to a special meeting of the Cabinet, perhaps followed by meetings with junior Ministers, on the government's strategy in the medium to longer term. This commitment might be more acceptable to a future Prime Minister, and easier to sell to Cabinet colleagues, if a future CPRS were slightly more political, with its head and some of its members known to be sympathizers of the party in power. Without a formal commitment, all the pressures of day-to-day government are likely to have the effect of pushing some future CPRS into fire-fighting and away from strategy.

In contrast to its work on strategy, the CPRS sustained its output of longer reports on particular problems until its demise. Generalizing about the quality of these reports is of course difficult. It is also hard to generalize on their value to Ministers. We are, however, convinced that the dismissive comments made by David Howell are unjustified. We have given numerous illustrations earlier in this book of reports which either at the time or later had some impact on Ministers' decisions or Whitehall thinking. The most difficult problem the CPRS faced in undertaking these studies, many of which involved investigations in depth, was lack of expertise leading to accusations of amateurishness. Denis Healey expressed doubts about the CPRS in this respect: 'I don't think it was terribly effective in my time because a group of intelligent individuals without responsibility or departmental support will very rarely persuade Ministers, who are advised by people with deeper knowledge than they have and responsibility, to override their own departments. It don't think that really worked' (Healey, 1986). The CPRS undoubtedly did find it hard to persuade Ministers to ignore their departments' advice, partly because of their doubts about the CPRS's credibility and partly because of their loyalty to their own officials. But the claim that departmental Ministers and officials always know best ignores two important facts: the use of outside expertise by the CPRS; and the high proportion of its reports whose subject areas crossed departmental boundaries in a context where Ministers and officials from different departments did not necessarily agree. Throughout its history, as we have shown, the CPRS used contacts outside Whitehall to provide expertise that it could not always supply from within its own ranks. The CPRS input was often fresh and valuable precisely because in general Whitehall made so little use of outside advice. One Civil Service ex-member of the CPRS suggested to us that, 'if the Civil Service had not been so desperately inward-looking I think the CPRS would have lost much of its comparative advantage'. The same person also commented that the CPRS's relative ignorance on a subject could be an advantage: 'It was very good to have people who could say "the way the Prison Service organizes its staff is quite terrible", ignorant of the hundred and one reasons why you could not expect prison officers to do this, that, or the other.'

It is possible that some of the studies carried out by the CPRS which covered the concerns of one department only could have been conducted by the department. This is particularly true of those departments which had their own policy or planning unit. But these units often had to contend with problems within their own departments similar to those experienced by the CPRS in Whitehall generally. They too could be criticized by their own department's management branches for lacking expertise, for interfering, or for producing unrealistic recommendations. But Denis Healey's objection to the CPRS does not apply to cross-departmental issues. The notion that departmental officials will have 'deeper knowledge' than a CPRS implies the existence of some kind of objective truth which a department can know. In fact, of course, truths about the world and about government policies, as perceived by departments, are highly subjective. The central position of the CPRS enabled it to see things in the round in the way that any single department was unlikely to do. Such a rounded view will rarely emerge from the familiar mechanism of an interdepartmental committee. There the relevant department subjectivities are pitted against each other. The outcome of such committees, as suggested at the beginning of this book, all too frequently lacked a radical cutting edge because of the need to seek lowest common denominator consensus. The potential strength of a CPRS report derived from the fact that the CPRS was licensed to take risks, and on the whole it was willing to use this license. It could afford to be radical. Sir Kenneth Berrill once said that the CPRS had a 'bank balance' of credibility which was worth building up only if there was something to spend it on. In other words it was not worth aiming just to become more and more credible but to become sufficiently credible in general to risk being incredible in particular cases.

It is probably a mistake to assess the success of the CPRS longer reports in terms of their immediate effects. It could even be argued that too ready and too immediate acceptance indicated simply that a report was too conservative in its recommendations. One civil servant ex-member of the CPRS suggested to us that

specific recommendations may often have had no obvious immediate results but I believe they often continued to work in a subterranean way until at some subsequent stage—months or even years later—departments started to put them forward as departmental wisdom without acknowledgement. I think this delayed action effect is true of some of the PAR activity in the early 1970s (e.g. in education), the review of overseas representation, some of the JASP work (e.g. demography or its implications), the 1980/1 unemployment study (when the Department of Employment put forward very similar ideas without acknowledgement within months), or even in a minor way Cashless Pay (a damp squib at the time, but something that encouraged the Department of Employment to focus on the absurdities of the Truck Acts or to take some later action).

We agree with this.

Sir Frank Cooper, formerly Permanent Secretary at the Ministry of Defence, has commented on the growth of cross-departmental policy problems:

The setting up of the very large departments created a more demanding role at the centre because their very existence sharpened up boundary problems. No structure is capable of eliminating boundary problems. But if the Cabinet Office is to do its job adequately and properly can it rely mainly on administrators seconded from other departments for a 2-year stint? Can it do without CPRS? Does it not need a significant analytical and questioning capability of its own, composed from mixed disciplines and including outsiders as well as insiders? (Cooper, 1986).

Throughout the CPRS's existence interdepartmental committees continued to operate. One role the CPRS could and did play was to provide more analytical support to the Cabinet Secretariat, which serviced and sometimes chaired these committees. This was one entry point available to it with respect to policy analysis and performance review, another area that needs examining in considering the CPRS's contribution.

As we pointed out in the early chapters in this book, the process of policy analysis and review in British government is not as strong as it should be. This

217

weakness is partly a reflection of characteristics of the system of government, such as the training and experience of civil servants, or the seemingly inevitable drift towards crisis management in the short term that has beset every government in recent years. It is partly a reflection of British political culture in a broader sense with its emphasis on pragmatism, gradual evolution, the avoidance of confrontation, and the reluctance to make anyone worse off in the course of bringing about improvements. In this context it was sometimes hard for the CPRS to be effective. And the nearer a government was to a general election the more true this was. Nevertheless, the activities of the CPRS helped to increase the attention paid in Whitehall to the processes by which decisions are made and to the need for more rational analysis of new policies and the operation of existing policies. Despite its weaknesses (and eventual demise), the PAR programme in which the CPRS played an important part, did help to develop experience and practice of policy analysis in Whitehall. The lessons of PAR subsequently informed the Rayner reviews, also run in part from the centre but on a rather different basis. The CPRS can certainly not claim all the credit for the change in climate towards the acceptance of more rigorous reviews of existing programmes, but it did contribute substantially to the increasing acceptability of queries to underlying assumptions, of fundamental questioning, of challenges to the conventional wisdoms. Its own work in this context took various forms. The best example was probably the CPRS's collective briefs on the outcome of PAR studies. But after PAR had been abolished the CPRS continued its analytical work through collective briefs on draft White Papers, draft responses to Select Committees, and the consideration of the Public Expenditure Programme.

The need for regular reviews of programmes is now widely recognized. The scope for improved policy analysis is still vast. By no means everything can be done from the centre. But the CPRS did, in our view, demonstrate the value of a central analytical capability, whether in supporting the Cabinet Secretariat, in keeping departments on their toes, or in supporting the Prime Minister in the tasks of 'chivvying' Ministers, as in the bilateral meetings held by Callaghan after he became Prime Minister about departments' individual programmes and possible internal inconsistencies within them.

It is a difficult question whether this central capability should serve the Prime Minister or Ministers collectively or the Prime Minister as head of the government and chairman of the Cabinet. The question raises the issue of the balance of power between the Prime Minister and his or her Cabinet. William Rodgers, a member of the Cabinet during the Callaghan government, has argued that the CPRS was bound to suffer the fate that eventually overtook it; that is, to become the short-term instrument of the Prime Minister rather than the long-term instrument of the Cabinet (Rodgers, 1986). It may also be the case that given Mrs Thatcher's style of Cabinet government, in which she leads from the front and takes many decisions in small *ad hoc* groups of Ministers rather than through the Cabinet and its system of committees, the expanded Policy Unit can fill the hole in the centre satisfactorily. But we do not believe that the characteristics of the CPRS under Thatcher derive from some inherent features of British Cabinet government. With a return to a more collective Cabinet decision-making process there would be a need for collective advice to Ministers of the kind given by the CPRS. There would also be a need for a Prime Minister's Policy Unit. The simultaneous existence, between 1974 and 1983, of the CPRS and the Policy Unit, playing different but complementary roles, demonstrated that they could work alongside each other and occasionally together. Since 1983 the Policy Unit under Mrs Thatcher has served her needs as a radical Prime Minister more effectively partly because it has been more in tune with her political beliefs than the CPRS, which sometimes found it difficult to give the kind of committed advice she wanted.

We also accept the need for changes in style, content, and mode of operation of the CPRS, to meet the needs of changing Prime Ministers and changing governments. One ex-member of the CPRS who served in it during Mrs Thatcher's premiership suggested to us that there had been an unfair tendency to see the Rothschild/Heath CPRS as the 'Platonic Ideal' and to castigate the later CPRS for failing to live up to this. He added that under Ibbs and Sparrow the institution had necessarily operated rather differently in an attempt to match the Thatcher style. He claimed that during this period the CPRS had become a useful part of the Whitehall machine, as was recognized almost unanimously by Permanent Secretaries at the time it was abolished. He went on to wonder whether, had it been allowed to survive, the CPRS might have helped the government avoid the sliding from banana skin to banana skin that had characterized it between 1984 and 1986. Mrs Thatcher would certainly dismiss such musings as rubbish. Whether with hindsight she will ever regret her decision to abolish it must await her memoirs.

Frank Cooper may have spoken for many of his peers in the senior Civil Service when he pointed out that 'the CPRS is not an easy concept but in my view its design and its inherent flexibility were readily adaptable to the style and needs of individual governments. Conviction, dogma and consensus are all very well but not one of them by itself is enough to get us to heaven. I deeply regret the passing of the CPRS' (Cooper, 1986).

The Leader of the Opposition, Neil Kinnock, has said that he would revive it:

I would restore either the CPRS or a body very much like it for those functions of review, of anticipation which is important in all systems of management and in order to take a strategic view and propose collective responses.

He went on to suggest that he might establish a small Prime Minister's Office.

But the moment that became a flattery agency then it would have lost all function at all which is why a conjunction of let's say three things: the Central Policy review function whatever it's called, a Prime Minister's Office, call it a unit whatever else and thirdly an element of the 'cabinet' system in the major departments of state would be needed (Kinnock, 1986).

Whether or not the CPRS as such is felt to have been effective, there can be no doubt that the problem which it tried to address—the 'hole in the centre'—still remains largely unsolved. Some future government, with a different Prime Minister, ought to try to deal with it. Such a government may not want to set up a body in any way resembling the CPRS, but it should certainly examine the role it played between 1971 and 1983. Whilst this short account of the history and work of the CPRS is by no means comprehensive, we hope it will provide some guide to a future Prime Minister wishing to strengthen advice at the centre.

Appendix 1 : Reports by the CPRS

PUBLISHED REPORTS
A Framework for Government Research and Development, 1971.
Energy Conservation, July 1974.
A Joint Framework for Social Policies, June 1975.
The Future of the British Car Industry, November 1975.
The Future of the United Kingdom Power Plant Manufacturing Industry, December 1976.
Population and the Social Services, April 1977.
The Review of Overseas Representation, August 1977.
Relations between Central Government and Local Authorities, September 1977.
Services for Young Children with Working Mothers, July 1978.
Vandalism, September 1978.
Social and Employment Effects of Micro-Electronics, November 1978.
Housing and Social Policies, Some Interactions, December 1978.
People and their Families, January 1980.
Education, Training and Industrial Performance, May 1980.
Cashless Pay, June 1981.

UNPUBLISHED REPORTS
The CPRS also produced unpublished reports on the following subjects, among others:
The Future of Concorde, 1971.
Government Policy towards the Computer Industry, 1972.
Lessons from Japanese Industrial Success, 1972.
Government Support to Industry, 1972.
Government Disengagement from the Management of Nationalised Industries, 1972.
Regional Policy, 1973.
Energy Policy, 1973.
The Future of London as an International Financial Centre, 1973.
Social Policy Priorities, 1973.
Race Relations, 1974.
Agricultural Policy, 1975.
Northern Ireland, 1976.
Prices and Incomes Policy, 1976.
Review of Overseas Representation Interim Report, 1976.
The Leisure Industry and its Economic Benefits, 1978.
Unemployment, 1978.
Alcohol Policies, 1979.

Government Support for Social Science Research, 1979.
Persistent Offenders, 1979.
Space Policy, 1980.
New Training Initiatives for Young People, 1981.
Nationalised Industries, 1981.
Reductions in Public Expenditure, 1982.
Pension Policies, 1983.
Higher Education and Industry, 1983.

Appendix 2 : CPRS Evidence to the House of Commons

House of Commons Expenditure Committee Inquiry into Developments in the Civil Service since Fulton

THE ROLE OF THE CENTRAL POLICY REVIEW STAFF IN WHITEHALL

A Note submitted by the Central Policy Review Staff (CPRS)

A. The Origins of the CPRS

1. In October 1970 the Government issued a White Paper on the reorganization of Central Government (Command 4506) which, among other things, announced the creation of a small multi-disciplinary central policy review staff in the Cabinet Office.

2. The White Paper defined the role of the CPRS as follows: 'Under the supervision of the Prime Minister, it will work for Ministers collectively; and its task will be to enable them to take better policy decisions by asking them to work out the implications of their basic strategy in terms of policies in specific areas, to establish the relative priorities to be given to the different sectors of their programme as a whole, to identify those areas of policy in which new choices can be exercised and to ensure that the underlying implications of alternative courses of action are fully analysed and considered.

3. The new staff will not duplicate or replace the analytical work done by Departments in their own areas of responsibility. But it will seek to enlist their co-operation in its task of relating individual departmental policies to the Government's strategy as a whole. It will therefore play an important part in the extended public expenditure survey process described below, and it will also be available to promote studies in depth of interdepartmental issues which are of particular importance in relation to the control of the development of the Government's strategic objectives.

4. The CPRS started work on February 1971 with Lord Rothschild as its head. He was succeeded by Sir Kenneth Berrill in October 1974.

223

B. *Its Size and Composition*

5. The CPRS usually has about sixteen members. At present it has eighteen. About half of these are career civil servants on short-term secondment from their Departments; the other half are recruited from outside the Civil Service—from universities, industry, financial institutions and international organizations. For both career civil servants on secondment from Departments, and for people brought in from outside Government, the normal length of stay in the CPRS is about two years. Some people have left after less than two years; some have stayed longer; and a few of those who have come in from outside Government have subsequently become established civil servants.

C. *The Role of the CPRS*

6. In broad terms the CPRS continues to carry out the remit given to it originally in Command 4506. Its main task is still to offer advice to Ministers collectively which will help them to relate their policies and decisions to the Government's strategy as a whole. But whereas most civil servants work within the broad framework of their Minister's policies, the CPRS is not a departmental institution and, to perform its task, needs usually to set its advice in much more general terms and sometimes put forward suggestions of a radical nature. The task of the CPRS is carried out in a variety of ways.

i. *Strategy Reviews*

At fairly regular intervals (in principle about every six months) the CPRS attempts to take stock, across the board, of the problems facing the Government, both in the shorter and in the longer term. These stock-taking exercises try to set out the objectives in the various parts of the Government's programme, the relationship between them and the constraints in achieving them; to identify gaps in the strategy, the new problems which are likely to emerge, and to suggest how these might be tackled.

The initial work of these stock-taking or strategy reviews is internal to the CPRS. The results are presented to Ministers in a variety of ways. For example, the CPRS may prepare a paper for the Cabinet which attempts a synoptic view of problems of Government strategy as a whole; normally the purpose of such a paper would not be to seek immediate executive decisions, but rather to give all Ministers an opportunity to have a broader debate than they would normally have in their Departments or at interdepartmental meetings, and to enable Ministers to indicate some general lines of policy and guidance on priorities, to be worked out in detail later. Alternatively, these strategy reviews may result in the presentation to the Cabinet of an analysis of a limited number of central policy issues which the CPRS internal stock-taking has highlighted as deserving a wide-ranging discussion by Ministers collectively. The frequency, timing and content of such strategy presentations will vary with circumstances.

These periodic stock-taking exercises also help in determining priorities for other CPRS work; they can suggest subjects which may require study in depth; or they can suggest what are the important areas of policy coming before Ministers on which the CPRS should be prepared to offer specific advice.

ii. *Major Studies*

Normally the CPRS is involved at any time in two or three major studies. The subjects of CPRS studies are kept confidential unless they involve widespread consultation outside Government. Those at present in hand which have been publicly announced are:

(a) The Review of Overseas Representation—which is considering the most suitable, effective and economic means of representing and promoting British interests overseas;

(b) a study of the Heavy Electrical Industry which is examining the problems arising from the mismatch between plant manufacturing capacity and prospective orders; and

(c) several studies under the general heading 'A Joint Framework for Social Policies', which are concerned particularly with the links between different but related social policies, for example the relationship between housing policy and other social policies.

Only three CPRS studies have been published. Energy Conservation (1974); A Joint Framework for Social Policies (1975); the Future of the British Car Industry (1975).

With such wide terms of reference, and a small staff, the CPRS has to be selective both in the subjects it studies, and in deciding whether or not to comment on a specific issue. There are some subjects which are of sufficient importance to justify continuing work of some depth, in order to ensure that when a particular issue comes up CPRS advice can be presented to Ministers (often at short notice).

The initiative for these in-depth studies may come from a direct remit from Ministers (usually a Cabinet Committee), interdepartmental discussion, or from the CPRS itself.

iii. CPRS Involvement in Programme Analysis and Review

Another aspect of the CPRS concern and involvement in the development of Government strategy and policy making is its participation in policy reviews. The CPRS is often associated with the more important departmental policy reviews. It has been involved from the outset in the system of programme analysis and review originally announced in the 1970 White Paper on the Reorganization of Central Government. This system has been adapted over the years; but the essential features have been a regular annual stock-taking leading to the selection of certain departmental activities for review in depth. These reviews have concentrated on assessing the effectiveness of particular departmental activities in addition to their intended objectives, and on examining whether the objectives were soundly based. The CPRS, together with the Treasury and the Civil Service Department, have participated both in the selection of these topics and in monitoring the progress of the reviews themselves. The particular contribution which the CPRS has been concerned to make in this process has been to encourage the selection of topics which concern a number of Departments rather than just one Department, and to ensure that a suitable range of options for future action is identified and that the results are adequately presented to Ministers collectively.

iv. The Preparation of Collective Briefs

The CPRS receives papers prepared for discussion in Cabinet and in Cabinet committees. It then decides whether or not to prepare a brief for Ministers on any issues raised in these papers; for example if it has been following a particular issue it considers whether a short CPRS paper might aid discussion.

Such briefs will sometimes simply try to tease out the threads of the arguments set out in the paper or papers before the Cabinet or Ministerial committees, mainly to make sure that the main issues and the wider and longer term implications of the options proposed are not lost among the detail. The briefs also provide comments other than from a departmental angle. The brief may take this process a step further in commenting on the action recommended by the Minister bringing the subject before his colleagues. These briefs, like the papers to which they relate, are circulated to all the Ministers who will be taking part in the discussion. About fifty such briefs are prepared each year but the rate is uneven; for example in one week in February the CPRS circulated six collective briefs but there have been weeks when there were no CPRS collective briefs.

v. The Special Role of the CPRS on Science and Technology Matters

Many of the studies undertaken by the CPRS have necessarily involved aspects of science and technology in the context of broader governmental policies, e.g. energy or industrial strategies. The CPRS recently assumed more specific responsibilities for the co-ordination of government policies in this field as described in the then Lord Privy Seal's Memorandum to the Select Committee on Science and Technology (Science Sub-Committee) 21 May 1976. Specifically, the CPRS now provides the central focus for advice and for initiating innovatory studies of a trans-departmental nature, tasks previously discharged by the Science Group in the Cabinet Office. Changes are being made to the staffing of the unit to meet this need: in particular, a Chief Scientist, CPRS, has now been appointed. It is also intended that the CPRS will play an active part in the work of the newly created Advisory Council for Applied Research and Development (ACARD).

D. Its Working Relationships

7. The CPRS is physically and constitutionally part of the Cabinet Office. It participates in the work of Cabinet committees and in a few cases provides the chairman for official committees. It has a close working relationship with the Cabinet Secretariat, particularly in identifying issues which will be coming before Ministers and where CPRS advice may be useful. In addition members of the CPRS are in daily contact with civil servants in other government departments mainly to obtain information which they require for their work but also to keep in touch with policy developments in those departments. The CPRS works with and through departments; but its conclusions and recommendations are its own. In general the working relationship between the CPRS and the rest of Whitehall is close and good.

8. The CPRS believes that it is important to keep in touch with a wide range of opinion outside Whitehall. The fact that half its members are recruited from outside the Civil Service often means that it can do this more easily than many other Government departments. Moreover the wide variety of its work brings it into contact with many different organizations and institutions. Finally, in undertaking studies of particular subjects the CPRS often makes use of outside consultants.

E. Conclusion

9. The CPRS is essentially an instrument to serve Ministers collectively and its prime function is to offer a view independent of individual Ministers or departments. If time

permits it normally checks with departmental officials to make sure of its facts, but it is not required to inform or consult a Minister before commenting on policy for which he is responsible. It must be prepared to offer advice which is not always acceptable and to see it rejected. To fulfil adequately their task of collective responsibility Ministers acting collectively often need advice from a non-departmental point of view. The CPRS is one channel for providing such advice. The CPRS is useful to the extent that Ministers find it so. The Head of the CPRS from time to time discusses the work of the CPRS with senior Ministers, to ensure that the CPRS is responsive to Ministerial needs and pre-occupations. But how successful it is, only Ministers can judge.

10. The impact of the CPRS on individual departments has been varied and usually indirect rather than direct. It has not for example ever attempted to act as a co-ordinator of departmental planning or research units. But the CPRS believes that in various ways whether by long term strategy papers, major studies, collective briefs, participation in PARs or interdepartmental committees it has, at a relatively small cost, both helped to improve the machinery for decision taking at the centre and helped departments to relate their individual policies to the Government's strategy as a whole.

26 October 1976

Appendix 3 : Calendar of Events, 1970–1983

1970

June	Conservatives under E. Heath win General Election	
Oct.	Publication of Cmnd. 4506 on Machinery of Government proposing, among other things, a new 'central policy review staff'	
Dec.		Lord Rothschild appointed first head of CPRS

1971

Jan.	Post Office workers' strike	
Feb.		CPRS starts work
June	Upper Clyde Shipbuilders declared bankrupt	CPRS 'strategy' presentation to Prime Minister
		Report on future of Anglo-French Concorde project
Aug.	Pound floated	First Cabinet 'strategy' meeting at Chequers
Oct.		First CPRS 'early warning' paper discussed by Cabinet

1972

Jan.	Treaty of UK acession to EEC signed	CPRS study of UK computer industry completed
	Miners' strike	
Feb.	Wilberforce inquiry recommends 22% pay increase for miners	
	Government declares state of emergency in light of miners' strike	
Mar.	Suspension of Stormont	
May		Cabinet 'strategy' meeting at Chequers
July		First meeting of Ministerial strategy group on nationalized industries

228

Calendar of Events, 1970–1983

Aug.	Government declares state of emergency in light of dockers' strike	
Sept.		CPRS Sunningdale seminar on lessons of Japan
Nov.		CPRS report to Ministerial group on nationalized industries suggests ways of disengaging from day-to-day involvement
Dec.		Lord Rothschild discusses CPRS on BBC television
		IBRO/CPRS report on London as a financial centre completed and leaked in press
1973		
Jan.	Britain joins EEC	Lord Rothschild meets Herman Kahn
19 Feb.		First meeting of Social Affairs Strategy Group
Mar.	European currencies floated against the £	CPRS featured in *Sunday Times* colour supplement
Apr.	Introduction of VAT	
May		CPRS energy policy report completed
June		IBRO report debated in Commons
		Cabinet 'strategy' meeting at Chequers
July	Northern Ireland Act provides for power-sharing executive	CPRS report to Ministers on social policy
Sept.		CPRS presentation to Ministers on public expenditure
		Rothschild's Wantage speech
Oct.	Outbreak of Middle East war. Cut in oil supplies; quadrupling of oil prices	
Nov.	Miners' overtime ban	Cabinet 'strategy' meeting fixed and cancelled
	Government announces 3-day week to start in January	
20 Dec.		Lord Rothschild 'to rest'
1974		
Jan.	Power-sharing executive established in Northern Ireland	CPRS race relations report (first version) submitted to Ministers
Feb.	Miners' Strike	
	General Election: Labour wins with no overall majority	
May	Northern Ireland executive resigns	CPRS race relations report (second version) submitted to Ministers

229

July		CPRS *Energy Conservation* report published
Sept.	Government announces decision to set up elected assemblies in Scotland and Northern Ireland	Sir Kenneth Berrill replaces Lord Rothschild as head of CPRS
Oct.	General Election: Labour wins with an overall majority of 3	
Nov.		Cabinet 'strategy' meeting at Chequers
Dec.	Year ends with industrial production down 3%, RPI up 19%, wages rates up 29%	
1975		CPRS report on agricultural policy completed
Feb.	Lome Convention signed	
May		CPRS proposals in *A Joint Approach to Social Policy* endorsed by new Ministerial committee
June	Referendum on continued British membership of EEC: 67% vote 'yes'	
	First landing of North Sea oil	
July	White Paper on inflation announces universal pay-rise limit of £6 per week	CPRS report *A Joint Framework for Social Policies* published
	Government takes majority share-holding in British Leyland	
Aug.	RPI shows 26.0% annual increase	
Nov.	Cash limits announced for public expenditure in 1976/7	CPRS report *The Future of the British Car Industry* published
Dec.	Unemployment reaches over 1 million	
1976		
Jan.		CPRS report on need for permanent incomes policy completed
		CPRS 'think-in' weekend at Civil Service College
Feb.	Public expenditure White Paper cuts spending by £1 bn. in 1977/ 8, and by £2.4 bn. in 1978/9, compared with previous plans	
Mar.	£ falls below $2.00 for first time	CPRS report on *Review of Social Services* presented to Ministers

Apr.	Budget: £1.3 million tax cuts subject to TUC agreement on new low pay norm	
	Harold Wilson resigns; James Callaghan replaces him as leader of Labour Party and Prime Minister	
June		Completion of interim CPRS report on overseas representation
early summer	Further £1 bn. to be cut from 1978/9 public expenditure	CPRS work on Cabinet Office briefs for Callaghan bilaterals with Cabinet colleagues
Sept.	IMF approached for £3.9 bn. stand-by credit	
Oct.	£ down to $1.57	New CPRS post of Chief Scientist filled
Nov.		CPRS paper presented to Chequers Cabinet on the national recovery programme
Dec.	Announcement of further cut £1 bn. in 1977/8 and £1.5 bn. in 1978/9 public spending, as part of agreement with IMF	Publication of CPRS report on UK power plant industry
6 Dec.		CPRS gives oral and written evidence to House of Commons Select Committee on the Civil Service
1977		
Jan.		CPRS 'think-in' weekend at Civil Service College
Apr.		Publication of CPRS report on *Population and the Social Services*
Aug.	Unemployment reaches over 1.5 million	Publication of CPRS report on *Review of Overseas Representation*
Sept.	Anti-inflation policies secure TUC support for '12 month rule' and government attempts to secure voluntary 10% limit on rises in earnings	Publication of CPRS report on *Relations between Central Government and Local Authorities*
Oct.		CPRS report on race relations (1973/4) leaked in *Guardian*
Nov.	Firemen's strike	

1978
Jan.

		With CPRS encouragement, ACARD starts work on micro-electronics
		Completion of CPRS Social Topic Notes on 'The Elderly' and 'Under Fives'
		CPRS gives evidence on Review of Overseas Representation to House of Commons Defence and External Affairs Committee
July	Scotland and Wales Bills (on devolution) receive Royal Assent	Completion of CPRS Social Topic Notes on 'The Family I' and 'Alcohol'
		Publication of CPRS report on *Services for Young Children with Working Mothers*
Sept.		Publication of CPRS report on *Vandalism*
		Publication of ACARD report on *Application of Semi-conductor Technology*
Nov.		Completion of CPRS report on *Social and Employment Effects of Micro-Electronics*
Dec.		Publication of CPRS report on *Housing and Social Policies*

1979

Jan.	Lorry drivers' strike	
Mar.	Referenda on devolution: less than 40% in favour means Scotland and Wales Acts not ratified	
	Labour government loses vote of confidence in House of Commons and resigns	
May	General Election: Conservatives win with overall majority of 43	CPRS report on alcohol policies completed but not published
June	Budget cuts income tax and raises VAT	
summer		CPRS report on government support for social science research
		CPRS report on persistent offenders
Oct.	Abolition of exchange controls	
Nov.	Minimum lending rate increased to 17%	

Calendar of Events, 1970–1983

Dec.	Lancaster House agreement on Rhodesia/Zimbabwe	
1980		
Jan.	Steelworkers' strike	Publication of CPRS report on *People and their Families*
Mar.	Announcement of medium-term financial strategy	
Apr.		Robin Ibbs replaces Sir Kenneth Berrill as head of CPRS
May		Publication of CPRS report on *Education, Training and Industrial Performance*
June	Britain becomes net exporter of oil	Completion of CPRS report on space policy
	Agreement on reduction of Britain's contribution to EEC	
Dec.	Unemployment reaches over 2.0 million	
1981		
spring		Completion of CPRS report on new training initiatives for young people
Apr.		Prime Minister invites Ibbs to study and report on relationships of nationalized industries with government
June		Publication of CPRS report on *Cashless Pay*
July		Completion of CPRS report on nationalized industries
Aug.	Minimum lending rate abolished	
Oct./Nov.	Unemployment reaches over 2.5 million	Establishment of Nationalised Industries Review Staff within CPRS
winter	Throughout year privatization of British Sugar, National Freight Corporation, parts of Cable and Wireless, and Crown Agents	Completion of CPRS report on Invergordon smelter
1982		
Apr.	Argentine forces land on Falklands: British task force dispatched	John Sparrow replaces Robin Ibbs as head of CPRS
May	British task force lands on Falklands	
summer		CPRS works with No. 10 Policy Unit on family policy

July	Surrender of Argentine forces in Falklands	Sparrow chairs interdepartmental committee on aerospace policy
	Northern Ireland Act provides for election of Northern Ireland Assembly	
Sept.	Unemployment reaches over 3 million	CPRS report on options for reducing public expenditure completed and leaked
1983		
Mar.		Completion of CPRS report on pensions
spring		Completion of CPRS report on higher education and industry
June	General Election: Conservatives win with overall majority of 144	CPRS abolished

Appendix 4 : Members of the CPRS, 1970–1983

Name	Period with CPRS	Current/last known occupation (as at July 1987)
Prof. John M. Ashworth	Oct. 76–Aug. 81	Vice-Chancellor, University of Salford
Ms Madeleine E. Aston	Sept. 71–Sept. 73	
Dr Leslie Atkinson	Oct. 77–Aug. 79	Senior Executive, British Petroleum Co. plc
Sir Alan M. Bailey	June 81–Nov. 82	Permanent Secretary, Dept. of Transport
Mr Tony W. Battishill	July 76–July 77	Chairman, Board of Inland Revenue
Mr Chris. B. B. Beauman	May 81–Apr. 83	Senior Executive, Morgan Grenfell & Co. Ltd
Sir Kenneth Berrill	Oct. 74–Mar. 80	Chairman, Securities and Investment Board Ltd.
Dr Tessa Blackstone	Sept. 75–Aug. 78	Master of Birkbeck College, University of London
Mr Peter W. Bocock	June 71–June 73	
Mr Stephen W. Boys Smith	June 77–May 79	Assistant Secretary, Home Office
Mrs June Bridgeman	Apr. 77–Apr. 79	Under-Secretary, Dept. of Transport
Dr John G. St C. Buchanan	Sept. 76–Sept. 77	Senior Executive, British Petroleum Co. plc
Sir John Burgh	Nov. 72–Mar. 74	Director General, the British Council
Mr F. E. Robin Butler	Feb. 71–May 72	Second Permanent Secretary, HM Treasury
Mr John Caines	Jan.–July 83	Permanent Secretary, Overseas Development Administration
Sir Peter Carey	May 71–Sept. 72	Chairman, Morgan Grenfell & Co. Ltd.
Mr James E. Cornish	Jan. 80–July 82	Phillips & Drew

Mr John M. Crawley	Feb. 73–Apr. 76 Feb. 79–Apr. 81	Deputy Secretary, Finance and Manpower Division, Inland Revenue
Mr Richard E. Crum	Sept. 71–Sept. 73	School of Economic and Social Studies, University of East Anglia
Mr Mark C. Dadd	June 77–Sept. 79	
Dr Peter T. Davies	June 82–July 83	Director, Advanced Technology Centre, Dept. of Engineering, University of Warwick
Sir Gordon S. Downey	July 78–May 81	Comptroller and Auditor General, National Audit Office
Mr Michael J. Elliot	June 82–July 83	Washington Correspondent, *The Economist*
Dr Anthony Fish	July 71–Feb. 72	Senior Executive, Shell Int. Petroleum Co.
Dr Richard J. Gibbs	Nov. 80–Nov. 82	DHSS
Mr 'Mig' I. Goulding	Jan. 75–June 77	Under-Secretary-General, the United Nations, New York
Dr David D. Green	Aug. 82–July 83	
John R. S. Guinness	July 72–Sept. 75 Nov. 77–Dec. 79	Deputy Secretary, Dept. of Energy
Mr Graham A. Hart	Apr. 82–July 83	Deputy Secretary, DHSS
Professor Michael Hart	Apr. 75–Oct. 76	Department of Physics, Manchester University
Dr Michael J. Harte	Apr. 73–Mar. 75	Under-Secretary, Ministry of Defence
Mr Nick J. Hartley	Nov. 78–Jan. 81	OFTEL
Mr Hector C. G. Hawkins	May 71–Aug. 77	Chief Economic Adviser, Standard Chartered Bank
Ms Carolyn A. Hayman	Mar. 78–May 80	Director, Korda & Co. Ltd.
Sir David Henderson-Stewart	Jan. 77–Dec. 78	Senior Executive, Audit Commission
Dr David G. B. Horne	Feb. 75–June 76	Senior Executive, British Petroleum Co. plc
Sir Anthony G. Hurrell	Jan.–Dec. 76	HM Ambassador, Kathmandu
Sir Robin Ibbs	Apr. 80–Mar. 82	Director, ICI plc, and Prime Minister's Adviser on Efficiency and Effectiveness
Ms Kate Jenkins	Jan. 76–July 78	Under-Secretary, the Efficiency Unit
Mr Michael A. Johns	Feb. 79–Nov. 80	Assistant Secretary, Board of Inland Revenue

Mr Peter J. D. Kind	Nov. 78–Mar. 80	Commission of the European Communities
Dr Nigel Kingsley	Aug. 77–Oct. 79	Senior Executive, Mars Electronics
Mr Trevor Knapp	June 77–June 79	Director-General, Marketing, Ministry of Defence
Miss Hilary Land	Oct. 78–Dec. 79	Reader in Social Administration, University of Bristol
Mr Andrew L. Likierman	Nov. 76–Dec. 78	Director, Institute of Public Sector Management, London Business School
Ms Maureen MacGlashan	Sept. 77–Nov. 79	Assistant Director, Research Centre for Int. Law, Cambridge University
Ms Eileen Mackay	Sept. 80–May 83	Assistant Secretary, Industry Department of Scotland
Mr Graham R. Mackenzie	May 81–Jan 83	Senior Executive, TI Group plc
Mr Anthony A. Maclean	Nov. 73–Aug. 74	
Mr William E. Martin	Mar. 81–July 83	Phillips & Drew
Mr R. Anthony J. Mayer	Feb. 74–Mar. 76	N. M. Rothschild & Sons Ltd.
Mr John F. Mayne	Feb. 71–Sept. 73	Deputy Secretary, DHSS
Mr Michael P. Mire	Oct.–Nov. 75	Consultant McKinsey & Co.
Dr Janet Morgan	July 78–Jan. 81	Adviser to the Board, Granada Group plc
Ms Kate Mortimer	Oct. 72–Oct. 78	Director of Policy, Securities and Investments Board Ltd.
Mr Anthony J. Neuberger	July 73–Jan. 75	Lecturer, London Business School
Sir Robin B. Nicholson	Nov. 81–July 83	Director, Pilkington Bros. plc
Mr Adrian R. D. Norman	June 80–May 81	Senior Executive, Arthur D. Little Ltd.
Mr John Odling-Smee	Nov. 75–July 77	Under-Secretary, HM Treasury
Mr David L. Pascall	Mar. 82–July 83	British Petroleum Co. plc
Dr William J. L. Plowden	Apr. 71–Apr. 77	Director-General, RIPA
Mr Stephen F. D. Powell	Oct. 74–Nov. 78	Economist, International Monetary Fund
Mr Richard E. S. Prescott	Dec. 80–Sept. 81	DHSS
Dr Ian A. Read	May 71–May 74	Senior Executive, Shell International
Mr Brian Reading	Nov. 71–Aug. 72	
Mr Peter Readman	Apr. 74–Dec. 76	Abercromby and Co.

Mrs Susanne Reeve	July 73–Dec. 74	The Secretary, Economic and Social Research Council
Mr Tom L. Richardson	Feb. 80–Dec. 81	Assistant Secretary, Economic Relations Dept., FCO
Dr John H. Rickard	Dec. 78–Nov. 82	Chief Economic Adviser, Dept. of Transport and Environment
Sir Adam N. Ridley	May 71–Aug. 74	Director, Hambros Bank Ltd.
Mrs Ann Robinson	Sept. 74–May 77	Assistant Secretary, DHSS
Mr Peter B. Rogers	July 73–Sept. 74	Director of Finance, IBA
Dr John Rosenfeld	Feb.–Sept. 72	Senior Executive, Shell International
Mr C. Richard Ross	Feb. 71–June 78	Vice-President, European Investment Bank
Lord Rothschild	Feb. 71–Sept. 74	N. M. Rothschild & Sons Ltd.
Ms Charlotte Rycroft	Dec. 81–July 83	Counsellor British Embassy, Ottawa
Mr Chris T. Sandars	Feb. 71–Mar. 74	Assistant Secretary, Ministry of Defence
Mr Anthony E. Smith	Nov. 79–May 82	Group General Manager, Cable Wireless plc
Mr Clive H. Smee	Jan.–June 83	Chief Economic Advisor, DHSS
Sir John Sparrow	Apr. 82–July 83	Director, Morgan Grenfell & Co. Ltd.
Mr Gerry B. Spence	Apr. 79–June 83	Cabinet Office
Mr John B. Stuttard	Dec. 81–July 83	Consultant, Coopers & Lybrand
Mr Brian A. E. Taylor	Jan.–June 83	Under-Secretary, Ministry of Defence
Mr Quentin Thompson	80–83	Director, Coopers & Lybrand
Mr Chris Turner	June–Nov. 81	Christian Salvesen Ltd.
Sir Alan B. Urwick	Sept. 73–Jan. 75	HM Ambassador, British Embassy, Cairo
Dr Paul R. Vaight	Nov. 79–Feb. 82	Divisional Manager, Corporate Planning, British Petroleum Co.
Sir Robert Wade-Gery	Jan. 71–Sept. 73	British High Commissioner, New Delhi (retired 1987)
Hon. William Waldegrave, MP	Mar. 71–Dec. 73	Minister of State, Dept. of Environment
Mr Gordon J. Wasserman	July 81–July 83	Under-Secretary, Home Office

Members of the CPRS, 1970–1983

Mr Ian William	Nov. 74–Jan. 77	Economic Adviser, DHSS
Mr Chris H. K. Williams	June 82–July 83	Associate Director, Coopers & Lybrand
Ms Jennifer Youde	Feb. 81–Feb. 83	CIN Management Ltd.
Mr David E. Young	May 75–July 77	Finance Director, John Lewis Partnership
Mr Robert Young	Apr.–July 83	Managing Director, Crane Ltd.

Bibliography

ADVISORY COUNCIL ON APPLIED RESEARCH AND DEVELOPMENT (ACARD) *The Applications of Semiconductor Technology*, HMSO, 1978.
—— *Industrial Innovations*, HMSO, 1979.
—— *Technological Change: Threats and Opportunities for the United Kingdom*, HMSO, 1980.
—— *Computer Aided Design and Manufacture*, HMSO, 1980.
ASHWORTH, John, 'Giving Advice to Governments: The role of the Chief Scientist in the Central Policy Review Staff'. Transcript of Proceedings of Meeting of the Royal Signals Institution, 23 November 1985.
BARNETT, Corelli, *The Audit of War*, Macmillan, London, 1986.
BELOFF, Max, 'The Think-Tank and Foreign Affairs', *Public Administration*, 55:4, 1977. Also published as an RIPA pamphlet, London, 1977.
BENN, Tony, 'Manifestos and Mandarins' in *Policy and Practice: The Experience of Government*, Royal Institute of Public Administration, London, 1980.
—— Letter to Tessa Blackstone, 28 October 1982.
BERRILL, Sir Kenneth, 'The Role of the Central Policy Review Staff in Whitehall', *Management Services in Government*, 32:3, 1977.
—— 'Strength at the Centre: The Case for a Prime Minister's Department', Stamp Memorial Lecture, University of London, 1980.
BLACKSTONE, Tessa, 'The Voices that drown in the Think-Tank', *The Times Higher Education Supplement*, 15 August 1980.
—— 'The Entrenched Generalists', *New Universities Quarterly*, 35: 3, 1981.
—— and PLOWDEN, W., 'Dear Mr. Ibbs . . .', *Observer*, 6 April 1980.
BLONDEL, Jean, *Government Ministers in the Contemporary World*, Sage Publishing, New York, 1985.
BOURNE, John, 'Heath has half-hour meeting with Lord Rothschild', *Financial Times*, 26 September 1973.
—— 'Rothschild takes rest', *Financial Times*, 20 December 1973.
BRUCE-GARDYNE, Jock, 'What use a Tank that Leaks', *The Times*, 22 June 1983.
CASTLE, Barbara, *The Castle Diaries, 1974–6*, Weidenfeld, London, 1980.
CHALFONT, Lord, 'Careless talk that could cost us dear', *The Times*, 8 August 1977.
CLARKE, George, 'Angry Mr. Heath rebukes Lord Rothschild over gloomy speech, but no demand for resignation', *The Times*, 26 September 1973.
CLARKE, Sir Richard, *New Trends in Government*, HMSO, 1971.
Cmnd. 4506, *The Reorganization of Central Government*, HMSO, London, 1970.
COLCHESTER, Nicholas, 'Professor Parkinson's Profession', *Financial Times*, 25 September 1975.

Bibliography

CONYERS, Tony, 'End Diplomatic Service Says Think-Tank', *Daily Telegraph*, 26 April 1977.

COOPER, Sir Frank, 'Changing the Establishment', *Political Quarterly*, 57: 3, 1986.

CPRS, Report on *Alcohol Policies in the United Kingdom* (1979), Stockholm, Sociologists Institutionen, Stockholm Universitet, 1980.

CROSLAND, Susan, *Tony Crosland*, Jonathan Cape, London, 1982.

DAALDER, Hans, *Cabinet Reform in Britain, 1914–1963*, Oxford University Press, 1964.

Daily Express, Leader: 'Why knock our diplomats?', 3 August 1977.

DAVIES, Michael, 'Can Think Tank Stay Free of Whitehall Grip?', *Observer*, 16 January 1977.

DELL, Edmund, 'Collective Responsibility: Fact, Fiction or Facade?' in *Policy and Practice: The Experience of Government*, Royal Institute of Public Administration, London, 1980.

—— 'Some Reflections on Cabinet Government by a Former Practitioner', *Public Adm. Bulletin*, 32, April 1980.

DEPARTMENT OF EDUCATION AND SCIENCE, 'The Development of Higher Education into the 1990s', Cmnd. 9524, HMSO, May 1985.

DEPARTMENT OF HEALTH AND SOCIAL SECURITY, 'Drinking Sensibly: A Discussion Document', HMSO, December 1981.

—— *Reform of Social Security*, Vols. i–iii, Cmnd. 9517, 9578, 9579, HMSO, 1985.

DEPARTMENT OF INDUSTRY, 'British Leyland the Next Decade', Report by Sir Don Ryder, HMSO, April 1975.

DONALDSON, Frances, *The British Council: The First Fifty Years*, Jonathan Cape, London, 1984.

DONOUGHUE, Bernard, *Prime Minister: The Conduct of Policy under Harold Wilson and James Callaghan*, Jonathan Cape, London, 1987.

DROR, Yehezkel, 'Think Tanks: A New Invention in Government' in Weiss, Carl (ed.), *Making Government Work*, Sage Publishing, New York, 1981.

—— 'Policy Analysis for Advising Rulers' in Tomlinson and Kiss (eds.), *Rethinking the Process of Operational Research and Systems Analysis*, Pergamon, Oxford, 1984.

—— 'Conclusions' in William Plowden (ed.), *Advising the Rulers*, Blackwell, Oxford, 1987.

DUNCAN, Sir Val (Chairman), *Report of the Review Committee on Overseas Representation, 1968–1969*, Cmnd. 4107, HMSO, 1969.

Economist, The, 'Think Tank's Damp Squib', 8 August 1981.

—— 'The Battle of Britain's Dinosaurs', 6 March 1982.

—— 'Mountains out of Molehills', 9 October 1982.

FOWLER, Derek, 'Management of objectives: BR's experience', *RIPA Report*, spring 1987.

FOX, James, 'The Brains behind the Throne', *Sunday Times Colour Supplement*, 25 March 1973.

GRAY, Andrew and JENKINS, Bill, 'Policy Analysis in British Central Government', *Public Administration*, 60: 4, 1982.

GREIG, Gordon, 'Too many men in Jim's army', *Daily Mail*, 29 December 1975.

GROSER, John, 'Government embarrassed by Rothschild warning of Britain as "poor nation"', *The Times*, 25 September 1972.

Guardian, Leader: 'Skirting the Old Lady', 5 June 1973.

—— Leader: 'Why the tank was junk, by Mrs. Thatcher', 18 June 1983.

HAWKINS, Hector, Review of Wilks, 1984, *Public Administration*, autumn, 1985.

HEALEY, Denis, in 'All the Prime Minister's Men', *Channel 4*, Brook Productions, 10 July 1986.

HENNESSY, Peter, 'Whitehall Hostility to Overseas Staff Inquiry', *The Times*, 26 April 1977.

—— 'The Firework that Fizzled', *New Society*, 3 January 1985.

—— *Cabinet*, Blackwell, Oxford, 1986.

—— MORRISON, Susan, and TOWNSEND, Richard, *Routine Punctuated by Orgies: the Central Policy Review Staff, 1970–83*, Strathclyde Papers on Government and Politics, No. 31, Glasgow, 1985.

HOME OFFICE, *Racial Discrimination*, Cmnd. 6234, HMSO, 1975.

HOSKYNS, Sir John, 'Whitehall and Westminster: An Outsider's View', *Parliamentary Affairs*, 36: 2, 1983.

—— 'Conservatism is not enough', *Political Quarterly*, 50: 1, 1984.

—— 'Thinking the Unthinkable', *The Director*, April 1986.

HOUSE OF COMMONS, Select Committee on Science and Technology, Session 1971–2, First Report: *Research and Development*, HMSO, 1972.

—— Expenditure Committee, Defence and External Affairs Sub-Committee, Session 1974–5, Eighth Report: *Diplomatic Manpower and Property Overseas*, HMSO, 1975.

—— Estimates Committee, General Sub-Committee, Session 1976–7, Report on *Developments in the Civil Service since the Fulton Committee report of 1968*, HMSO, 1977.

—— Expenditure Committee, Defence and External Affairs Sub-Committee, Session 1977–8, Report on *The CPRS Review of Overseas Representation*, HMSO, 1978.

—— Treasury & Civil Service Committee, Session 1985–6, Seventh Report, *Civil Servants and Ministers: Duties and Responsibilities*, Vol. ii, 1986.

HOUSE OF LORDS, Debate on the CPRS Review of Overseas Representation, *Hansard*, 23 November 1977.

HOWELL, David, 'Marks & Spencer and the Civil Service: A comparison of Culture and Methods', *Public Administration*, 59, 1981.

—— in 'The Quality of Cabinet Government', Radio 3 interview with Peter Hennessy, 21 February 1985.

HUNT, Lord, 'Cabinet Strategy and Management', Paper given to RIPA/CIPFA Conference, Brighton, 6 June 1983.

HURD, Douglas, in 'All the Prime Minister's Men', *Channel 4*, Brook Productions, 24 July 1986.

INTER-BANK RESEARCH ORGANISATION, *Future of London as an International Finance Centre*, HMSO, 1973.

ISSERLIS, A. R., 'The CPRS and After', *Policy Studies*, 4: 3, 1984.

JAMES, Simon, 'The Central Policy Review Staff, 1970–83', *Political Studies*, 34, 1986.

JAY, Peter, 'Plan for "task force" to advise Government on new policies for future development of City', *The Times*, 30 November 1972.

JENKINS, Peter, 'Think Tank suggests an end to the FO', *Guardian*, 25 April 1977.

JENKINS, Simon, 'The battle for Britain's dinosaurs', *The Economist*, 6 March 1982.

KINNOCK, Neil, in 'All the Prime Minister's Men', *Channel 4*, Brook Productions, 10 July 1986.

LORD PRIVY SEAL, Memorandum 25 to House of Commons Select Committee on Science and Technology, 1976.

Bibliography

MACHINERY OF GOVERNMENT COMMITTEE, Report, Cmnd. 9230, HMSO, 1918.

MACHINERY OF GOVERNMENT GROUP, First Report to Mr Heath, 6 February 1969.

MACDOUGALL, G. D. A., 'The Prime Minister's Statistical Section' in Chester, D. N. (ed.), *Lessons of the British War Economy*, Cambridge University Press, 1951.

—— 'The Machinery of Economic Government: Some Personal Reflections', in Butler, D., and Halsey, A. H. (eds.), *Policy and Politics: Essays in Honour of Norman Chester*, Macmillan, 1978.

—— *Don and Mandarin: Memoirs of an Economist*, John Murray, 1987.

MACKINTOSH, John, 'The Think-Tank should have remembered what foreign policy is for', *The Times*, 22 August 1977.

MANPOWER SERVICES COMMISSION, 'A New Training Initiative', A consultative document, MSC, 1981.

MARKS, Laurence, 'Rothschild and his Think Tank', *Observer*, 30 September 1973.

MELTSNER, Arnold, J., *Policy Analysts in the Bureaucracy*, University of California Press, 1976, 1986.

MORISON, Ian, 'Steering the City through confusing cross-currents of change', *The Times*, 28 November 1972.

New Society, 'Observations', 7 June 1979.

NORTON-TAYLOR, Richard, 'Whitehall fears on Think Tank', *Guardian*, 17 June 1983.

PHILLIPS, Melanie, 'Think Tank's race warning', and 'The great race report opt-out', *Guardian*, 24 October 1977.

PLIATZKY, Leo, *Paying and Choosing*, Blackwell, Oxford, 1985.

PLOWDEN, Lord (Chairman), *Report of the Committee on Representational Services Overseas*, Cmnd. 2276, HMSO, 1964.

—— and ROBERTHALL, Lord, 'Strengthening the Cabinet Office': Memorandum submitted to Mr. Edward Heath, n.d. [1968].

PLOWDEN, W., 'The British Central Policy Review Staff' in Baehr, P. and Whittrock, B. (eds.), *Policy Analysis and Policy Innovation*, Sage, London, 1980.

—— 'Collective advice to Ministers on Decision-making' in *Collective Decision Making in Government*, Public Finance Foundation, London, 1985.

—— (ed.), *Advising the Rulers*, Blackwell, Oxford, 1987.

POLLITT, C., 'The CPRS, 1970–1974', *Public Administration*, 52: 4, 1974.

RODGERS, William, The government we deserve: Can Whitehall function better?, abstract of paper presented at RIPA Conference, September 1986.

ROGALY, Joe, 'The Case for rescuing the Think Tank', *Financial Times*, 21 February 1976.

ROTHSCHILD, Lord, *Meditations of a Broomstick*, Collins, London, 1977.

—— *Random Variables*, Collins, London, 1984.

—— 'Epistle to a Prime Minister' in Hennessy, Morrison, and Townsend, 1985.

—— Letter to William Plowden, 14 May 1986.

SHARP, Baroness (Evelyn), Letter to William Plowden, 3 September 1982.

SPANIER, David, 'Foreign Office denies overstaffing change', *The Times*, 30 December 1975.

STOCKHOLM UNIVERSITY, 'Alcohol Policies in the United Kingdom', April 1982, reprint of Alcohol Policies, CPRS, 1979.

STUART, Frederick, 'Drink up men—the party's over', *Daily Express*, 30 October 1975.

THOMAS, Yvonne, 'Who do they think they are . . . ? How dare they? Etc., Etc.', *Daily Mail*, London, 11 April 1978.

Times Educational Supplement, 'Barriers down in a quest for social security', 23 May 1975.

Times, The, Leader: 'Emptying the Tank', 18 June 1983.

TURNER, John, *Lloyd George's Secretariat*, Cambridge University Press, 1980.

WALDEGRAVE, William, *The Training of Leviathan: Conservatism and the Future*, Hamish Hamilton, 1978.

WALKER, Peter, 'Too wet, too shallow, *and* out of their depth', *Daily Mail*, 5 August 1977.

WALLACE, William, 'After Berrill: Whitehall and the Management of British Diplomacy', *International Affairs*, 54: 2, April 1978.

WASS, Douglas, *Government and the Governed: The BBC Reith Lectures 1983*, Routledge and Kegan Paul, London, 1984.

WIENER, Martin, J., *English Culture and the Decline of the Industrial Spirit, 1850–1980*, Cambridge University Press, 1982.

WILDING, Richard, 'The Professional Ethic of the Administrator', *Management Services in Government*, 34: 4, 1979.

WILKS, Stephen, *Industrial Policy and the Motor Industry*, Manchester University Press, 1984.

WILLIAMS, Shirley, 'The Decision Makers' in *Policy and Practice: The Experience of Government*, Royal Institute of Public Administration, London, 1980.

YOUNG, Hugo, 'A curse of orthodoxies', *Sunday Times*, 26 June 1983.

—— and SLOMAN, Anne, *The Thatcher Phenomenon*, BBC, London, 1986.

Index